Operating Systems

Design and Implementation

Operating Systems

Design and Implementation

Raymond W. Turner

Senior Scientist, GHG Corporation
Houston, Texas

Macmillan Publishing Company
New York
Collier Macmillan Publishers
London

Macmillan Publishing Company
866 Third Avenue, New York, New York 10022

Collier Macmillan Canada, Inc.

Library of Congress Cataloging in Publication Data

Turner, Raymond W.
  Operating systems.

  Bibliography: p.
  Includes index.
  1. Operating systems (Computers) I. Title.
QA76.76.063T87 1986   001.64'2   84-7240
ISBN 0-02-421820-0

Printing: 1 2 3 4 5 6 7 8   Year: 6 7 8 9 0 1 2 3 4 5

ISBN 0-02-421820-0

Preface

This text is written to provide computer science students in-depth answers to five questions.

1. What is an operating system?
2. How do operating systems work?
3. What features of operating systems are available to programmers and how can these features be used to assist with the development of complex software systems?
4. What are the various resource management options generally available for meeting installation specific needs?
5. How does the operating system support interfaces to both programs and external equipment and what is involved in providing new interfaces?

By addressing these questions, this text also introduces the student to a large number of data structures and algorithms which have applicability to a wide range of software systems. For example, basic concurrent programming principles and methods are addressed in a manner easily related to nonoperating system environments. Input and output techniques may be extended to data base applications. And the general nature of the dynamic memory management presentation makes these techniques applicable to any system requiring runtime management of available memory. For those involved in a minioperating system implementation project, the detailed data structure and algorithm specifications presented in the following chapters provide a complete software design suitable for implementing a basic operational operating system kernel.

Operating system analysis courses typically concentrate on theories and strategies of resource management and conflict resolution and generally cover a broad spectrum of capability. Often, however, they do not expose students to the complex system environment of detailed design and implementation. An operating system programming environment requires the application of knowledge from data structures, assembler language, and computer architecture, as well as operating system concepts.

It is unreasonable to cover the necessary breadth of the classical operating systems course at a code and data format level of detail. This text is therefore structured to cover the vertical gap between the preceding undergraduate courses and the operating systems course. This is an operating systems programming

v

techniques book, focusing on one simplified environment with a solution to each of the basic problems of

implementing multiprogramming,
managing memory,
communicating with input/output devices,
synchronizing and communicating with processes,
managing time,
processing various classes of interrupts, and
scheduling the processor.

Rationale for this rather narrow set of topics and limited operating system capability is four-fold.

1. Most of the important aspects of operating systems can be examined in detail without necessarily learning the structure and functions of a complicated full-featured operating system.
2. An introduction to the concepts of operating systems is provided for those who will continue with studies of full featured operating systems.
3. Many techniques needed by more sophisticated applications can be isolated and learned independently of any operating system.
4. A substantive set of system programming topics suitable for a one semester systems software development course was desired. (Other pseudo-system programming areas such as language translation and data base management systems are left to other courses.)

The subject of dynamic memory management is covered as an extension of a data structures course. Those techniques of memory management which have practical utility in contemporary systems and executive controlled applications are examined and contrasted. Program segmentation and overlaying is discussed, as these techniques are important to software operating on small systems. Next, swapping processes between main memory and secondary storage and paged memory systems are considered.

In the first three chapters, a framework for a hypothetical and limited multiprogramming mock operating system, MOS, is defined. Subsequent chapters build on this framework so that in the end all functions treated have been addressed with respect to a consistent and reasonably realistic environment similar to those presented in many contemporary minicomputers. About a hundredth of the structural complexity of a real operating system is involved in learning MOS organization.

Chapter 4 covers the problems of low level input and output using both direct and indirect input and output operations and techniques for using direct memory access controllers and channels. Initially, a uniprogramming environment is assumed in an I/O example performing card to disk spooling. Chapter 5 then extends the environment to multiprogramming with system call and I/O interrupts. Appropriate extensions are made to previously defined data structures and new functions are added. All of the techniques are integrated into a logically consistent MOS environment.

The basic problems of subprocessing, concurrency, and communication are addressed in Chapter 6, while coordination, race conditions, and deadlock are examined in Chapter 7. Solutions to several concurrency problems are developed in such a way as to extend the student's repertoire of programming techniques. Chapter 6 also covers process traps and techniques for application program handling of errors and exception conditions.

Chapter 8 introduces the interval timer and techniques for maintaining the time of day and for supporting time dependent process events. Use of timer services in time dependent applications and real-time processing are also discussed. The timer management services are used to support time sharing of the processor in Chapter 9. In this chapter, the final system component, the process dispatcher, is defined. (Several times in earlier chapters, the phrase ''Call the dispatcher to . . .'' is used to leave a process in some blocked condition and select another process to run.) This approach has been taken so as to develop a complete set of requirements for this key component of MOS in a systematic and obvious way.

For those who intend to use MOS as a design basis for a project implementation of a minioperating system, an alternative chapter sequence might be considered. Although the text builds concepts from Chapter 2 through Chapter 9, an ''inside out'' development can occur by beginning with the chapter sequence 1, 9, 6, and 2. This will provide an overall system perspective and a base containing the dispatcher, basic concurrent processing capability, and memory management. The remaining units consisting of Chapter 3, the Chapter 4 and 5 pair, Chapter 7, and Chapter 8 can be covered in almost any order.

Major operating system functions not addressed in this text are file systems, and the scheduling of batch jobs. File systems is a very large topic when covered in-depth. This system component allows logical access to collections of data maintained on secondary storage. Each collection, or file, can be accessed and manipulated in a variety of ways, all independent of the physical location of the data on the storage media. A typical file system can be viewed as an extensive layer of services separating programs from the basic I/O capability of the operating system and hardware. Use of these services is similar to the use of lower level system functions and they are implemented using basically the same techniques and data structure philosophy.

As interactive use of computers increases, a lower percentage of work is run unattended in batch mode. While the discipline of scheduling batch work received much study in the 1960s and 1970s, many installations provide only minimal batch support today.

MOS is designed to support batch processing, but this is not the focus of the text. Simplifying the system structure and logic by reducing the range of supported functions allows a detailed study of fundamental techniques applicable to systems. From a systems programming aspect little is lost by minimizing coverage of file systems and job scheduling.

Each chapter contains a selection of graded problems. The five general types of problems are classified, and identified, as follows.

[DS] Data structure illustration and manipulation similar to examples presented in the chapters. Frequently, these problems require functional tracing of the algorithms to insure understanding of the techniques.

[Alg] Algorithm design, modification, and/or extension. These problems generally require that alternative strategies be investigated or more realistic error recovery methods be developed.

[Ana] Analysis and comparison of techniques and alternatives. These problems generally require an in-depth examination of techniques in order to justify and explain their applicability or performance.

[OS] Study and use of features available in the system used to support programming assignments of the class. These are generally problems which allow students to compare MOS with the system used by their laboratory computer.

[MOS] Moderate sized programming projects requiring use of the MOS I/O simulator (see Appendix B).

As stated earlier, one of the objectives of this text is to assist in the development of the skills necessary to use systems programming techniques to the maximum benefit. The material and problems suggested in the chapters are therefore biased in this direction. To assist in this mission, a simulator of the MOS hardware and software I/O environment has been developed. This teaching aid is compatible with the design used in the text and is available directly from the author in FORTRAN source form for copy costs. Appendix B provides a student overview of interfaces to the simulator.

It is not through the efforts of just the author that a book is written. The support, encouragement, suggestions, and above all the patience of friends and associates is indispensable. I sincerely thank all of those who provided their support. First, I would like to thank the several hundred students who have taken CSCI 4534 using various drafts of the text. They have not only provided support and suggestions but have also provided the means to test presentations, examples, projects, and homework problems. Without these students the book would never have been written. Earl Ellisor, Anthony Lekkos, and Dennis Taylor taught sections of the course through which they were able to provide insights, perspectives, and alternatives which I would not have otherwise considered. Earl and Anthony were particularly patient and helpful while working with the initial draft of the manuscript. A special thanks goes to Barbara Lawson who helped me immeasurably through her reviews, teaching efforts, suggestions with problem development and solutions, and assistance with the simulator. David Burris also provided many excellent review comments and references and extensive help developing problems for several chapters. Finally, I am appreciative of the patience and moral support of Kathryn, Karen, and Steve and the proofreading and typing support of Kathryn and P. C.

R. W. T.

Contents ▬▬▬▬▬▬▬▬▬

Appendix

CHAPTER 1

Introduction

This is a book about operating systems and systems programming. What is systems programming? Some claim that it is programming done by "systems programmers" working for a computer manufacturer developing software delivered with the computers. If this definition is accepted, not only is operating system development encompassed by systems programming, but also the development of text editors, BASIC interpreters, COBOL compilers, linkage editors, scientific subroutine libraries, word processors, data base management systems, and so on. As a matter of fact, since most manufacturers have many standard industrial and commercial software applications packages available to enhance the marketability of their products, development of such programs as general ledger, inventory control, and energy management might also be considered systems programming.

Obviously, this definition is too broad to define topics to be covered adequately in a single-semester course. How about defining systems programming as the development of "nonapplications" programs? But what is an applications program, as opposed to a systems program? It is a program that executes under the control of the operating system, generally in a nonprivileged mode. But under this definition, all programs listed in the preceding paragraph, except the very heart of the operating system itself, could be considered applications. Should text editors and compilers be classified as applications programs? Systems programming might, therefore, relate to the programming of the operating system itself and nothing more. Thus it follows that the only "systems programmers" are the programmers who develop or maintain operating systems.

Now we have a definition that is probably too restrictive. For the purposes of this text, **systems programming** will be defined as programming that uses techniques similar to those commonly found in operating systems, even though the use may not be in direct support of the operating system. Generally, these techniques will be used to develop software that can provide a programming

1

environment to others: for example, operating systems, file systems, compilers, interpreters, assemblers, linkers and loaders, and some data base management systems and utility software. Thus a systems programmer might be a person who possesses many of the skills of operating system developers but who is applying them in support of software of any flavor.

In the following chapters, the analysis of these techniques and the implementation of related software will be considered in the light of operating systems alone. There are many operating systems currently operational. Since their implementation details depend on the host hardware and the intended principal use of the computer, the actual code has little similarity from computer to computer. However, the general techniques are the same across most systems. Therefore, in the following chapters we discuss operating system programming techniques in terms of elements of the nucleus of a Mock Operating System (MOS), which is adequately realistic and reasonably representative of contemporary minicomputer operating systems.

MOS is greatly simplified in the extent of its capability and thus its design. For example, typical full-featured operating systems rely on 50 or so significant data structures for their mechanization. MOS has 10, all of which are comparatively small. This magnitude of simplification is typical of that used in defining the problems and developing solutions for various MOS components presented in subsequent chapters. The penalty for such simplification is a more limited set of supported features and occasionally the inability to resolve an obscure intrasystem conflict. Generally, a section in each chapter addresses the implications of these simplifications and suggests alternative approaches.

This is intended to be a very practical text with emphasis placed on understanding and analysis of the general problems facing systems programmers and the definition of data structures and the design of algorithms to solve those problems. All algorithms are presented in a structured English-oriented Process Design Language (PDL), defined in Appendix A. The syntax and semantics of the PDL are intended to be intuitively obvious to the reader and to be independent of the machine and implementation language. The PDL includes many structures provided by modern procedural languages such as Pascal. Examples of straightforward translation into very basic assembler, FORTRAN, and Pascal are included in Appendix A.

1.1
OPERATING SYSTEMS

What is an operating system, and why study it and the related programming techniques? An **operating system** is a collection of programs that control the use of computer resources, provide standard communication interfaces, and provide for continuous operation of a computer. Resources include memory, the processor, secondary storage, other input/output (I/O) devices, the clock, and many software items, such as service programs and global data structures.

The study of operating system techniques is important for several reasons.

1. To make maximum effective use of a tool, such as a computer, we must have an understanding of the environment related to its use. If we are to

implement a complex, on-line, multiuser scheduling or reservation system, it is necessary to have a thorough understanding of the memory and processor allocation strategies, the techniques used to access the disks and terminals, and the efficiencies and costs associated with various alternatives when they exist.

2. Many services are provided by operating systems. To be really effective in implementing applications, we should have an understanding of all available functions and the implications of their use.

3. When new equipment is to be acquired or existing equipment applied to new applications, someone must provide reliable evaluations of the proposed configurations and possibly modify and/or extend existing operating system components to meet new needs. For example, suppose that you are asked to assess the applicability of a given computer system to a new function that requires interfacing custom made equipment. First, the manufacturer's hardware and software must be evaluated, then estimates made for interfacing equipment. Finally, you may be faced with the job of actually implementing the software for the interfaces, perhaps within the budget constraints of typically optimistic estimates.

4. Many operating system programming techniques have direct applicability to common applications. For instance, an inventory control program may have very significant memory management problems for large data areas. Or a multiuser, on-line filing system may need to address data access conflicts between programs executing concurrently. An attached processor might need to be managed and shared among several executing programs. All these problems have direct counterparts within most operating systems. Learn the techniques, and use them to the benefit of your application.

MOS is a typical **multiprogramming system.** By this we mean that within the computer at any one time, there exists a set of executing programs that operate almost independently of each other, cooperate via synchronization signals, and compete for various resources.

Within the limits of MOS, the techniques for accomplishing the following topics are addressed:

General multiprogramming.
Memory management.
Program segmentation and overlaying.
Program swapping and paging.
System service calls.
Input and output.
Interrupt handling.
Concurrent processing.
Communication and coordination between processes.
Process-trap handling.
Time management.
Processor management (process scheduling and dispatching).

The remainder of this chapter provides a high-level overview of the structure and capabilities of MOS and a computer hardware environment to host it.

1.2
MOS OVERVIEW

An abstract view of MOS is that of a traffic signal located at a multiway intersection controlling access paths to managed resources and processes, as shown in Figure 1-1. Processes are central to the concept of modern operating systems. A **process** is a single execution of a program that is identifiable and controllable by the operating system (MOS in this case). It is a customer to which the operating system provides services. From the system point of view, it is an indivisible execution that can be performed concurrently with other processes. For example, each execution of a compiler, text editor, or user program is a process. If three users are using the editor program at a given instant, there exist three independent executions of the same program, and therefore three processes, one supporting each user.

Processes are the fundamental units of sequential work managed by MOS. They may or may not correspond to total user jobs. For example, a job might include compiling, linking, and executing a program. This requires a sequence of three program executions or steps: a compile step followed by a link step followed by execution of the application program with the user's input data. MOS will complete such jobs as sequences of processes, one for each of the steps in the job. In this environment some processes may be using programs that are also being used to service other processes. It is very likely that more than one execution of the compiler and linker will be in progress at any instant, even though there is only one compiler program and one linker.

The resources managed by the traffic controller/operating system are the computer system input/output devices, such as card readers, disks, and printers, the central processing unit (CPU), the clock or interval timer, and main memory. None of these resources are directly available to the users (the processes) on demand. Rather, each process must proceed through a standard interface to the control functions of MOS (the traffic signal) and then use the resources only when permission is granted. Similarly, MOS can temporarily suspend the use

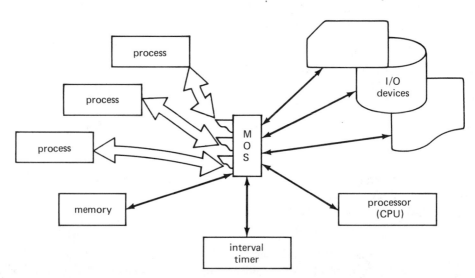

FIGURE 1-1   Major Components of the MOS Environment

of a resource by one process in favor of another, just as a traffic signal can suspend the traffic flow from one direction at an intersection in favor of flow from another direction.

I/O devices are simply external sources or destinations of data for the various processes and for MOS. They include such equipment as disks, tapes, printers, card readers, and terminals. Generally, processes do not access these devices directly; rather, MOS transfers data to and from them for the processes.

Unless otherwise stated, all discussions are limited to managing a single **processor** system, that is, a single CPU that executes noninterruptible instructions. (Interrupts are discussed at length in Chapter 5.) The CPU will never stop executing in the middle of an instruction. For example, the CPU can be switched from one activity to another after it has completed a multiplication operation and before it starts a subsequent addition, but it cannot switch activities in the middle of the multiplication. This mode of operation allows the environment of an activity to be saved by only considering registers visible to the programmer. Any internal CPU registers used to accomplish an instruction need not be a concern of any software, MOS or user written.

The **interval timer** shown in Figure 1-1 is a high-speed, precision countdown clock that signals the processor when a requested time interval has expired. The interval timer is in many respects similar to a common kitchen timer. With the support of this device, MOS manages all time-related activities.

The fourth managed resource is memory. **Memory** is the place of residence of the program that contains the currently executing instruction as well as any referenced data. Memory can be viewed as a contiguous array of randomly addressable, high-speed storage elements containing program instructions and data. As we shall see, not all programs currently active need to be totally within memory at any given time. Some may be temporarily on secondary storage when not actually using the processor. Other programs may have needed subprograms in memory while presently unneeded ones remain on secondary storage. Instructions can be fetched and executed only from memory; thus at least part of a program must actually reside in memory at the time its instructions are executed.

Considering the total environment, the MOS capability is sufficient to

Initiate and terminate processes.

Allocate memory to processes.

Move processes between memory and secondary storage.

Allocate memory for various internal services.

Control input/output operations and handle interrupts from the associated devices.

Provide a general multiprogramming environment by controlling allocations of the processor and other resources.

Provide for the communication and synchronization of multiple processes executing concurrently.

Allow activities to operate in a time-dependent manner.

The remaining chapters each concentrate on a specific aspect of operating system responsibility and present details of how MOS provides each function. The order of presentation is such that a comprehensive overview of the operating system is not needed to understand the function of the early components; however, a glimpse of the basic structure of the complete system follows. This

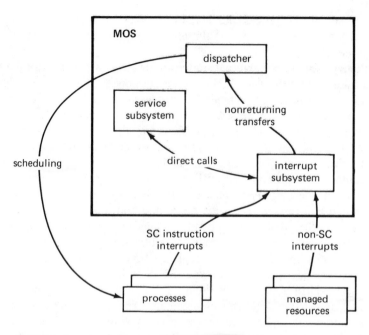

FIGURE 1-2 Basic MOS Components and Their Relationships with User Processes and Managed Resources

view will allow each subsequent topic to be placed in proper perspective as it is developed.

Figure 1-2 shows the major program components of MOS and the control paths between them, and Table 1-1 lists these components, their constituent elements, and the chapters in which each element is discussed. Notice from the figure that the only direct communication by user programs (processes) is with the interrupt subsystem. This is a typical restriction placed on user environments by the hardware and operating system and is justified in the interest of computer system integrity. By controlling the communication and access paths, the operating system is able to ensure the validity of each request for a

TABLE 1-1   Elements of MOS

MOS Component	Major Elements	Chapter(s)
Dispatcher	System list management	9
	Process scheduling	9
	Process swapping	3, 5, 9
	Time sharing	8, 9
Interrupt subsystem	Initial-phase handlers	5, 6, 8
	Second-phase handlers	5, 6, 7, 8
Service subsystem	Memory management	2, 3
	I/O-device management	4, 5
	Process synchronization	6, 7
	Process communication	6
	Process trap handling	6, 8
	Timer management	8

resource or service and thus protect both itself and other user programs and data from erroneous or malicious user programs. Processes cannot unilaterally acquire memory, manipulate the timer, transfer data to or from I/O devices, or communicate with each other. They may only request that such actions be performed on their behalf by MOS. A special interrupt-generating instruction is used to implement this interface. In MOS a **system call** (SC) instruction is assumed to exist for this purpose.

There is no direct path between processes and I/O devices. When a process needs to read a record, it executes an SC instruction, requesting MOS to perform the read for it. MOS first checks the request, then performs the operation, and eventually schedules the process to run again. The SC instruction is the service request mechanism in the MOS computer. Upon receiving the SC interrupt, the interrupt subsystem calls modules in the service subsystem to accomplish the functions requested.

As shown in Figure 1-2, the interrupt subsystem can also be invoked via managed resources such as the CPU, I/O devices, and timer. This path allows physical resources to signal the occurrence of significant events that require action by the software. It is by this path that the timer indicates its expiration, the printer signals that it has run out of paper, and the CPU switches control to MOS when a process attempts to execute an invalid instruction.

In addition to the protection from activities of the processes provided by the required use of the SC instruction, another layer of protection exists due to the centralization of list management and process scheduling functions. All elements of MOS invoke the dispatcher for updating process control list structures and for selecting the next process to use the CPU. The interrupt subsystem passes control to the MOS dispatcher upon completion of its functions, thus allowing centralized list updating and scheduling to be performed. Basically, all user programs can be thought of as executing as subprograms of the dispatcher program.

It is through the modules of the service subsystem that both MOS and the processes communicate with most resources. Within this element are standard functions for accomplishing input and output, starting logical timers, initiating processes, and communicating with processes. MOS sees only the basic resources of the computer system. It creates a higher-level machine for the process execution environment through the many functions provided by the service subsystem, each of which is available through a system call.

1.3
MOS DATA STRUCTURES

Let us now preview the forthcoming data structures of MOS. Ten global structures, around which MOS is designed, will be defined in detail. Figure 1-3 shows the nine structures that are created and maintained by the software and the access paths and linkages between them. (The remaining structure is a hardware-dependent interrupt vector which is not connected directly to the other structures. It serves as the tie between the host hardware and MOS and is treated in detail in Chapter 5.) As indicated by their names, each structure is assigned the basic task of representing the state of some event or element of the computer system and controlling its activity.

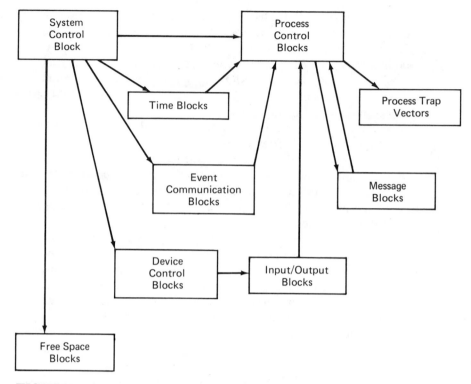

FIGURE 1-3   Functional View of the MOS Data Structure

Each manufacturer has its own operating system design based on the data structure organization best suited to the host equipment. MOS encompasses simplified but typical structures which are sufficient for instructional purposes. Names are selected to be functionally descriptive and do not necessarily parallel those of any particular manufacturer.

The **system control block** (SCB) is the master table through which the other structures are accessed. It is largely the domain of the dispatcher, although minor manipulation is done by other MOS elements. The SCB is to the entire operating system as the process control blocks are to their respective processes and device control blocks are to their related devices.

Process control blocks (PCBs) are used to maintain the status of each process within the computer and to track its assigned resources. The PCB is the control point through which MOS defines and governs the actions of a process. Connected to the PCBs are **message blocks** used by processes to communicate with each other. Also connected to each PCB is a **process-trap vector** (PTV), which allows the process to request permission to handle asynchronous activities or events normally processed by the operating system. For example, the PTV allows a process to maintain control when an arithmetic error or fault occurs and to be notified when a message has arrived from another process.

Similarly, **device control blocks** (DCBs) are used to manage input/output devices. They are to a device what the PCB is to a process, each describing the characteristics and state of an external device. **Input/output blocks** (IOBs) are used to track the progress and status of individual I/O operations. Since there may be many requests for access to a device, each I/O operation has its own IOB which relates it to the originating process. (An input/output operation is a device activity such as the reading of a record.) Each DCB may have many IOBs connected to it, each of which points to the process requesting the I/O operation.

As process events occur that are significant to MOS, **event communication blocks** (ECBs) are used to notify the dispatcher so that appropriate actions can be taken. For example, when a job starts or stops, these events must be communicated to the dispatcher, since they affect the set of processes competing for control of the CPU, the scheduling of which is a function of the dispatcher. All communications with the dispatcher are via ECBs.

Time blocks (TBs) are associated with interval-timer-related activities. They are approximately the timer equivalent of input/output blocks in that they relate timer operations to requesting processes. Note that there is no device control block for the timer since it is not considered an external device, is operationally much simpler than an input/output device, and the characteristics of the only timer connected to the computer do not vary. (The characteristics of input/ output devices are neither standard nor constant.)

The final structure shown in Figure 1-3 is the **free-space block** (FSB). This structure is used to keep track of available memory, that is, memory that is not currently allocated.

1.4
HOST HARDWARE ENVIRONMENT

The major components of the host hardware are shown in Figure 1-4. The single processor is connected to the interval timer, memory, and I/O devices through I/O controllers. Instructions executed by the CPU are capable of changing and reading appropriate timer registers. The timer, in turn, can interrupt the CPU when its count reaches zero. I/O controllers are used to physically connect devices to the CPU and to memory. Controllers provide a standard electrical and instruction interface for a wide variety of nonstandard I/O devices. In addition, they can relieve the CPU of some of the details of device communications.

Both the CPU and the I/O controllers may access memory. The controllers are said to have direct memory access (DMA) in such a configuration. Once

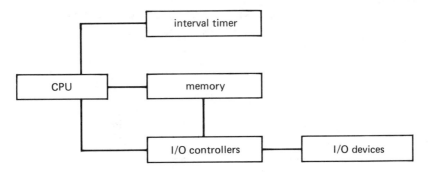

FIGURE 1-4 Basic Hardware Components

an I/O operation has been initiated by a CPU instruction, DMA allows transmission of data between memory and the devices without the use of CPU registers. When necessary, the I/O controllers can interrupt the CPU to signal significant events in the I/O environment, just as the timer signals its expiration event.

Throughout this text, the computer central processor is assumed to contain several general-purpose registers and several special-purpose registers. The main special register is called the **processor status word** (PSW), which defines the state or condition of the CPU at any given time. As shown in Figure 1-5, the PSW contains a **program counter** (the rightmost field) which generally specifies the address of the next instruction to be executed and a **condition code** which indicates the results of the last data operation performed. The condition code is assumed to differentiate between positive, negative, and zero values and to indicate error conditions, such as arithmetic overflow. The other fields of the PSW are the memory address map bit, interrupt bit mask, execution state bit, and run- or wait-state bit.

Chapter 3 will discuss memory partitioning and memory address mapping in conjunction with two other processor registers, the base and limit registers. The memory address map bit of the PSW will indicate whether this capability is enabled or disabled.

The interrupt mask is used to enable and disable various processor interrupt classes. In the MOS computer, this mask is a bit vector that can be used to prioritize the various classes of interrupts recognized by the processor. It also ensures that the processing of an interrupt can be completed before another interrupt of the same class is allowed. For example, the telephone system can block additional calls to a number until the first call is completed. (There is much more on interrupts in Chapters 5, 6, and 8.)

Placing the CPU in either the privileged system state or the normal process execution state will also be introduced in Chapter 5. For now it is sufficient to realize that there are certain instructions which generally must not be executed by programs of the user community, lest the integrity of the system be com-

run/wait	sys/proc	mask	map	condition code	program counter

Run/wait	Bit that indicates whether the processor is running or waiting (i.e., executing an instruction or not)
System/process	Bit that indicates operation in either the system state or process state, with the primary objective being the authorization to execute privileged instructions
Mask	Bit string that specifies which interrupt classes are enabled (e.g., I/O or timer interrupts)
Map	Bit that indicates whether or not memory address mapping is enabled
Condition code	Bit string that indicates the results of the last operation
Program counter	Address of the next instruction to be executed or of the current instruction if an error occurs

FIGURE 1-5 Processor Status Word Contents

promised. In the case of the MOS computer, all instructions that relate directly to input and output, modify the memory-mapping registers, or change the leftmost four fields of the PSW register are restricted to system-state use. The major significance of this restriction is that user programs may not perform I/O directly or manipulate memory protection or interrupt mask bits; MOS will perform these functions for such programs on request via the SC instruction interrupt interface. It is ultimately through the system/process-state bit, and the memory address mapping function, that MOS is able to protect itself and the processes from unauthorized use and access.

The last field of the PSW is the processor run- or wait-state bit. In all computer systems there are times when no programs are ready to execute. On these occasions, there are three basic ways of ''doing nothing.'' If provided by hardware, the processor can be placed in an interrupt-enabled state, which does nothing but wait for the occurrence of the next interrupt. This is what MOS does. Many processors have such states, and some indicate this state by the value of a run/wait bit in the PSW. Other processors execute a halt instruction explicitly but have no PSW wait bit to set. There are also processors that have no CPU wait state. In this case, when there is no useful work to be done, the operating system simply executes a single instruction loop to await the next event. An assembler instruction of the form

```
SPIN BRANCH SPIN    (equivalent to "label GO TO label")
```

accomplishes such a function. Regardless of which option is used, interrupts should be enabled so that productive work can be performed when it becomes available.

1.5
AN ALTERNATIVE SOFTWARE STRUCTURE

Figure 1-2 presented a software organization known as a **monolithic operating system structure.** MOS was shown to exist as an integrated program behind a wall, the gate through which is the SC instruction. All software external to MOS operates as application processes controlled by MOS.

There is an opposing system design philosophy which places much of the operating system itself into the process environment. In such a structure, only the dispatcher and those elements of the interrupt and service subsystems needed to create and sustain the process environment remain in the original configuration. This core of fundamental software elements is referred to as the **kernel** of the operating system.

Figure 1-6 illustrates a kernel-type structure for MOS. As will become apparent in subsequent chapters, there are often significant advantages to implementing selected system functions as processes. The principal advantage is concurrency of operation. **Concurrency** in a computer system refers to the support of multiple activities during the same period. In multiprogramming systems, processes operate concurrently, although with only one CPU they do not execute instructions simultaneously. (The cylinders of an automobile engine operate concurrently, but they receive their ignition spark serially, not simultaneously.)

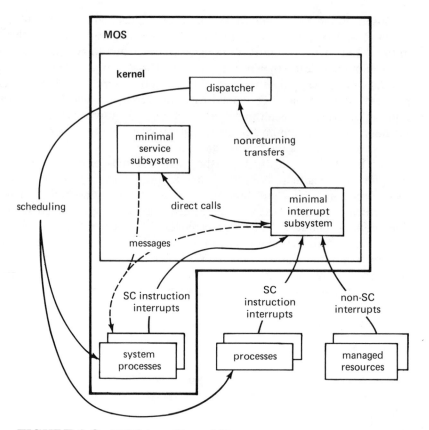

FIGURE 1-6   MOS in a Kernel Structure

Generally, system activities either within a monolithic operating system or within a kernel do not operate in a truly concurrent fashion as do the processes. Overall concurrency is therefore somewhat reduced during periods of operating system activity. Removing appropriate MOS elements from the kernel and making them processes therefore tends to offset this loss of parallelism, increase multiprogramming, and promote more productive computer operation. (One intent of multiprogramming is to keep as many activities as feasible going at once.)

In the remaining chapters each MOS function and its supporting data structures are presented using the monolithic structure of Figure 1-2. Then, for those functions that are candidates for execution as system processes, the alternative concurrent implementation is discussed and advantages and disadvantages presented.

PROBLEMS

1. Why must processes access the MOS service subsystem modules via the interrupt subsystem? Why not allow direct calls from the programs? [Ana]

2. Explain the differences between uniprogramming and uniprocessing. [Ana]

3. Explain the differences between multiprogramming and multiprocessing.
[Ana]

4. Give three examples of the benefit of multiprogramming on a single-user, uniprocessor system such as a home computer. [Ana]

5. List three examples of why processes need the capability to communicate with each other. [Ana]

6. Why must processes communicate via the service subsystem? Why not allow direct communication? (Consider the mechanics of direct process-to-process communication.) [Ana]

7. Refer to the high level language reference manuals for your multiprogramming computer system and locate the sections on system service functions. (These services will generally be callable via an intermediate library function that will execute the system call instruction for your program.) List and briefly summarize the interface for services

   a. To open a file, read a record, and close the file.
   b. For obtaining the current date and time of day.
   c. For starting and communicating with another process. [OS]

8. Refer to the processor manual and determine how your computer does nothing: that is, how a system wait state is implemented. [OS]

9. Why do computers provide for operation in either process or system mode?
[Ana]

10. Determine which instructions are privileged in your system. Why is their use restricted, and what does each of them accomplish? [OS]

11. MOS system services are invoked via a system call (SC) instruction. What software interrupt mechanism does your computer use to access services from the process environment? What is the assembler language format of such calls? [OS]

12. How many service functions are available to the assembler language programmer from your operating system? Code an example call to one service from each of the categories listed in problem 7. [OS]

13. Write a high-level-language program using low-level I/O function calls to the service subsystem to copy a file (see problem 7). [OS]

14. Write a program to fetch the time of day in milliseconds using a system service call (see problem 7). [OS]

15. Write a program to time 25 data transfer operations to disk. Run the program at different times of the day during a workday. Explain any variations in measured elapsed time. [OS]

16. What is the memory access speed of your computer; that is, how long does it take to fetch an instruction or data item? [OS]

17. What is the average instruction execution speed of your computer in millions of instructions per second (mips)? How long does it take to copy a data value from memory into a general register, to add the integer contents of two registers, and to divide the contents of a register by an integer value in memory? [OS]

18. Throughput is defined as the amount of useful work accomplished in a given period of time. It is frequently measured in jobs or processes per

hour. Discuss the impact of multiprogramming and multiprocessing on throughput. [Ana]

19. Assume three general categories of processes: primarily I/O work, primarily CPU work, and mixed. What effect do the proportions of these processes have on throughput? [Ana]

20. Simple process scheduling might involve running the highest-priority process until it finishes or until it is waiting for an event such as an I/O operation to complete, then running the next-highest-priority process, and so on. How does process priority assignment affect throughput, given an even mix of process types from problem 19? [Ana]

21. Turnaround time is defined as the elapsed time between submittal of work and receipt of results. Discuss the impact of multiprogramming and multiprocessing on mean turnaround time. [Ana]

22. For the categories of processes in problem 19, what effect does the mix of these processes have on mean turnaround time? [Ana]

23. How does process priority assignment affect mean turnaround time, given an even mix of process types from problem 19? [Ana]

CHAPTER 2

Multiprogramming and Basic Memory Management

The chief rationales for multiprogramming systems are improved resource utilization and decreased response time. Keeping the CPU, memory, and input/output devices productively busy tends to maximize the total amount of useful work accomplished in a given time. This is called maximizing **throughput.** **Response time** is the period between making a request and having the results available. Decreasing response time tends to increase the productivity of both interactive users and users submitting batch work.

To see the benefit of multiprogramming, consider a computer with 128K of available memory, a disk, a terminal, a card reader, and a printer. Let JOB1, JOB2, and JOB3 have the attributes shown in Table 2-1 and be submitted for execution at the same time. It is evident that serially processing this collection of jobs would result in gross underutilization of all resources when averaged over the required 30-minute time period. (JOB1 completes in 5 minutes, JOB2 completes 15 minutes later, and JOB3 completes only after 30 minutes has elapsed.) By assuming minimal processor requirements for JOB2 and JOB3 and continuous disk and printer use by JOB3, the average resource utilization,

TABLE 2-1 Sample Job Attributes

	JOB1	*JOB2*	*JOB3*
Type of job	Heavy compute	Heavy I/O	Heavy I/O
Duration	5 min	15 min	10 min
Memory required	25K	50K	40K
Need disk?	No	No	Yes
Need terminal?	No	Yes	No
Need card reader?	No	No	No
Need printer?	No	No	Yes

TABLE 2-2   Effects of Multiprogramming on Resource Utilization

	Uniprogramming	*Multiprogramming*
Processor utilization	17%	33%
Memory utilization	30%	67%
Disk utilization	33%	67%
Card reader utilization	0%	0%
Printer utilization	33%	67%
Elaspsed time	30 min	15 min
Throughput rate	6 jobs/hr	12 jobs/hr
Mean response time	18 min	10 min

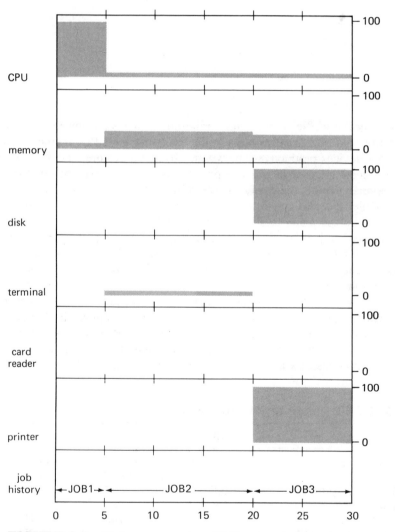

FIGURE 2-1   Uniprogramming Utilization Histogram

throughput, and response times are shown in the uniprogramming column of Table 2-2. Device-by-device utilization histograms are shown in Figure 2-1.

Now suppose that the jobs are run concurrently under MOS or some other multiprogramming operating system. Since there is little resource contention between the jobs, all three can run in nearly minimum time while coexisting with the others in the computer (assuming that JOB2 and JOB3 are allotted enough processor time to keep their input and output operations active). JOB1 will still require 5 minutes to complete but at the end of that time JOB2 will be one-third finished and JOB3 half finished. All three jobs will have finished within 15 minutes. The improvement is evident when examining the multiprogramming column of Table 2-2, obtained from the histograms shown in Figure 2-2.

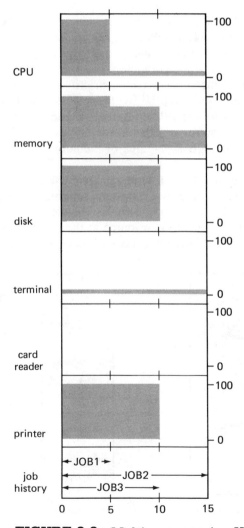

FIGURE 2-2 Multiprogramming Utilization Histogram

Effective resource use is obviously dependent on actual job mix. There are certainly mixtures that do not lend themselves to multiprogramming: for example, three compute-bound jobs. However, in general, multiprogramming gives users better turnaround, that is, faster service, and makes better use of expensive equipment.

2.1
PROCESS MANAGEMENT AND BASIC DATA STRUCTURES

Recognizing that a multiprogramming system is generally in continuous operation, with jobs continually starting and ending, the 15-minute period of concurrent processing of the sample jobs of Table 2-1 might result in memory configured as shown in Figure 2-3. Each program execution must be controlled by MOS. To accomplish this, MOS will need to maintain various facts regarding the processes (executions). This information is typically gathered into a table called a control block. In MOS this structure is called a **process control block** (PCB). A PCB is typically a few hundred bytes in size and is used to list the attributes and describe the current state of a single process. There is one PCB for each process existing in the computer system at any given time.

For now a PCB will contain the process name, priority, state (what it is doing), and identification of all resources used by the process. The priority of the process will determine when it is scheduled to receive control of the CPU and perhaps when it will gain control of other resources as well. The only resource presently tracked in the PCB is the area of memory occupied by its program.

Initially, processes will have two states: running and ready to run. As shown in Figure 2-4, transitions between these two states are determined by process scheduling policy as implemented in the MOS dispatcher (Figure 1-2). A process will be running if it has control of the CPU resource at the current time. The running process is referred to as the **current process.** Processes that are ready

FIGURE 2-3   Typical Changes in Memory Configuration for Multiprogramming

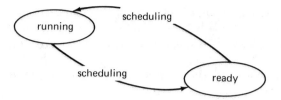

FIGURE 2-4   Transitions Between Process States due to Scheduling

to run but, due to scheduling policy, do not have control of the CPU (i.e., are not the current process) reside in a queue of ready processes called the **PCB ready queue.** As the complexity of MOS increases with increased function, many additional PCB lists will be needed.

MOS will need its own control block to keep pointers to the various lists and to track the total system state. A master table of pointers to other structures is normally found in an operating system. In MOS this table is called the **system control block** (SCB). The SCB resides at a fixed location in memory and serves to maintain the state of MOS itself. It contains pointers to other operating system data structures as well as information related to them. The SCB is principally a sequential list of head nodes for other lists.

The SCB has pointers to the PCBs of the current and ready processes as shown in Figure 2-5. In this example three processes exist and all are ready to make use of the CPU. Using its scheduling policy, the dispatcher has selected JOB1 to be the current process (currently using the CPU), thus leaving JOB2 and JOB3 on the ready queue. (In MOS all PCB lists are maintained in doubly linked structures to facilitate arbitrary node removal and queuing operations.)

Returning to the example three-job environment and associated memory configuration of Figure 2-3, it can be seen that not all memory is utilized at any one time and that a mechanism must exist to track available memory space. Unallocated memory is one of the resources of the operating system; therefore, a head node to a list of **free-space blocks,** the FSB list, exists in the SCB to track the unused space.

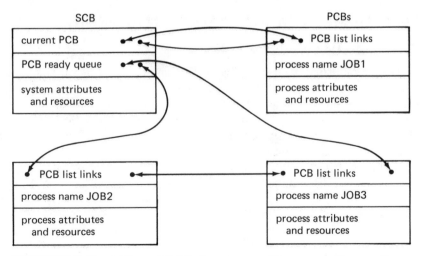

FIGURE 2-5   SCB and PCB Structures Corresponding to Process States

With this very simple environment of multiple programs executing concurrently, we have identified two needs for dynamically allocating memory. First, when a job enters the system, a PCB must be created, completed, and established in the appropriate list. Since the number of processes and PCBs existing at any time is unknown, space will be acquired dynamically for them. Conversely, when a process terminates, the space for its PCB will be released and made available for reuse by another process.

The second need for dynamically allocated memory is for space into which programs can be loaded and executed. Such program areas are typically large blocks of unpredictable size which may not even be constant for the duration of the process. The initial size of each program is determined by the number and type of instructions and the space for declared data. In addition, some programs will be written to have dynamic data, space for which will be acquired during execution. For instance, an assembler may reach a point at which the symbol table overflows. To continue processing it must request additional space for symbol data. The operating system must be able to service such requests.

Additional demands are placed on memory management functions when more processes are active than will actually fit in memory. This condition is normal in multiprogramming systems and requires the hardware and operating system to cooperate in creating **virtual memory.** Virtual memory is the appearance of having more memory in a computer than really exists, with the ability for processes to use that memory automatically, that is, without specific effort to do so. A simple way of providing the illusion of more memory is to shift programs and pieces of programs continuously between memory and secondary storage. With this strategy the program for a process is placed in memory, executed for a few milliseconds, and then copied back to disk. Its memory area is then used to load the program for some other process which is allowed to execute briefly, and so on. Such techniques demand that memory management functions reclaim vacated spaces as well as allocate new spaces for programs coming in from secondary storage.

2.2
DYNAMIC MEMORY MANAGEMENT STRATEGIES

2.2.1   Trying to Use a Linked Stack

Having established the need for allocation and recovery of variable sized areas of memory, let us now turn to the analysis of some of the strategies available. As a first approach, consider the simple technique of maintaining free space blocks in a linked stack. Deviation from strict stack operations will of course be needed since if the size of the top block on the stack is inadequate, subsequent blocks should be examined.

Suppose that an area of 10 words of available storage is initially structured into a single FSB and indexed by the pointer AVAILABLE:

The first two words of each FSB are used as link and size fields, respectively.

Now let a request be made for three words of storage. There are two reasonable choices from which to assign this space.

1. The first three words may be allocated, leaving a new FSB consisting of the last seven words of the initial area.
2. The last three words may be allocated, thereby shortening the existing FSB from 10 to seven words.

(It is obvious that the three words should not be taken from the middle of the FSB. Such an action would leave two small, separate blocks rather than one large one. This is called memory **fragmentation.** Generally, the more fragmented memory becomes, the less likely future allocation requests will be satisfied and the less efficient system operation becomes.)

If allocation is from the front of the block, three data value assignments must be made to update the stack: new link and size fields must be created in the fourth and fifth words and the AVAILABLE pointer must be changed to index the new FSB position.

However, if the second option is used and allocation occurs at the rear of the FSB, only one assignment need be made: the length of the FSB is decremented by three. Thus, for efficiency, the latter option is used, resulting in the configuration

Recalling that we have assumed a stack-type organization whenever possible, returning the three words to the availability pool would result in the very efficient add-to-top operation, producing

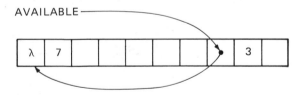

At this point any request for more than three words forces the strict stack technique to be abandoned in order to increase the chances of satisfying such requests. For example, a request for allocation of five words must take the last five from the node of size seven, producing

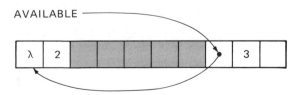

Even this simple example now produces a fragmented mess when the five-word area is released and placed on the top of the stack.

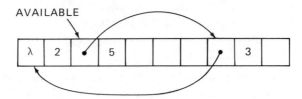

All 10 words are available, but the list structure hides this fact. No request for more than five words can be immediately satisfied even though none of the ten words in the space is in an allocated state. The available space has been fragmented into pieces too small to be used. Satisfying a large request would necessitate reorganization of the list to combine adjacent free blocks into a larger single unit. This "garbage collection" can be continuously accomplished as part of the normal returning of space if the stack strategy is abandoned.

2.2.2 Ordering the List by Block Address

If the FSB list is ordered by increasing address of the list nodes, it will appear as

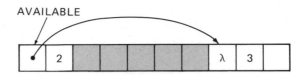

prior to releasing the middle five words. Now releasing this area makes the coalescing of adjacent areas a simple matter.

If the ordered FSB list is traversed until the insertion point of the new block is located and if a pointer to the previous node is maintained, the condition

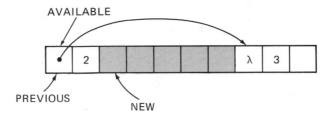

can be efficiently transformed into

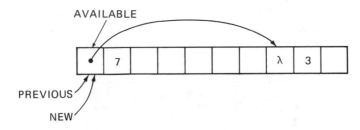

by the logic

> **If** PREVIOUS + size(PREVIOUS) = NEW, i.e., the new node is adjacent to the previous node
> **Then**
> >   Append the new block to the end of the previous FSB by increasing size(PREVIOUS)
> >   Set NEW pointer to PREVIOUS pointer value
> **EndIf**

This state can be further improved by the successor logic

> **If** NEW + size(NEW) = link(NEW), i.e., the new (and possibly combined) node is adjacent to its successor in the FSB list
> **Then**
> >   Append the successor to the new FSB by increasing size(NEW)
> >   Remove the successor from the FSB list
> **EndIf**

These two collection operations produce

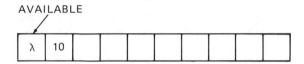

AVAILABLE

(Note that if either of these tests fails, additional logic is necessary to insert the new node into the list.)

2.2.3   Selecting a Free-Space Block

Best-Fit Method

Now that a mechanism for recovering space and combining it with adjacent FSBs has been defined, several heuristics for selecting an FSB from which to allocate space may be investigated. An obvious candidate strategy is to fit the allocation request into the smallest adequately sized block, that is, to minimize the residual space when an FSB of exactly the desired size is not in the list. (Notice that a residual of at least two words must be left to support formation of an FSB from the unused space.)

This **best-fit** method of allocation examines the FSB list for an exact match with the size of the requested area. If no match is found, but blocks exist of at least the required size plus two words, the new area is allocated from the rear of the smallest FSB of adequate size. This choice minimizes the residual and leaves the larger blocks untouched and available for future requests of large areas.

A few characteristics associated with the best-fit technique are important.

1. In general, one would not expect to find an FSB of exactly the desired size, so the entire FSB list must be searched to locate the smallest adequate FSB; thus a list of n blocks requires time proportional to n for allocation.

2. The search time could be cut by about one-half if the list were ordered by FSB size rather than by location, but such an ordering preempts the gains made in coalescing adjacent free areas and is thus not desirable. (Section 2.6 considers size ordering under a different set of circumstances.)

3. As we shall see later, this method tends to cause a proliferation of very small, perhaps unusable blocks which simply lengthen the list and further increase the search time. (Elson [1975] refers to this as the "tax the poor" method.)

4. Reasonably efficient use of available memory space is normally achieved; that is, the likelihood of satisfying a large number of requests is generally better with best-fit than with the methods that follow.

Worst-Fit Method

If minimizing the residual is not particularly attractive, how about maximizing it with the hope of keeping unusably small blocks from forming? The **worst-fit** method examines the list for the largest block, with a residual of two words or more. It allocates from the large blocks, hopefully leaving them large enough to be used again. Alas, the pendulum has now swung too far in the other direction. Worst-fit has the following characteristics.

1. The entire list must still be examined to guarantee that the largest block is located (it should, however, be a shorter list than with best-fit) requiring time proportional to n.

2. Traversal time could essentially be eliminated by ordering the list by nonincreasing FSB size, since the largest block would always be at the front of the list. However, the advantage for space combination is again lost with size ordering of the list.

3. Worst-fit will tax the rich until there are no large blocks, making it less likely that large requests can be satisfied at all.

4. This method tends to make very poor use of space. Its packing of allocated areas into memory is generally inefficient.

First-Fit Method

A disadvantage of both of these strategies is the search time when address ordering of blocks is used. Searches can be shortened if the first adequately sized block encountered is used without regard to residual considerations. In other words, when an adequate block is located, take it. The performance characteristics of this **first-fit** method are as follows.

1. Only part of the list is normally searched. A time proportional to $n/2$ would be expected except for item 3 below, which causes time related to n/c; $1 < c < 2$.

2. The list should not be ordered by size, either nonincreasing or nondecreasing, since this causes first-fit to degenerate to either best-fit or worst-fit, depending on which ordering is used. FSB combination is also complicated by abandoning the ordering-by-node-address organization.

3. Tests by Knuth [1975] indicated a tendency toward congregation of small, potentially useless FSBs near the front of the list, due to the repeated examination of this area. The FSB list will tend to lengthen with large blocks congregating near the rear, as can be seen in the data presented in Table 2-3.

   4. Efficiency of space utilization is intermediate between best-fit and worst-fit.

Even though first-fit tends to degrade with time due to the lengthening of the list by the small blocks, it consistently requires less time to run than do the previous two methods.

First-Fit-with-a-Roving-Pointer Method

It is the observation of small block collection near the front of the list that leads to a simple modification to first-fit allocation that makes a quantum leap to a dramatically faster strategy. If both small and large blocks were distributed more or less uniformly throughout the list, the search for an adequate block would terminate earlier. The small blocks associated with the first-fit method originate as residuals from repeatedly examining the nodes near the front of the list. This constant traffic further reduces their size as adequate blocks are located. The front of the list is simply worn out from continuous use. By observing this pattern we see a hint of the solution: skip the small block area by entering the list at a different point, thereby shortening the search and distributing the wear.

The **first-fit-with-a-roving-pointer** strategy begins each search at the point in the list where the previous search ended, that is, at the point of last success. This is accomplished by remembering the predecessor of the FSB selected for allocation. When invoked again, the algorithm begins its search with the node following this predecessor. When the end of the list is detected, the search skips to the front and continues until either successful allocation is accomplished or the original roving-pointer position is encountered. Completely cycling the list indicates an exhaustion of possibilities. These changes produce a circular FSB list with a roving pointer indicating the current starting point of the search, as shown in Figure 2-6.

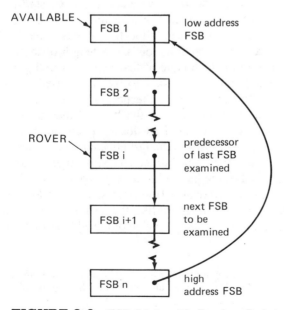

FIGURE 2-6   FSB List with Roving Pointer

The significant characteristics of this modified first-fit method are as follows.

1. The average length of the search is dramatically reduced to less than three examinations per execution (see Table 2-3 and Knuth [1975]).[1] The search time is therefore nearly constant and independent of the length of the list.

2. There is no advantage to ordering by size; therefore, areas being released should be inserted in order by address to facilitate coalescing with neighbors as described previously.

3. Since the same portions of the FSB list are not repeatedly assaulted and pounded to dust, there are fewer small blocks and those that are formed tend to be uniformly distributed throughout a generally shorter list. An area of the list in which large blocks have been depleted is allowed to rest and be rejuvenated, while the rover moves slowly through the rest of the list.

4. Space utilization is generally somewhat less efficient than simple first-fit, which is in turn less efficient than best-fit [Nielsen, 1977].

2.2.4   Returning a Block

Having produced a time-efficient allocation strategy, let us now consider the cost of returning released areas of memory to the FSB list. As demonstrated earlier, it is highly desirable to maintain the list in order of increasing block address. The simplest method of locating the appropriate position within the FSB list at which to insert a new block is by the normal technique of adding to an ordered linked list; that is, traverse the list from the beginning, remembering the predecessor, until the appropriate node position is located. The expected time cost of this free-space technique is therefore proportional to $n/2$. Thus the time for releasing space is on the same order as allocating space by the simple first-fit technique. This is a disappointing observation since we have substantially improved the allocation time by using a roving starting point. There is a large imbalance between the cost of allocating an area and the cost of returning it to the pool of available space. Allocation time is a small constant, but time for releasing space is a linear function of the length of the list.

An important spin-off from the technique of first-fit-with-a-roving-pointer is the ability to improve search times necessary to return released areas to the location-ordered FSB list. Notice that with the previous method, there exist two points of entry into the list: the head of the list and the current roving-pointer position. Since the list is ordered by location, all nodes having an address less than the rover (predecessor to the last allocation point) are between the head of the list and the rover, and all nodes with larger addresses are between the rover and the end of the list. With these two pointers, search times can be reduced again simply by comparing the address of the released area to the roving-pointer value and then either starting the search at the head of the list or at the rover, depending on the relative value of the address of the released area.

---

[1] Knuth's tests were run using the roving-pointer technique combined with the boundary-tag method described in Section 2.4. He observed an average of 2.8 node examinations per allocation request.

The speed imbalance is not removed but it has become less pronounced. Allocating a block using the first-fit-with-a-roving-pointer method requires an average of two to three node examinations, while returning the area requires approximately $n/3$ examinations, where n is the number of nodes in the list. (See Knuth [1975] for a derivation of expected release time.)

2.3
DYNAMIC MEMORY MANAGEMENT ALGORITHMS

Now consider the mechanization of the first-fit-with-a-roving-pointer method. In general, each FSB has three parts: a link field to the next FSB in the list, a size field to indicate the total amount of space contained in the FSB (including the size and link fields), and an unused area equal to the size of the FSB less the two previous fields.

Algorithms for adding to and removing from linked lists are frequently simplified if the list is never allowed to be completely empty. Typically, this is accomplished by defining a head node which is always accessible and which is never removed from the list (the "empty" list thus being a list containing only the head node). An appropriate structure for the FSB head node has three fields, the first of which is a link to the first real FSB in the list, the second a size field always containing a zero (to prevent allocation of this node), and a third field containing the current value of the roving pointer.

Figure 2-7 illustrates the logical configuration of the FSB list for the example of the preceding section just prior to returning the area of five words. (Recall that from an initial node of 10 words, blocks of three and five words had been allocated from the rear, and the block of three then released.) Notice that the list has been made circular to facilitate switching back to the front of the list once the last node has been examined. Since the last FSB examined in the example was the node with size = 2, which is preceded by the head node, the rover currently points to the head node.

Algorithms 2-1 and 2-2 present the detailed logic for allocating and returning space. Notice that care has been taken to specify allocation sizes with a minimum of two words and to leave nonzero residuals of at least two words. These minimums are established to guarantee adequate space for creation of FSB elements containing the required link and size fields.

In practice, the operating system memory management services do not depend on valid input to maintain the integrity of the FSB list. All inputs must

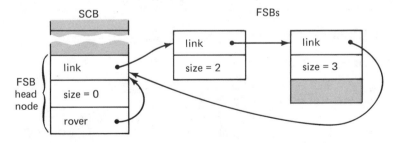

FIGURE 2-7 Free-Space Block List Organization

Begin GET_MEMORY

> Allocate space from a list of FSBs using the first-fit-with-a-roving-pointer technique
>
> Input   — SIZE of area desired (must be two or more words)
>   — SCB containing the FSB head node as defined in Figure 2-7
>
> Output — STATUS of the GET_MEMORY operation
>   — LOCATION of the area, if allocation is successful
>   — FSB list structure is modified
>
> Assume — Minimum allocation of two words in order that a returned area may be structured into an FSB (see Algorithm 2-2)

Default STATUS to failure
Initialize PREVIOUS pointer to ROVER from the head node

Do

> Set CURRENT to link(PREVIOUS)
>
> **If** the current block is adequate, i.e., size(CURRENT) = SIZE or size(CURRENT) ≥ SIZE + 2
> **Then** [Allocate space from the current block]
>
>> Set LOCATION to the last SIZE words of the block, i.e., to CURRENT + size(CURRENT) − SIZE
>>
>> **If** all of the block is needed, i.e., LOCATION = CURRENT
>> **Then** [Delink the FSB from the list]
>>> Set link(PREVIOUS) to link(CURRENT)
>> **Else** [Shorten the FSB]
>>> Decrement size(CURRENT) by SIZE
>> **EndIf**
>>
>> Save a new roving-pointer value in the head node, i.e., set ROVER to PREVIOUS
>> Change STATUS to success
>
> **Else**
>> Advance PREVIOUS to CURRENT to continue searching
> **EndIf**
>
> **Until** an area is allocated or the list is exhausted, i.e., STATUS = success or CURRENT = ROVER
> **EndDo**

End GET_MEMORY

Algorithm 2-1   First-Fit-with-a-Roving-Pointer Allocation

be validated. The normal action upon detection of incorrect conditions is to abort execution of the calling process.

Code to validate the input SIZE is essential. In addition, when the tests for adjacency with neighboring blocks are made, the FREE_MEMORY routine should also test for overlapping blocks; that is, does the new area extend beyond the starting address of the successor or begin before the end of the predecessor?

Begin FREE_MEMORY

Release space and return it to a location ordered
list of FSBs

Input   – LOCATION of the area being returned
         – SIZE of area being returned (must be two
             or more words)
         – SCB containing the FSB head node as
             defined in Figure 2-7

Output – FSB list structure is modified

Assume – Minimum allocation of two words in order
             that a returned area may be structured
             into an FSB
         – Head node has a smaller address value than
             any node in the FSB list, thus preventing
             it from being merged as a successor to
             some new FSB
         – LOCATION and SIZE are valid and blocks do
             not overlap

[Locate the insertion point in the FSB list]
Initialize a NEW index to the node at LOCATION
If the area goes in the front part of the list, i.e., NEW < ROVER
Then
    Initialize PREVIOUS to point to the head node
Else
    Initialize PREVIOUS to ROVER from the head node
EndIf
Initialize CURRENT to link(PREVIOUS)
While the insertion position is not found, i.e., CURRENT < NEW and
    CURRENT ≠ FSB head node
Do
    Advance PREVIOUS to CURRENT
    Advance CURRENT to link(PREVIOUS)
EndDo
[Merge the new area with its predecessor or create a new FSB]
If the predecessor is adjacent to the new area, i.e.,
    PREVIOUS + size(PREVIOUS) = NEW
Then [Merge with predecessor]
    Set NEW to PREVIOUS
    Increment size(PREVIOUS) by SIZE
Else [Create a new FSB and link it to the predecessor]
    Set size(NEW) to SIZE
    Set link(PREVIOUS) to NEW
EndIf
[Merge the new area with its successor or link the new area to it]
If the new area is adjacent to the successor, i.e.,
    NEW + size(NEW) = CURRENT
Then [Merge the area with its successor]
    Set link(NEW) to link(CURRENT)
    Increment size(NEW) by size(CURRENT)
    If ROVER will no longer be valid, i.e., CURRENT = ROVER
    Then [Update roving pointer in head node]
        Set ROVER to NEW
    EndIf
Else [Link the new FSB to its successor]
    Set link(NEW) to CURRENT
EndIf

End FREE_MEMORY

Algorithm 2-2   Releasing Space with a Roving Pointer

2.4
BOUNDARY-TAG METHOD

The techniques of Section 2.3 concentrated on time efficiency when allocating space, given the constraint that free blocks were ordered by location to facilitate coalescing when adjacent. As indicated by the summary tables in Section 2.5, a very time efficient allocation strategy was developed, but the releasing of space required much more search time than did allocation. This disparity exists because address ordering was maintained within the list. Let us now return to the initial assumption for allocation and release of space: the linked stack.

2.4.1   A Return to the Modified Linked Stack

Maintaining the FSB list in a stack obviously has the minimum release time, since it simply links the FSB to the top of the stack in a constant amount of time. But if this approach is followed, how can adjacent FSBs be combined efficiently, or, more explicitly, how can one detect that a neighbor of a new FSB is also available, since address ordering does not exist?

Consider the environment of an available block of memory:

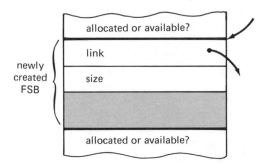

Is it adjacent to other available blocks? The two previous algorithms depend on the node addresses and sizes to determine the state of neighboring blocks of memory. Specifically, if the location of the predecessor in the list plus its size equaled the location of the new FSB, all space between the origin of the predecessor and the FSB was contained within the predecessor. Detection of this condition allowed the predecessor to be extended to encompass the new block. If the FSB list is not ordered by location, this logic is obviously inadequate.

So how can the state of neighboring blocks be determined efficiently if address ordering of the FSB list is abandoned in favor of a simple stack structure? The key is to be able to examine the areas of memory physically adjacent to the new FSB to determine the state of the neighbors. To do this, all areas must be labeled or tagged to indicate their state. Since a block can be a predecessor of one new FSB and a successor to another, it may be examined from either end. Tags must therefore appear at both ends of each block, for example,

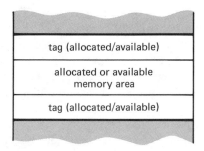

tag (allocated/available)

allocated or available
memory area

tag (allocated/available)

When the memory release routine needs to determine the state of memory adjoining a new area, it can simply examine the tag located in the word immediately in front of the new block and the tag located in the word immediately beyond the block. Thus the ability to determine the allocation state of all blocks of memory is provided.

Now suppose that a new FSB is determined to have neighboring blocks which are also available. As seen earlier, the new block should be combined with these adjacent FSBs. But to coalesce with the predecessor area requires changing the size field in the front of the predecessor, while combining with the successor area requires delinking that FSB from the list. Both of these actions reintroduce the potentially expensive search loop into the free algorithm, elimination of which was the very reason the stack approach was revived.

Consider merging with the predecessor. The previous technique of changing the size of the predecessor would work if the size field of that block could be located. Thus, information for locating the front of an FSB is needed at the back of the block, in addition to the tag indicating status. With this information the size field of the predecessor can be located and incremented to reflect the merge.

As for merging with the successor, if examination of the front tag of a successor block in memory indicates adjacent available memory, how is it combined with the new block? The size of the new (and possibly merged area) can be incremented easily enough, but recall that the successor must be removed from the FSB list also. (Refer to the successor logic in Algorithm 2-2.) Delinking a block from a linked linear list requires the location of the previous node in the list so that its link field can be changed to skip the removed node. How do we efficiently locate the predecessor of a node? The problem is much easier if the list is doubly linked, with each node containing pointers for locating both predecessor and successor list nodes. Thus efficiency objectives dictate that the free-space blocks in a stack should not only contain size and tag fields, but also link fields to both the predecessor and successor in the stack.

From this analysis the final form of the free-space blocks for the boundary-tag method of memory management is determined to contain

1. A front boundary tag indicating an available state.
2. The size of the FSB including all management fields.
3. Predecessor and successor link fields to other FSBs in the stack.
4. Unused space, if any.
5. Information to locate the front of the FSB when examined from the rear (either the size or a pointer to the front of the block).
6. A rear boundary tag indicating an available state.

Two of these items are of a binary nature. The tags indicate either allocated, "on," or available, "off." For space efficiency, these tags may be combined with other information in the blocks to reduce the space overhead of FSBs and thus reduce the size of the minimum allocation and minimum residual. (Recall that unallocated space from an FSB must be of sufficient size to allow it to be formed into an FSB itself and that returned space must also be at least this minimum size.)

The success of this method depends on reliably determining the state of all memory by examination of the tags adjacent to the boundaries of a new block. Thus allocated blocks must also contain tag information. The appropriate information for allocated blocks is thus:

1. A front boundary tag indicating an allocated state (the size may also be included at no cost in space, since a whole word is needed for tag integrity anyway).
2. Allocated space as required by the application.
3. A rear boundary tag indicating an allocated state.

Figure 2-8 summarizes the complete structure necessary for supporting the boundary-tag technique of dynamic memory management. As usual, it is desirable to prevent combination of the head node with any adjacent FSB. The mechanism to prevent this is the setting of the tags of the head node to "al-

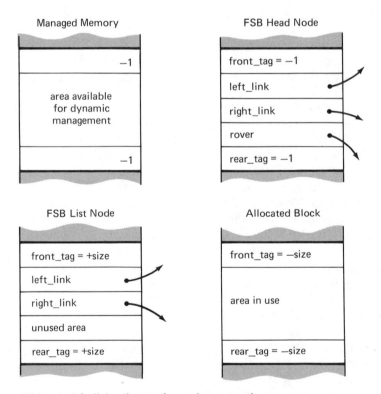

Where the left_link points to the predecessor node in the FSB list and right_link points to the successor node.

FIGURE 2-8 Data Structures for Boundary-Tag Technique

located''; thus, even though the head node is linked into the FSB list, it has a permanently allocated state and will never be joined to any adjacent free area.

x   It is also important to prevent examination of memory that is beyond the range of the space being managed, since the contents of such areas are undefined. This can be accomplished by establishing ''allocated'' tag words at the address extremes of the managed space. These values signify that memory beyond the tags is permanently allocated.

2.4.2 Implementing the Boundary-Tag Technique

Let us now turn to the algorithms implementing the boundary-tag technique by use of an example. Suppose that memory is initially configured into a single FSB and that five consecutive allocation requests have been received. The physical structure of memory and the logical organization of the FSB list would be

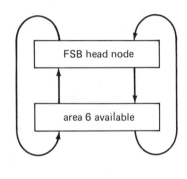

If area 2 is now released, the free algorithm, TAG_FREE_MEMORY, would examine the boundary tag at location(area 2 − 1) and determine that the preceding space is allocated and thus not in the FSB list. A new FSB for area 2 would therefore be formed and added to the top of the stack. Subsequent examination of the tag at area 2 + size(area 2) (i.e., the front of area 1) would also fail to locate a neighboring FSB, so no nodes would be deleted from the list. The physical and logical states would thus be

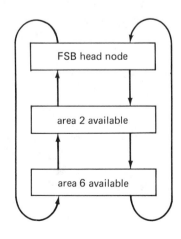

Notice that no search loops were utilized in this operation. All referenced fields were accessed directly.

Now let area 5 be released. Examination of location(area 5–1) reveals the presence of an existing FSB, area 6. Using its size, contained in the rear_tag field, locates the origin. The physical predecessor is now increased in size to include the new area. (Area 6 has grown to include area 5.) The link structure of the stack is unchanged since subsequent examination of location(area 5 + size(area 5)) indicates an allocated area 4.

Next, area 3 is released. This causes a new FSB to be created and added to the stack since no FSB exists for the area physically preceding area 3. Examination of the following area does, however, reveal an FSB, area 2, which is then merged with the newly created FSB, area 3, and delinked from the list. The structure is now

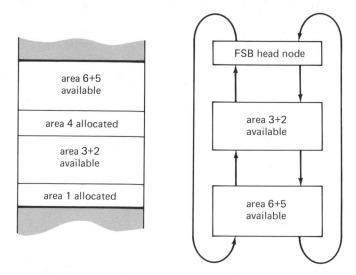

Should area 4 now become available, the stack would be reduced to a single FSB element plus the head node through the following sequence of steps.

1. Examination of location(area 4-1) detects an FSB, area 6 + 5, so area 4 is merged with that block.
2. Examination of the location following this combined block, that is, location(area 6 + size(area 6 + 5 + 4)), detects another FSB, area 3 + 2. This block is combined with block area 6 + 5 + 4.
3. Removal of the old area 3 + 2 from the list completes the operation.

Again, no list traversal was necessary for releasing the four blocks and coalescing when appropriate.

Algorithms 2-3 and 2-4 present the detailed logic for accomplishing dynamic memory management using the structures defined. They combine the approach of first-fit-with-a-roving-pointer with the structure of the boundary-tag technique. Notice the striking similarity to Algorithms 2-1 and 2-2. Differences are primarily in linked list management, using a double-linked structure rather than a single linked one, and in the maintenance of the boundary tags. (A significant point in the tag maintenance functions is the required overallocation of the requested area by two words of memory. This overallocation is needed to

Begin TAG_GET_MEMORY

⎡ Allocate space from a list of FSBs using the
first-fit-with-a-roving-pointer technique for
blocks containing boundary tags

Input — SIZE of area desired (must be two or
more words)
— SCB containing the FSB head node

Output — STATUS of the TAG_GET_MEMORY
operation
— LOCATION of the usable area, if
allocation is successful
— FSB list structure is modified

Assume — The environment and structures defined
in Figure 2-8 and a minimum allocation
of two words in order that a returned
area may be structured into an FSB
— A minimum nonzero residual of four
words is required ⎤

Set the EFFECTIVE_SIZE to SIZE plus two more words for tags in the allocated
area
Default STATUS to failure
Initialize CURRENT to ROVER from the head node

Do

    Set CURRENT to right_link(CURRENT)
    If the current block is adequate, i.e., front_tag(CURRENT) = EFFECTIVE_SIZE
        or front_tag(CURRENT) $\geq$ EFFECTIVE_SIZE + 4
    Then [Allocate space from the current block]

        Set LOCATION to the last EFFECTIVE_SIZE − 1 words of the block,
            i.e., to CURRENT + front_tag(CURRENT) − EFFECTIVE_SIZE + 1
        If all of block is needed, i.e., EFFECTIVE_SIZE = front_tag(CURRENT)
        Then [Delink the FSB from the list]
            Set right_link(left_link(CURRENT)) to right_link(CURRENT)
            Set left_link(right_link(CURRENT)) to left_link(CURRENT)
        Else [Shorten the FSB]
            Decrement front_tag(CURRENT) by EFFECTIVE_SIZE
            Set new rear_tag(CURRENT) to front_tag(CURRENT)
        EndIf
        Set both tags(LOCATION) to allocated, i.e., address LOCATION-1 and
            LOCATION + EFFECTIVE_SIZE − 2 to − EFFECTIVE_SIZE
        Save a new roving-pointer value in the head node; i.e., set ROVER
            to left_link(CURRENT)
        Change STATUS to success

    EndIf

    Until an area is allocated or the list is exhausted, i.e., STATUS = success
        or CURRENT = ROVER
    EndDo

End TAG_GET_MEMORY

ALGORITHM 2-3   Boundary-Tag Method of Allocation

Begin
TAG_FREE_MEMORY

> Release space and link it in to a stack of tagged FSBs
> Input   – LOCATION of the area to be returned
>   – SCB containing the FSB head node
> Output – FSB list structure is modified
> Assume – The environment and structures defined in Figure 2-8
> Note   – Use of boundary tags requires that entire areas be released as a unit
>   – Since the tags also contain the size of the areas, no input SIZE is needed

Set the origin of the NEW FSB to LOCATION − 1, i.e., to the front_tag
Set the EFFECTIVE_SIZE to -front_tag(NEW)

If the area preceding NEW is also an FSB, i.e., rear_tag(NEW-1) > 0
Then [Combine the NEW block with its physical predecessor]
    Set NEW to the beginning of the predecessor, i.e., to NEW - size stored
        at NEW-1, which is rear_tag(previous node)
    Increment front_tag(NEW) by EFFECTIVE_SIZE
    Set rear_tag(NEW) to front_tag(NEW)
Else [Add the block as a new FSB at the front of the list]
    Set front_tag(NEW) to EFFECTIVE_SIZE
    Set rear_tag(NEW) to EFFECTIVE_SIZE
    Set left_link(NEW) to point to the FSB head node
    Set right_link(NEW) to right_link(head node)
    Set left_link(right_link(head node)) to NEW
    Set right_link(head node) to NEW
EndIf

Set SUCCESSOR to point to the area just beyond the NEW FSB, i.e., to
    NEW + front_tag(NEW)
If the new, possibly merged, block is adjacent SUCCESSOR, i.e.,
    front_tag(SUCCESSOR) > 0
      Then [Merge SUCCESSOR with the NEW block and remove the SUCCESSOR from FSB list]
    Increment front_tag(NEW) by front_tag(SUCCESSOR)
    Set rear_tag(NEW) to front_tag(NEW)
    Set left_link(right_link(SUCCESSOR)) to left_link(SUCCESSOR)
    Set right_link(left_link(SUCCESSOR)) to right_link(SUCCESSOR)
    If ROVER will no longer be valid, i.e., ROVER = SUCCESSOR
    Then [Update the roving pointer in the head node]
        Set ROVER to NEW
    EndIf
EndIf

End TAG_FREE_MEMORY

ALGORITM 2-4   Releasing Space with Boundary Tags

support tag field formation in the allocated areas.) Algorithm 2-3 parallels Algorithm 2-1 to the extent possible. For example, GET_MEMORY ensured nonzero size residuals of two or more words for FSB formation and TAG_GET_MEMORY similarly demands residuals of four or more words. However, since block sizes are automatically maintained in the boundary-tag method, any block of sufficient size could be allocated and if a one-, two-, or three-word residual remained it could just be appended as an overallocation reflected in the size field. Finally, observe that the TAG_FREE_MEMORY routine has no search loop and is thus exceedingly fast (see the test results presented in Table 2-3).

2.5
COMPARISON OF ALGORITHM PERFORMANCE

2.5.1 Other Methods

There are other strategies for dynamic memory management which have not been covered here: for example, the buddy system, described by Knuth [1975], and release-match and age-match, analyzed by Beck [1982]. Under proper circumstances these methods may out perform even best-fit in efficiency of memory utilization. However, achieving high efficiency frequently depends on the availability of application-specific knowledge of such memory usage characteristics as the size and/or frequency distributions of future allocations, how long each allocated block is to be retained, and in what order blocks are to be released.

One such method is a variation of the basic first-fit: the **double-ended-first-fit** method. This approach maintains the FSB list as a location-ordered doubly linked list and uses a threshold value to decide in which direction to search the list. Allocation requests for sizes less than the threshold are serviced by searching from the front of the list, while searches for sizes larger than the threshold start from the rear. There are two rationales behind this method. First, large blocks congregate in the rear area of the FSB list when using the simple first-fit method. Searching the list in reverse would locate them quickly. Second, if allocated areas are segregated by size, there will be a tendency to reduce the mixing of small and large blocks as they are allocated and released. Overall, an average search of about one-fourth of the list is expected.

2.5.2 Testing the Various Techniques

Table 2-3 presents data resulting from tests of all techniques discussed in this chapter. The tests used both uniformly distributed and normally distributed random data. Requests were issued for block sizes between two and 100 words and allocated blocks were held for times between one and 100 program cycles. The durations were independent of block size. Each test operated for 1000 cycles. During each cycle two pseudorandom numbers were generated. The first number determined the size of the allocation request and the second the number of cycles the block was to be held before being released. A time-ordered queue of release requests was then built. Each cycle therefore consisted of two parts: allocation of a block and release of all blocks queued to expire during that cycle.

After the 400 cycles, performance counters in the search loops were reset. This permitted accumulation of statistics during the last part of the tests only, when the FSB list had reached a more or less equilibrium state. The same pseudorandom number sequence was used in testing all methods. As can be seen in the summaries, the data distribution had little effect on the relative performance of the algorithms.

TABLE 2-3 Comparison of Dynamic Memory Management Techniques
a. Using Uniformly Distributed Data

Method	Final FSB Node Sizes (Left to Right, Top to Bottom)					FSBs < 10 Words	Maximum Number of Allocations		Cycles Per:		Speed Improvement Relative to Best-Fit	Minimum Space Required
							Of 50	Of 100	Get	Free		
Best-fit	1270	2	31	25	333	9	50	23	20.0	11.5	—	3790
	3	5	7	9	268							
	308	3	44	12	22							
	19	253	154	32	2							
	7	7										
Worst-fit	162	72	65	189	24	0	45	17	22.5	12.0	−10%	4588
	224	193	164	125	164							
	46	135	192	249	227							
	56	184	144	144	57							
First-fit	6	3	4	7	12	7	48	23	11.5	12.3	24%	4113
	5	29	23	11	44							
	10	2	5	41	47							
	89	58	15	23	111							
	24	2247										
Double-ended-first-fit*,†	6	4	8	5	4	8	49	23	5.9	6.6	60%	4048
	5	4	6	47	15							
	44	2200	66	140	39							
	56	22	20	67	10							
	47											
First-fit-with-a-roving-pointer	3	29	87	86	13	1	46	19	1.4	8.5	69%	4151
	44	27	138	96	145							
	355	701	29	86	317							
	384	83	42	151								
First-fit-rover using boundary tags	46	31	162	180	673	1	44	19	1.6	1.0	92%	4356
	125	183	29	33	27							
	86	23	215	331	289							
	282	6‡										

b. Using Normally Distributed Data

Method	Final FSB Node Sizes (Left to Right, Top to Bottom)	FSBs < 10 Words	Maximum Number of Allocations — Of 50	Of 100	Cycles Per: Get	Free	Speed Improvement Relative to Best-Fit
Best-fit	1967 299 17 8 42 / 8 2 4 48 142 / 3 23 44 22 16 / 92 3 4 2 53 / 3	9	48	22	21.9	12.0	—
Worst-fit	244 167 247 199 223 / 164 159 207 132 11 / 207 100 311 169 129 / 133	0	49	22	17.9	9.4	19%
First-fit	13 4 9 6 11 / 26 5 18 8 50 / 46 5 26 27 14 / 22 11 49 43 110 / 2299	6	48	23	11.4	12.0	31%
Double-ended-first-fit [*][†]	9 11 4 14 23 / 1927 359 267 70 5 / 19 21 23 49	3	51	24	5.4	6.0	66%
First-fit-with-a-roving-pointer	8 60 68 75 182 / 108 158 173 147 25 / 32 20 1189 136 421	1	49	21	1.1	5.4	81%
First-fit-rover using boundary tags	260 64 1420 91 84 / 205 24 41 43 25 / 7 130 275 31 9[§]	2	45	20	1.3	1.0	93%

[*]Using the optimum threshold for the given test data (see Table 2-4 for the uniformly distributed data).
[†]One word less total available space due to an extra link field in head node.
[‡]Ninety-five words in use as tags of allocated blocks and a larger head node.
[§]Ninety-three words in use as tags of allocated blocks and a larger head node.

Of particular interest are the columns of Table 2-3 that summarize block sizes, speed improvement when compared to best-fit, and the minimum space required to complete the tests successfully. Best-fit produced the largest number of small blocks (fewer than 10 words), while worst-fit and the various first-fit techniques generated very few such blocks. This contributed to the execution speed differences seen between best-fit and first-fit.

The fourth and fifth columns tabulate the number of consecutive average and large size allocations (50 and 100 words) which could still be satisfied at the end of the test. The number of such potential allocations is related to the memory packing efficiency and to the degree of fragmentation produced by each algorithm. In this category of comparison the roving-pointer methods performed worse than the other methods, indicating that they sacrificed space utilization to gain part of their speed.

2.5.3   A Choice of Methods

From the data presented, we are drawn to the conclusion that best-fit, first-fit-with-a-roving-pointer, and the boundary-tag method are the preferred techniques, depending on the relative importance of speed and memory utilization. Best-fit and the double-ended-first-fit method tended to provide superior utilization of memory, as evidenced by the number of large requests that could still be satisfied at the end of the test. (Memory fragmentation was less than with the other methods.) With uniformly distributed data, these methods were also found to satisfy the test set of allocation requests using a smaller total area of managed storage (see the last column in Table 2-3a).

Considering algorithm speed, the two roving-pointer techniques were observed to complete the tests significantly faster than best-fit and somewhat faster than did the double-ended method. The double-ended approach is attractive in its relatively efficient use of memory while maintaining a reasonable speed improvement over best-fit. Notice, however, that the results presented for this method are based on the optimal threshold value for the data involved. Table 2-4 shows the parametric analysis results of varying the threshold to determine the values producing minimum search times. For reasonably random requests, this value could be continuously computed by the algorithm; however, nonrandom or cyclic data could have very adverse effects on the performance of the double-ended method.

Since the search time for releasing blocks of memory is eliminated in the boundary-tag method, it is by far the fastest technique. However, this method suffers a rather severe integrity exposure. For the boundary-tag technique to function properly, all tags, both in allocated and available blocks, must be accurately maintained. If space is allocated for controlled operating system use, this exposure is minimal and the advantages therefore probably outweigh the risks. Depending on the uncontrolled applications to maintain tag integrity is, however, out of the question.

If memory is allocated in blocks corresponding to physical page boundaries and if memory protection is available, the other methods can shield the vital FSB management fields from overstore errors by application programs. However, the tags of allocated blocks for the boundary-tag method must obviously be in the same memory page as the assigned space and therefore are vulnerable to destruction by application errors. This problem, accompanied by the com-

TABLE 2-4   Effects of Threshold Value on Double-Ended Method for Uniformly Distributed Data

Threshold Size	Cycles Required Per:		
	Get	Free	Get/Free Pair
30	7.0	7.7	14.7
35	6.7	7.5	14.2
40	6.3	6.9	13.2
45	6.2	6.8	13.0
48	5.9	6.6	12.5 ← minimum
50	6.1	6.7	12.8
55	6.2	6.7	12.9
60	6.4	6.9	13.3
65	6.6	7.1	13.7
70	6.7	7.2	13.9

paratively high space overhead for management of small blocks, limits the usefulness of this very fast technique.

A compromise method is therefore that of first-fit employing a rover. It has a significant speed–performance advantage over the best-fit method but not the small block space overhead or tag integrity problems of the boundary-tag method.

Notice that any of these methods can fail with adequate space on the FSB list but with no sufficiently large single block to accommodate a request. In many applications, existing allocated blocks can be shifted in memory, thus compacting all allocated areas into one end of the managed space and combining all FSBs into a single large area at the other end. When compaction is possible, the requesting process need not be aborted when space becomes overly fragmented. For instance, if a large fourth job were to attempt to start at the 11-minute point in Figure 2-3, it might not fit into either of the available memory blocks. Shifting JOB2 to either end of memory would result in a single large area in which the new job could more likely be accommodated.

This is obviously not an appropriate action within the operating system itself, however, since most allocated areas will contain addresses of, and pointers to, other areas. If the target areas are shifted, all referencing pointers must be corrected. Since this requires intimate knowledge of the contents of allocated areas, such compaction is generally not practical.

2.6
CONCURRENCY IN MEMORY MANAGEMENT

As a final note on dynamic memory management strategies, consider the relative urgencies of requests to the GET_MEMORY and FREE_MEMORY services. When MOS or a process needs memory, it can usually be assumed that the need is immediate and that meaningful processing cannot continue until the request is satisfied. We therefore conclude that, other things being equal, the faster the allocation algorithm, the better the performance of both the requesting program and the system. But what about releasing storage? What is the urgency of a free request?

Once a program no longer needs an allocated area, it returns it to the availability pool as a matter of orderliness and to restock the memory resource on which this and other programs depend. But the timeliness of release operations is not critical to the continued operation of the caller. This observation leads to an implementation that executes the FREE_MEMORY service as a separate, low-priority system process whose input requests are queued until serviced.

For example, if three processes all release blocks of memory to a low-priority process, FREE_MEMORY, the high-priority SC service portion of the release operations could be as simple as adding the addresses and sizes of the areas to a list of pending release requests. After the constant-time queuing operations are complete, these high-priority processes can continue with their normal functions, leaving the memory management operations to a later time. Eventually, when each of these processes is suspended, pending the completion of I/O or some other event blocking further progress, the operating system can schedule the execution of the low-priority FREE_MEMORY process, which will examine its list of release requests and methodically place the released blocks back into the pool. Thus the time required to release storage by processes is minimal. The major portion of the release-space operation occurs when the CPU would otherwise be idle. In summary, a multiple-process version of dynamic memory management might only perform free-space management when the CPU has nothing better to do.

The Hewlett-Packard 3000 computer MPE IV operating system uses this approach coupled with a best-fit allocation strategy. It attempts to gain maximum use of available memory while servicing memory requests rapidly. With FREE_MEMORY executing as a low-priority process, where efficiency is not a major concern, the FSB list can be maintained in size order, thus reducing the expected execution time of the GET_MEMORY service [Busch, 1981].

An obvious performance exposure for this approach occurs when the user processes are CPU bound and FREE_MEMORY rarely gets executed. Eventually, the available memory pool will be depleted and execution of FREE_MEMORY must be forced by the operating system to replenish the available memory pool.

PROBLEMS

1. Given 22 words of memory with a head node in the first two words, illustrate the state of memory after each of the following steps if the best-fit method of memory management is used. Maintain the FSB list in location order. Explain the reasons for any rejected requests.

   a. Initialize the space such that 20 words are available.
   b. Allocate area A of three words, area B of five, area C of three, and finally area D of three.
   c. Release area B.
   d. Allocate area E of three words, then area F of two.
   e. Release area A and area C.
   f. Allocate area G of two words.
   g. Release area F.
   h. Allocate area H of three words.   [DS]

2. Work problem 1 using the worst-fit method.   [DS]

3. Work problem 1 using the simple first-fit method. [DS]

4. Work problem 1 using an area of 37 words containing a five-word head node at the front and managing space with the boundary-tag method. [DS]

5. Design a sequence of requests similar to that of problem 1 that can be satisfied by the simple first-fit method but not by the best-fit method.
   [ANA]

6. Design a sequence of requests similar to that of problem 1 that can be satisfied by the best-fit method but not by the simple first-fit method.
   [ANA]

7. [Angier, 1983] Produce a random queue of 20 jobs using the procedure described below, then use the best-fit and first-fit-with-a-roving-pointer methods to produce time–space graphs of memory as jobs from the queue are processed. Assume that 35 units of memory are available and that only the next job in the queue can be placed in memory. If sufficient space is not available, the job must be delayed until some other job or jobs terminate. Analyze the behavior of the two strategies as follows.

   a. Define a measurement for effective utilization of memory.
   b. Using this metric, determine which strategy performs "best."
   c. Define a measurement for the degree of fragmentation.
   d. Using this metric, determine which strategy has the lowest fragmentation.
   e. All things considered, determine which strategy was "better" for this set of jobs. What characteristics of the job queue or the strategies caused this performance?

   Use the following technique to create the queue of jobs, labeled A through T, with independent space and time requirements.

   (1) *Memory space*: Roll two six-sided dice and use the sum of the top faces. (This approximates a normal distribution.)
   (2) *Time requirement*: Roll one die and double the result, thus approximating a uniform distribution. [ANA]

8. Design an algorithm for best-fit allocation of memory given a noncircular, location-ordered FSB list similar to that of Figure 2-7. [Alg]

9. Design an algorithm for worst-fit allocation of memory given a noncircular, location-ordered FSB list similar to that of Figure 2-7. [Alg]

10. Design an algorithm for releasing areas of memory and returning them to a noncircular FSB list ordered by nondecreasing size similar to that of Figure 2-7. (Do not overlook the need to reorganize the list when existing FSBs are combined.) [Alg]

11. Design a TAG_FREE_MEMORY algorithm, maintaining the FSB list in order of nondecreasing size for use with a best-fit version of TAG_GET_MEMORY. [Alg]

12. Design an extended version of the FREE_MEMORY algorithm that does not depend on the validity of user inputs. Assume that the head node of Figure 2-7 has been extended to include the minimum and maximum addresses of managed memory. (Do not overlook the fact that valid release requests may leave single words allocated between them which may be subsequently returned.) Discuss the implications of various error handling options. [Alg]

13. Implement and exercise programs using the best-fit and first-fit-with-a-roving-pointer strategies with uniformly distributed size and duration requests in the range 2· · ·1000 and 1· · ·1000, respectively. Instrument your modules and execute 10,000 cycles, resetting the search loop counters after the first 4000 cycles. Analyze your results and explain the speed differences from the data presented in Table 2-3. [ANA]

14. Work problem 13 with normally distributed data. [ANA]

15. Implement and exercise programs using the best-fit and first-fit-with-a-roving-pointer strategies with a Poisson distribution of size and duration requests in the range 2· · ·100 and 1· · ·100, respectively. Instrument your modules and execute 1000 cycles, resetting the search loop counters after the first 400 cycles. Analyze your results and explain any speed differences from the data presented in Table 2-3. [ANA]

16. Code and execute an assembler routine that acquires, then releases, space dynamically from the operating system of your computer. [OS]

17. Frequently a bit map is used to manage the allocation of disk sectors, each bit in the map indicating the status of one sector. This technique, by its very nature, automatically combines adjacent free areas of disk in a location-ordered structure. Design an algorithm for best-fit allocation of contiguous sections of disk. [Alg]

18. Work problem 17 using a first-fit-with-a-roving-pointer method. [Alg]

19. Use the double-ended-first-fit method to manage memory for process initiation only. In this problem each starting process must have a PCB of 100 words and a variable-size program area of 2000 words or more. There is a one-to-one correspondence between PCB allocation and release and program area allocation and release. Design the DE_GET_MEMORY and DE_FREE_MEMORY algorithms. [Alg]

20. Since the only pointers to a program area in problem 19 are from the corresponding PCB, it is feasible to reorganize memory when fragmentation prevents additional allocations from being satisfied. Assume that each PCB contains the LOCATION and SIZE of the corresponding program area. Specify the DE_PACK algorithm to compact allocated program areas into the rear area of managed memory while adjusting PCB pointers. [Alg]

21. Write subprograms consistent with the MOS simulator defined in Appendix B to implement one pair of dynamic memory management modules from the following table. Verify your code by independent tests with a driver program. These memory management modules can then be used to support additional MOS simulator programming assignments from Chapters 4 and 5. [MOS]

| GET   Memory Options | FREE Memory Options | |
	Algorithm 2-2	Problem 12
Algorithm 2-1	a	b
Problem 8*	c	d
Problem 9*	e	f

*Adapt these algorithms to the circular FSB list supported by the simulator.

CHAPTER 3

Multiprogramming and Virtual Memory

Chapter 2 addressed the problem of keeping the CPU and external devices busy by using extended amounts of memory to load multiple programs, thus permitting basic multiprogramming. Given sufficient memory, enough work can be initiated to ensure full utilization of other resources. But providing huge amounts of computer memory is not always cost-effective. Providing 10 megabytes or so of memory to support concurrent execution of a few dozen input/output-intensive processes may not be the best way to approach the problem of keeping a fast CPU busy.

To provide a high degree of multiprogramming in a limited amount of memory, less space must be occupied by the average program. Since the programs are presumably written with some care for efficiency, they probably do not contain large quantities of unnecessary instructions and data. The operating system and memory management hardware, therefore, must assume the task of fitting the set of executing programs into less memory.

Executing a set of concurrent processes in less memory than the sum of their individual requirements is accomplished by creating the appearance of more memory than actually exists in the computer. The operating system, and, when appropriate, special hardware features, create a memory space for each process that is larger than that actually assigned to the program.

In this chapter we present four common techniques for creating more memory space: program overlaying (which requires action on the part of the programmer) and three types of **virtual memory** (created without the explicit knowledge of the programmer). Techniques covered in the area of virtual memory are process swapping, program segmentation, and demand paging. Since they are indispensable to a multiprogramming system, the fundamental topics of program relocation and memory protection are also discussed.

45

3.1
Program Overlaying

Given the necessity of executing a large program in a smaller area of memory, the classical solution is to overlay part of the program. **Overlaying** is a technique by which only a part of a program is resident in the available portion of memory at any one time. Later, when some other part of the program is needed, it is copied into the memory area previously occupied by some of the original portion, thereby overlaying that portion. This technique is applicable to any environment in which the individual programs must reduce their demands to meet relatively small memory constraints.

As an illustration, assume that the seven subprogram modules of a program and their memory requirements are

Module	Size
MAIN	3,000
SUBB	2,000
SUBC	6,000
SUBD	4,000
SUBE	3,000
SUBF	6,000
SUBG	8,000
	32,000

and that the logical dependency relationships are defined by the intermodule calls shown in Figure 3-1. This program can be partitioned into portions that are not needed concurrently and placed into an overlay structure such that it only requires the amount of memory of the longest path from the MAIN routine to a subordinate subroutine. (MAIN and all intermediate modules in the path to the currently executing subroutine must be resident in order to continue their processing when called modules end their functions.)

If the program does not involve recursive calls, its structure can be represented as a tree with the main program placed at the root. Each module called by the main program becomes a subtree of the root. Now each of these routines is viewed as a root and the procedure is repeated. Construction of the dependency tree ends when there are no more modules to consider. Following this

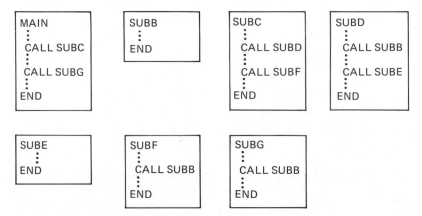

FIGURE 3-1   Example Program Module Structural Dependency

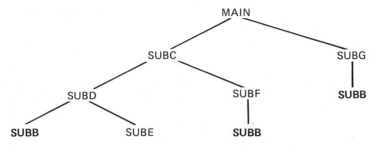

FIGURE 3-2   Tree Structure Representation of Program Dependencies

procedure, the program of Figure 3-1 has the tree structure represented in Figure
3-2. Notice that SUBB appears three times, reflecting the fact that there are
three modules which contain calls to SUBB. (Any module called from multiple
modules will appear as a subtree of each of the calling modules.)

Since most relocating linkers do not support generation of multiple copies
of an object module offset to different origins, the tree must be factored to
migrate modules with multiple occurrences to positions common to all calling
routines. The only common position for those modules calling SUBB is in the
root. SUBB is therefore placed in the root together with MAIN. It will thus
always be in memory when needed, regardless of the source of the call.

Figure 3-3 shows the resulting overlay plan and the corresponding sizes of
the various subtrees of the structure. As shown, it is possible to run the example
program in 18,000 units of memory (the length of the longest path, as indicated
in the figure). Possible contents of the reduced program area of memory are

> MAIN and SUBB;
> MAIN, SUBB, and SUBC;
> MAIN, SUBB, SUBC, SUBD, and SUBE;
> MAIN, SUBB, SUBC, and SUBF; or
> MAIN, SUBB, and SUBG;

depending on which, if any, subroutine call has been made from MAIN. At

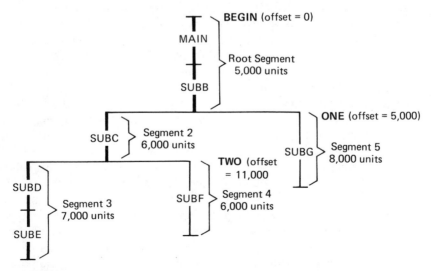

FIGURE 3-3   Example Program Static Overlay Structure

any given time, only one of these sequences of program modules will be resident in the 18,000-unit area of memory.

The specification of an overlay structure is generally the responsibility of the programmer and is defined to the linker via a set of input commands. For the IBM Linkage Editor [IBM Systems Reference Library, 1969] the commands for the example given above are

```
ENTRY BEGIN
      INSERT MAIN,SUBB

OVERLAY ONE
      INSERT SUBC

OVERLAY TWO
      INSERT SUBD,SUBE

OVERLAY TWO
      INSERT SUBF

OVERLAY ONE
      INSERT SUBG

INCLUDE MODULES
```

The names of the overlay origins, BEGIN, ONE, and TWO, are labels and refer to the relative levels in the structure at which the included module segments are to be loaded when called. These labels and their relative address values are also shown in Figure 3-3.

As the linker executes and constructs the load module file for a program, it also builds a subprogram directory in the file. Meanwhile, it replaces those calls to routines in lower-level overlay segments with calls to the overlay loader function of the operating system. (Lower-level overlay segments are those further removed from the root segment than the calling routine.) Each of the replacing calls supplies an identifier for the requested module.

When call statements are executed, the overlay loader is invoked as an intermediate step in the call activity. It uses the directory from the load module file to locate the overlay segment on secondary storage, copies it into memory at the appropriate address, then branches to the module specified by the original code. As execution proceeds, portions of the program are thus loaded on demand as part of the call invoking a routine in that segment.

For performance reasons, some overlay loaders maintain an indication of the residence state of each overlay segment. This prevents unnecessary reloading of segments already in memory when iterative calls are made. Of course, any module called that is not in memory will be fetched by the overlay loader. (For a more complete treatment of program overlaying, including implications of iterations, conditional executions, and delay times associated with fetching overlays from secondary storage, see Yourdon and Constantine [1979].)

Many computer systems do not follow this approach of automatically calling the overlay loader. Input/output to secondary storage is explicitly required each time an overlay segment is fetched. When this activity is performed automatically, it has the effect of hiding the input/output overhead from the programmer. Since cyclicly fetching overlays during program execution can have a degrading effect on performance, many systems require explicit execution of the overlay loader by the calling program before issuing the subprogram call

[Interdata, 1977]. All points of increased overhead are therefore readily apparent to the programmer. This approach does, however, increase the cost of program modification since any program whose overlay structure is to be changed must not only be relinked but also edited to modify the overlay fetch calls and recompiled as well.

Program overlay techniques apply to both uniprogramming and multiprogramming environments. They can be used any time a program is too large for its assigned area of main memory.

3.2
Memory Partitioning, Program Relocation, and Memory Protection

If multiple programs are to be resident in memory and share the CPU, the operating system must decide where to place them and each program must have its memory references offset or relocated to the origin of the area to which it is assigned. A simple approach to concurrently executing such programs is achieved by partitioning memory into several fixed areas with a single process assigned to each area. In this environment, large programs must be overlaid in order to fit into smaller partitions, just as if each of those partitions represented the total main memory of the computer. This technique was used in the old IBM MFT system, **multiprogramming with a fixed number of tasks** or processes.

In simplest form, each program executing under an MFT-type system could be relocated by the linker to execute in one and only one partition. This approach, however, has the obvious drawback of the inability to use currently unoccupied partitions in order to reduce a backlog of jobs waiting for occupied partitions.

Practical implementation of the MFT approach therefore requires a **memory address mapping** hardware capability and control of this capability by the operating system. In its simplest form, memory mapping may be implemented with an **address base register** and a **limit register** within the CPU. Each time the operating system passes control to an active process, it first loads the base register with the beginning address of the associated partition and then the limit register with either the size or ending address of the partition, depending on the hardware.

With this method the linker relocates each program relative to memory address zero; thus all addresses within the program become offsets from the origin of the assigned memory partition. At instruction-execution time the hardware adds a bias to all memory references. Any program can therefore execute in any of the partitions, provided that it will fit into the area.

Each time an address is calculated by the CPU, the partition relative address contained in the instruction is compared to the limit register value. A value equal to or exceeding the limit is rejected as an error since the reference extends beyond the partition. Values that do not violate the limit are added to the base register contents to produce an actual real memory address. Figure 3-4 illustrates this logic for a 1500-word program loaded at starting address 1000 in memory.

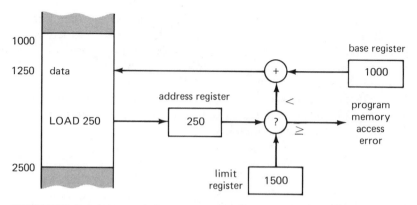

FIGURE 3-4 Application of the CPU Base and Limit Registers

The memory address mapping function of the CPU may be enabled (activated) or disabled by the map bit in the PSW (see Figure 1-5). It will be enabled when instructions from a process are executing and usually disabled when MOS is executing. This allows MOS to have free access to all of memory. Conversely, while a process is executing, memory beyond the mapped area is protected from access.

The memory protection feature is an automatic benefit of relocation techniques that use base and limit registers. Since negative addresses do not exist, areas less than the base address value are obviously unreachable. Also, since the CPU will signal a program error interrupt when a relative address is greater than or equal to the limit register value, areas beyond the assigned block of memory are similarly protected by the mapping hardware.

Returning to the MFT philosophy, to achieve reasonable utilization of memory, an MFT-type operating system usually supports partitions of different sizes with various classes of programs assigned to each. Thus large programs may

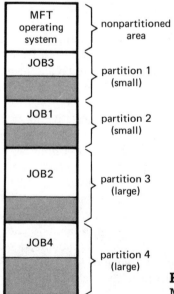

FIGURE 3-5 Fixed-Partition Multiprogramming

be executed in the large partitions, minimizing the amount of overlaying, while the smaller programs run in the small partitions, thus not wasting the large amounts of unused memory that would result from their execution in the large partitions (see Figure 3-5).

The MFT approach provides a very limited operating environment, however. Utilization is said to be limited by the **degree of multiprogramming,** which is constrained by the number of fixed partitions and the corresponding maximum number of concurrent processes. This condition can be relieved if the area of memory available for program execution is treated as a single resource and managed by a dynamic memory management strategy such as GET_MEMORY and FREE_MEMORY of Chapter 2. Now when a process needs memory for its program, the required amount of contiguous memory can be obtained on demand from the GET_MEMORY service. With this approach, any number of processes can be supported, up to the capacity of memory. The actual limit on the number of processes is dependent on the number and sizes of the active processes.

This approach is similar to that employed by the **IBM MVT** operating system, **multiprogramming with a variable number of tasks** (processes), popular in the early 1970s. In MOS, memory mapping with the variable number of dynamic partitions is implemented by using the GET_MEMORY and FREE_MEMORY services and memory address mapping.

3.3
Process Swapping in MOS

Thus far, we have discussed the practical sharing of memory under the control of mapping hardware, the reduction of memory requirements of individual programs by overlaying parts of the programs, and the packing of many programs into memory at once by dynamically creating partitions of the correct size. Given a sufficiently fast CPU, a computer with only one or two megabytes of memory may still be underutilized due to an insufficient number of active processes. This condition arises frequently in systems supporting many interactive users. The speed disparity between a million-instruction-per-second CPU and the human suppliers of input data may require a very high degree of multiprogramming to utilize the CPU fully. Effective CPU utilization is therefore dependent on increasing the degree of multiprogramming beyond that supportable by a reasonable amount of real memory.

By using secondary storage as an overflow area for the main memory, theoretically any number of processes may be activated in an extended dynamic partition system. When memory is full and additional processes need to be started, processes currently in memory, but not ready to execute, can be temporarily copied to secondary storage, their memory confiscated and returned to the FSB list, and allocation requests for the new processes satisfied. At some later time, processes copied, or swapped, to the secondary storage can be returned to main memory and their execution resumed. This is the technique used by most minicomputer operating systems and is adopted for use by MOS.

If the swapping is accomplished frequently enough, and with sufficiently fast secondary storage devices, interactive users will hardly perceive the delays in their transactions. Fifty or more processes may exist in a computer that can

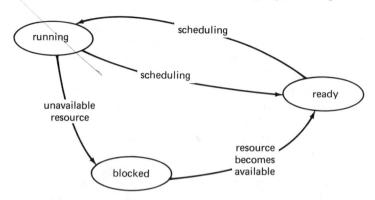

FIGURE 3-6   Basic Process State Transitions

only support a dozen or so programs in memory at any time. (See problems 17 and 18 for the impact of swapping on system performance.)

Three features are needed in the MOS data structure to accommodate this multiprogramming and swapping approach. First, the PCB structure must contain two fields in which to save the base and limit registers when its process is not in control of the CPU. When time comes to resume a suspended process, the register values are then reloaded from the PCB by the MOS dispatcher.

These PCB fields also serve another purpose. If the process is swapped to secondary storage, the base register value will be nil in the PCB, indicating that the process is no longer resident in memory. The limit field retains the length of the program area so that the required memory size can be determined when attempting to swap the process back into memory.

The third new PCB field contains the secondary storage address: the location of the area of disk containing the image of the program to be swapped into memory. Generally, a single area of disk will be allocated for the duration of a process to accommodate the swapping of the program for the process.

We now also need a new process state, **blocked,** and a PCB list to accommodate processes in this state. Processes that cannot make use of the CPU due to a missing resource will be placed in the blocked list. (A common example of blocking a process is the delay associated with interactive input of data.) Figure 3-6 illustrates the expanded state transition diagram, including the blocked state. (More detail on process states and transitions is provided in Chapter 5.)

Figure 3-7 provides an example of the MOS approach to swapping processes. In this example, two processes are currently memory resident and two others have been swapped to secondary storage. JOB1 is executing; therefore, copies of the values contained in the base and limit fields of its PCB are also in the CPU base and limit registers. All memory addresses referenced by JOB1 are checked and mapped by the hardware. The PCB for JOB2 contains the mapping register values to be loaded when it reaches the current state. Values for the base register for JOB3 and JOB4 will not be established until these processes are swapped back into memory.

With this structure, a simple technique for initiating a new process can be defined for MOS.

1. The program load module file is located on disk and the program size determined.
2. A PCB is allocated using the GET_MEMORY service.

3. A swap file of adequate size is created on secondary storage and the program image is copied into it from the load module file.
4. The PCB is completed by
   a. Clearing the base register field.
   b. Storing the program size in the limit register field.
   c. Placing the secondary storage address in its field.
   d. Adding the PCB to the ready queue.
5. When the PCB nears the front of the ready queue, its program will automatically be swapped into memory so that execution can begin.

Starting a process is thus a simple task of making it look like a continuing process that has been temporarily swapped out. It will then compete for memory with the other processes and eventually be swapped in for execution.

Next, consider a simple algorithm for managing partitions and swapping processes between memory and secondary storage. Suppose that this function is invoked once it has been determined that a program needs to be brought into memory. Such a determination might result when the PCB for a process nears the front of the ready queue, thus becoming a candidate for execution by the CPU in the very near future. The function of the algorithm is to acquire sufficient space for the program and then copy it into the allocated area. Algorithm

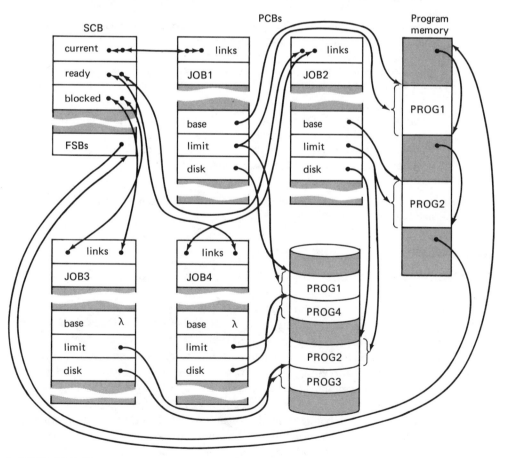

FIGURE 3-7 MOS System with Process Swapping

Begin SWAP_IN
⎡ Attempt to bring the program for a specified process
into memory from a swap area of secondary storage
Input   – PCB of the process needing memory
        – SCB and associated lists
        – Process swap file
Output – Base field of the input PCB
        – Base field of PCBs for processes swapped out
          to accommodate the specified process
        – Swap files of processes removed from memory
Assume – No errors occur during input/output operations ⎤

Determine the amount of memory required for the process from the limit
register field of the input PCB

Do ⎡ Attempt to bring the program into memory or locate an
area of memory to confiscate ⎤

Call GET_MEMORY to request the needed space
If allocation was successful
Then [Swap the program into memory]
    Locate the program on secondary storage
    Copy the program image into the allocated area
    Set the PCB base register field to the origin of the allocated area
Else
    Look for a process to swap out (consider blocked processes first,
        then ready processes of lower priority)
EndIf
If swap-in was not accomplished and a process to swap out was located
Then [Move the identified process to secondary storage]

    Copy the program area of the located process to secondary storage
    Call FREE_MEMORY to return the vacated area to the available memory
        pool and merge it with any adjacent free areas
    Clear the base register field of the located PCB to indicate that
        the process is no longer in memory
EndIf

Until swap-in occurs or the search for processes to remove from memory
    is exhausted
EndDo

End SWAP_IN

ALGORITHM 3-1   Simple Approach to Process Swapping

3-1 defines such a procedure. The step "Look for a process to swap out" uses
process blocked states, priority, or other attributes of existing resident processes
as necessary to determine the appropriateness of removing a process and swapping it to secondary storage. (Blocked refers to process ineligibility to run due
to its waiting for the completion of pending events, such as input/output operations from the terminal.) (An alternative logic structure for SWAP_IN appears
as an example in Figure A-3 of Appendix A.)

Simplifications have been made for instructional purposes. In practice, candidate processes would not actually be copied to secondary storage until it had
been ascertained that such swapping would actually result in satisfying the
demand for memory; that is, if enough space could not be identified, no swap-

ping would occur. Similarly, processes not contributing directly to the formation of the memory area to be used by the incoming program need not be removed from memory.

3.4
Program Segmentation

A moment of reflection on the composition of computer programs and on the swapping procedure reveals that swapping performs considerably more output than necessary, and that the probability of acquiring memory upon request has not been maximized. It is possible to use memory more effectively by sharing memory among resident processes while reducing demands for input/output to secondary storage devices supporting swap operations.

Programs consist of two major elements: code and data. Of the data, part is constants and part variables. Under normal conditions and good programming practice, the code and constants are not modified. Thus each time they are copied back and forth to secondary store, the same values are involved, unlike the variable areas, which change as the program execution progresses. Programs may therefore be divided or segmented into two basic parts: a **pure** or unchanging segment and an **impure** or variant segment. (Some manufacturers refer to these parts as **reentrant** and **nonreentrant** segments.) If the PCB is extended to include a pair of base and limit register fields for each segment type, and if the hardware supports additional segmentation with a second set of mapping registers, the pure and impure parts of the program can be treated as independent elements and need not be located physically adjacent to each other. Now, rather than requesting a single large area for an entire program, two smaller areas of the same total size may be required. The program pure segment can reside in one area of memory, under the control of one set of base and limit registers, while the impure is in another area being controlled by the other set. Chances are greatly increased that the allocation requests will be successful and that fewer processes will be swapped out to make room for the segments.

This method of segmenting a program requires a mechanism for identifying which of the two segments contains the memory location being referenced by the address. A common approach is to partition the address field into two parts: a segment identifier and a displacement within the segment of the referenced item. Assuming that the pure segment is designated as segment number 0 and the impure segment as number 1, typical program address references would be resolved as shown in Figure 3-8. The only differences between this example and that of the unsegmented program of Figure 3-4 are the expanded form of the instruction address fields and the selection of the appropriate segmentation register pair for address translation. Once the proper segment has been established, the CPU address register, base register, and limit register function as defined previously.

If a copy of the program pure segment is continuously maintained on secondary storage, even when the process has been swapped into memory, output operations for this part of the program can be eliminated altogether. The secondary copy of the pure segment is always valid by definition. Now, the swap procedure must copy only the impure segment to secondary storage, then re-

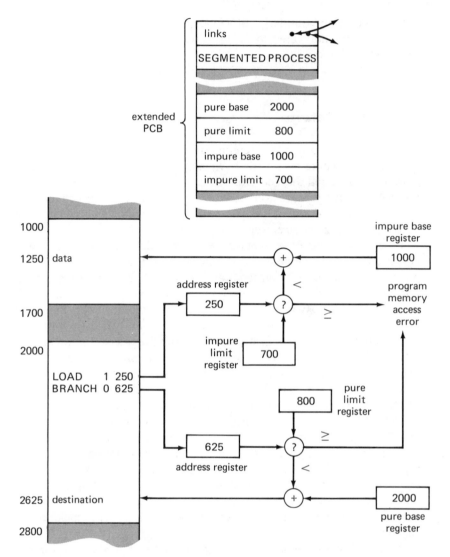

FIGURE 3-8   Address Translation in a Segmented Program

lease the memory area occupied by both the impure and pure segments. The entire computer system now runs more efficiently because smaller blocks are requested, thus perturbing system operation to a lower degree, and because less output is required to remove a process from memory.

A third benefit of program segmentation is the ability of processes concurrently executing the same program to share the pure segment. With this feature, if two or more users are each executing the same program (e.g., a text editor), there will be several distinct copies of the data, one for each user, but only a single shared copy of the pure segment (code and constants). This is possible because all copies of the pure segment are by definition identical. Now an even more efficient operation is realized since the requirement is not for several complete programs, but rather for one shared pure segment and an impure segment for each process. Figure 3-9 illustrates this example. Notice that the illusion has been created that each user has a complete copy of the editor program, when actually only a data segment is exclusively the user's.

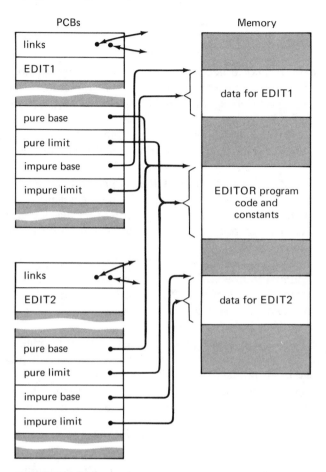

FIGURE 3-9 Segmentation of an EDITOR Program into Pure and Impure Areas

In human experience, consider the baking of two similar cakes (the editing of two files). There are two bakers (processes), each following a common and unchanging recipe (editor program instructions) but using different pans, utensils, and ingredients (data). The bakers can proceed independently of each other just as do the EDIT processes in Figure 3-9. Resources unique to the bakers are duplicated, but they are able to execute asynchronously from a common set of shared instructions. They need only one cookbook and one area of the counter (memory) on which to place it.

Sharing pure segments places two additional requirements on the basic segmentation capability. First, a count of the number of resident processes currently using (mapped to) each pure segment must be maintained. Only if and when this count reaches zero may a pure segment be removed from memory as part of a swap-out operation.

Also, sharing pure segments is generally less effective if the programs are overlayed. This is because the pure segment of overlayed programs usually includes instructions and constants from the root segments only, since different processes normally do not require the same overlay segments of a program to be in memory at the same time. Overlaid portions are, therefore, normally relegated to the impure segments of a program.

3.5
Paged Memory Systems

We have examined four major aspects of program memory management. All have direct implication on improved utilization of the CPU, memory, and other resources. Overlaying, partitioning and hardware relocation, swapping, and segmentation each individually support more efficient utilization. Combinations of these techniques offer even higher degrees of utilization. By using the entire set, as is frequently done, very effective utilization can occur in moderate sized memory environments.

Overlaying a program addresses the fact that larger and larger programs generally require smaller and smaller percentages of their total memory space during an interval of time. By folding the program into an overlay structure, currently unused sections can remain on secondary storage rather than idly occupying valuable memory.

Run-time relocation of a program by memory address mapping hardware allows instant and automatic preparation of a program for execution in any available block of memory of adequate size. There is no need to relocate the addresses in the program load module by software prior to loading it into memory.

When swapping is provided, those processes that will not be making productive use of memory in the near future are displaced in favor of processes that can use memory more productively. When combined with dynamic partition creation and program relocation by hardware, it is possible not only to have multiple processes in memory and active at once, but to have many more processes waiting, on secondary storage, ready to resume execution on short notice. More processes can be executing concurrently than could ever be practically fit into memory simultaneously.

By recognizing that much of a program is static during execution and that multiple executions of the same programs can occur concurrently using identical copies of static portions, segmentation reduces memory requirements so that even less total memory is needed to support a given work load. When adequate hardware and operating system features exist, programs can be partitioned and loaded into discontiguous areas of memory, as well as share static segments. The objective of systems supporting most, or all, of these features is the concurrent accommodation of processes whose total memory requirements exceed actual available memory.

There are still other techniques and combinations of techniques applicable to this area of system management. They require significantly more advanced hardware and operating system functions than could be presented with an introductory system such as MOS. Frequently, knowledge of the implementation details of these systems are of limited value to programmers unless a performance analysis and system tuning effort is under way. The remainder of this section provides an overview of some of these options, while omitting most implementation detail.

Dynamic creation of partitions for placing programs or program segments into memory produces what is known as **external fragmentation** of memory. Partitions are allocated for the exact sizes required, but residuals, frequently small ones, exist between the allocated areas. This external fragmentation results because free space blocks, from which the partitions are allocated, are

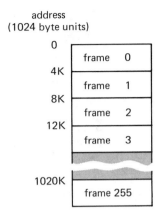

FIGURE 3-10   A One Megabyte Memory
Divided into 4096-Byte Frames

rarely the same size as the requested partitions. When no free-space blocks of
sufficient size to satisfy a memory request for a new program or segment exist,
some entire program or segment, of less relative importance (perhaps a process
of lower priority), may be swapped to secondary storage.

3.5.1 Frames and Pages

A different approach is to allocate all storage in multiples of some predefined
increment such as 512, 2048, or 4096 units of memory. Memory is thus permanently divided into **frames** of fixed size as shown in Figure 3-10. Next,
each program or program segment is automatically viewed as a collection of
pages that correspond to the memory frame size exactly. (The last page of each
program segment will generally contain an unused area, since the lengths of
segments will rarely be exactly an even multiple of frame size.) Figure 3-11
illustrates the division of a 15K segmented EDITOR program into 4K pages.

Since page/frame sizes usually are a power of 2, each address value can be
viewed not as a single binary value of 20 bits, for example, but as a 4-bit
segment number, a 4-bit page number, and a 12-bit displacement into the page.
In the example of Figure 3-11, a branch instruction referencing relative location

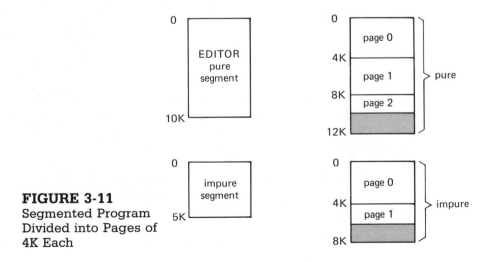

FIGURE 3-11
Segmented Program
Divided into Pages of
4K Each

6000 in the pure segment (0000 0001 011101110000 in binary) divides into segment 0, page 1, and displacement 1904:

segment	page	displacement
0000	0001	011101110000

Similarly, if the impure segment is defined to be segment number 1, a reference to location 1500 in that segment will appear as

segment	page	displacement
0001	0000	010111011100

producing segment 1, page 0, and displacement 1500.

If a separate memory address mapping base register existed for each page of the program, the contents of individual pages could be loaded into discontiguous memory frames. The program of Figure 3-11 could then be loaded into any five available memory frames.

Such a paged memory approach has two major advantages from a memory management perspective: several small requests are more likely to be satisfied than one or two large ones, and free-space management reverts to a simple strategy of managing constant-sized nodes. Any page can fit into the first available frame. (Note that this approach has traded external fragmentation for **internal fragmentation.** The unused memory space is now internal to the allocated areas of memory, although it occurs only in the last page of a segment, as shown in Figure 3-11.)

The ability to divide programs to this level and to load each page without regard to the placement of other pages exceeds the capability of the base and limit register philosophy presented earlier. A program of size S would require at least

$$\left\lceil \frac{S}{\text{page size}} \right\rceil$$

pairs of mapping registers and could require more if the program were segmented. A large program of 350K bytes, a compiler for example, would require 88 base registers if each mapped to only 4K bytes. This would dictate a very expensive CPU and would require a considerable amount of time whenever the set of registers had to be saved or loaded.

A common alternative is to have a table of segments for each process and a set of **page tables** for each segment. The page tables reside in memory and serve the purpose of memory address mapping registers. Each entry in the page table provides the function of one base register. They are maintained by the operating system to map the address of each program page into a memory frame. When the program is loaded, the operating system simply stores the frame number of the nth page of a segment in the nth element of the page table.

Increased hardware capability is needed to dynamically translate a segment, page number, and displacement into a real memory address corresponding to

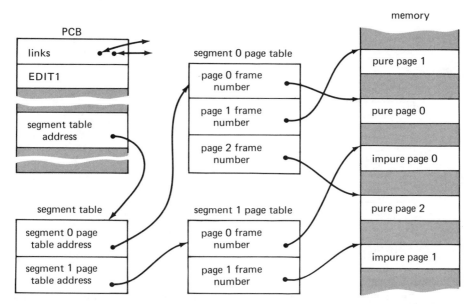

FIGURE 3-12 Structure for Dynamic Address Translation via Segment and Page Tables

a frame number and displacement. As with memory address mapping, this translation must occur each time memory is referenced. It is, however, more complicated when the CPU base registers do not exist, since the translation must occur by accessing the segment and page tables, which are themselves located in memory. Figure 3-12 illustrates relationships of these tables and frames of memory.

3.5.2 Special Paging Features

If **dynamic address translation** of segment and page numbers into frame numbers were the only new hardware feature associated with paged memory systems, the computer would run much slower than its potential. This results from the fact that the translation process itself requires two accesses to memory, one for the segment table, and one for the page table entry, assuming that the address of the segment table is itself contained in a CPU register. Once these two memory references have been made and translation completed, the CPU is ready to perform the actual requested access. Because of the additional memory accesses, this extension alone is counterproductive to the objective of improved resource utilization, since each instruction referencing memory requires at least three memory accesses when being executed.

IBM [1972] solves this problem with a small array of high-speed **associative registers.** Each of these registers contains the segment, page, and frame numbers of a recently translated memory address for the current process. The address translation hardware automatically keeps the results of recent translations in the associative registers. Each time memory is accessed, the hardware begins a simultaneous examination of the array of associative registers and a translation via the segment and page tables described previously. Thus two methods are racing to determine the actual memory address, as shown in Figure 3-13. If

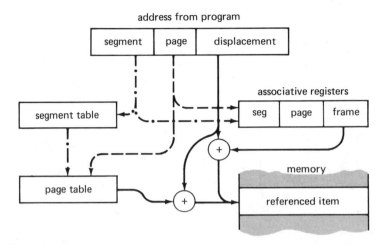

FIGURE 3-13   Simultaneous Address Translation and Lookup

the page is in an associative register, it will be found almost immediately and the slower translation via the tables will be halted; otherwise, translation will continue. The resulting frame, and the corresponding segment and page numbers, will be saved in an associative register for future use. Due to the natural clustering of memory references by most program modules, once a program has started executing, relatively few of its memory references will require slow translation via the segment and page tables. Most accesses will receive their frame numbers from an associative register.

An additional feature is frequently present in contemporary paged and segmented paged systems: virtual storage by **demand paging.** By adding still more memory management hardware and operating system functions, a "swapping" of pages between memory and secondary storage can occur on demand (i.e., upon reference a page will be brought into memory). With this approach, the pages of a program are not only loaded into discontiguous areas, but many program pages (even those not in overlay segments) do not necessarily reside in memory while the program is executing. Only those pages actually in use (being referenced during a short period of time) will be resident. It is actually possible to execute a program if only a page or two of the program can be loaded.

The operating system of a demand paged computer system must manage the paging activities and the translation and look-up hardware must detect references to pages not currently loaded. Such references generate a page fault interrupt to signal page management software, which then locates the referenced page on secondary storage and loads it into memory. If necessary, an occupied frame is vacated, or paged out, to accommodate the request.

As described in Section 3.3, when MOS needs memory for an important process that is currently swapped out, some other processes are swapped to secondary storage, vacating memory. This allows the specified process to be loaded. The VAX/VMS operating system [DEC, 1980b] uses a similar philosophy in addition to a demand paging function. When paging activity reaches very high levels, or when a sufficient number of pages cannot be kept in memory for active processes, entire sets of pages for other processes are swapped to secondary storage. VMS thus swaps processes as discussed in earlier sections; however, even when processes are resident in memory, they will be demand paged. Programs for processes are thus rarely entirely memory resident, since having a swapped-in state merely makes them eligible to compete for memory frames with other processes.

PROBLEMS

1. Diagram the structure and specify the IBM Linkage Editor commands for overlaying the program below so that it will fit in a 10,000-unit area of memory. [Ana]

Module	Size	References
MAIN	1000	A, B, and C
A	2000	None
B	3000	A and D
C	2000	E, F, and G
D	2000	H
E	1000	F
F	2000	None
G	3000	F
H	1000	None

2. Specify the linker commands appropriate for your computer system to overlay the program presented in Figure 3-1. Construct a test program following this structure, link it using the overlay commands, and execute the program. [OS]

3. Assume that memory exists for executing processes from address 20K to 120K-1, that it is managed by swapping unsegmented programs using variable-sized partitions, and that six programs are to be run in this space. In decreasing order of priority, the sizes of the processes are

JOB1	20K
JOB2	40K
JOB3	20K
JOB4	20K
JOB5	30K
JOB6	30K

Initially, JOB2 is in memory beginning at location 20K, JOB4 begins at 70K, and JOB6 begins at 90K. Other memory is on the FSB list. Also, JOB2 is blocked, JOB3 is blocked and swapped to secondary storage, JOB4 is current, and JOB6 is ready. Other processes have not yet been started.

   a. Illustrate the initial configuration of the SCB, PCBs, managed memory area, and secondary storage.
   b. Describe the events and illustrate the results when JOB3 becomes unblocked and then JOB1 is initiated.
   c. Describe the events and illustrate the results when JOB2 becomes unblocked and then JOB5 is initiated. [DS]

4. Specify the requirements for a pseudo-FREE_MEMORY algorithm, P_FREE_MEMORY, and the complete design of a new version of

SWAP_IN which only removes those processes that contribute directly to the formation of a contiguous area of memory for the swap-in of the specified process. Be sure to state all assumptions necessary for the proper execution of this new technique.   [Alg]

5. Extend the MOS data structures to support program segmentation into pure and impure segments with sharing of identical pure segments among processes. Your structure must support swapping of segments when requests for memory exceed capacity.   [DS]

6. Using the structure of problem 5, extend SWAP_IN to handle segmented programs with sharing of pure segments.   [Alg]

7. Explain why SWAP_IN should be used to reload a process before it reaches the front of the ready queue; that is, why not wait until a process is to become current before swapping it into memory?   [Ana]

8. SWAP_IN should probably be a high-priority system process with privileges to disable memory address mapping. What are the advantages of running this function as a process rather than as part of the MOS dispatcher? Why should it be allowed special privileges?   [Ana]

9. Assuming that SWAP_IN is a process, as described in problem 8, develop two separate heuristics for when the dispatcher might schedule SWAP_IN. Compare the expected results of the two options.   [Ana]

10. Write a reentrant subprogram for adding a supplied node to the rear of a singly linked circular queue, given the address of the pointer to the rear of the queue. This module must contain only instructions and constants, and all communications should be via the parameter list. Be sure to state all usage requirements.   [OS]

11. Assume that a program has been partitioned to fit into memory frames of 4K words each with an 11K pure segment and a 13K impure segment ($K = 1024$). Assume further that the host CPU contains only four associative registers. Illustrate the specific contents of all PCB related data structures and the associative registers at the beginning of execution of the instruction at relative displacement 7000. (This instruction is reached via the BRANCH at 2004.) Your illustration should combine the structures of Figures 3-12 and 3-13. Describe the translation of all addresses associated with the second LOAD instruction.   [DS]

Relative Displacement	Operation	Segment Number	Displacement
2000	LOAD	1	1776
2002	ADD	1	10020
2004	BRANCH	0	7000
.	.	.	.
.	.	.	.
.	.	.	.
7000	LOAD	1	5432

12. Illustrate reasonable configurations of the structures, including segment tables and page tables, for problem 3 if a demand paging approach is taken using pages of 10K each.   [DS]

13. Design a minimal set of extensions to the segment and page tables and associative register contents and any new data structures necessary to support demand paging. Remember that some pages may not be in memory when reference is requested and that some frames may need to be vacated to allow page-in operations. [DS]

14. Discuss the conditions under which overlaying programs in a process swapping environment would be beneficial. What are the effects (if any) of segmenting on these conditions? [DS]

15. Discuss the merits of overlaying programs in a paged memory system. What are the effects (if any) of demand paging on your conclusions?

[Ana]

16. Determine the mechanism for making a process nonswappable (or to fix certain of its pages in memory) in your computer system. When should these functions be used? [OS]

17. Give examples and explanations of when throughput is reduced in a multiprogramming computer system that is using

   a. The MFT philosophy of memory management.
   b. Dynamic partitions with swapping of processes.
   c. Demand paging. [Ana]

18. Assume three general categories of processes: primarily I/O work, primarily CPU work, and mixed. What effect do the proportions of these processes have on throughput given limited memory managed by the SWAP_IN strategy? [Ana]

19. For the categories of processes in problem 18, what effect does the mix of these processes have on turnaround time given limited memory managed by the SWAP_IN strategy? [Ana]

CHAPTER 4

Basic Input/Output Programming

Thus far we have introduced the concept of the shared computer, and its operation in a multiprogramming environment, primarily from the view of managing the memory resource. Some basic concepts of processes and processor management have been used, but many important aspects were omitted. In this chapter the concepts of input/output management and shared external devices are addressed. As with the earlier topics, the organization and extension of MOS will serve as a simplified example of operating system design.

4.1
Direct Input and Output

Communications between the central processor and peripheral devices are usually through an intermediate electronic device called an input/output controller. **Controllers** provide standard hardware interface mechanisms to the software as well as providing the actual electronic paths to the devices. They have a wide range of capabilities or "intelligence" and support varying numbers of physical devices and modes of operation.

For simplicity, controllers, and their associated input/output devices will be classified into two general categories: those requiring direct input/output operations and those supporting indirect input/output operations. **Direct I/O** requires intensive service by the CPU in that each unit of data, usually a byte or word, must be transferred to or from memory by explicit actions of the CPU. That is, the CPU, under control of an I/O-oriented program, is utilized in presenting the individual data atoms to the controller for output or receiving them from the controller and storing them in memory when input. This mode of data transfer is sometimes referred to as **programmed input/output.** By contrast,

indirect I/O is accomplished independently of the CPU, once initiated. In this environment the controller is sufficiently powerful to move all data between memory and the devices without the aid of the CPU.

4.1.1 Input/Output Architecture

Figure 4-1 provides an architectural framework from which to discuss both types of input and output operations within MOS. In this simple architecture, all components are interconnected by a single bus. The **bus** is a multiple conductor cable containing a set of address lines, a set of control lines, and a set of data lines. Depending on the number of data lines, the bus can simultaneously move all bits of a byte, half-word, word, or double word as an indivisible data unit or atom.

Each device has a physical address on the bus by which it is accessed. For example, if the first controller is capable of interfacing eight devices, I/O device addresses zero through seven might be supported by the first controller, while addresses eight and higher would be accessed through other controllers.

Direct I/O controllers functionally contain three internal registers for each device connection as shown in Figure 4-2. The registers are accessible by the CPU and are used for control and status information and for staging data for transmission. These registers are generally accessed by either special I/O instructions or by a memory-mapping technique. If a single bus architecture exists, each addressable system component must have a unique address. Since both controller registers and memory are repositories for data, and since each register or memory cell has its own address within the address range of the CPU, **memory-mapped I/O** creates the illusion that the controller registers are actually part of memory.

If the controllers are connected to the CPU via a separate bus, an I/O bus, some CPU instructions will access memory using the memory bus while others will access the controllers via the I/O bus. Interfacing with these controllers thus requires execution of special I/O instructions. Since the **I/O instruction interface** is conceptually simpler, we will investigate it first.

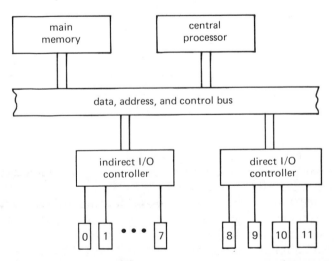

FIGURE 4-1 Typical Single Bus I/0 Configuration

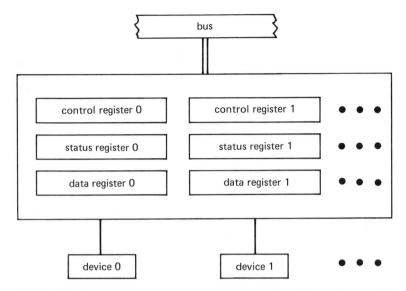

FIGURE 4-2 Functional Register Set of a Direct Controller

With this technique a few special CPU instructions exist expressly for communicating with I/O controllers. As a minimum, the ability to load from and store into the various controller registers must exist. In simplest form this may include **IN** and **OUT** instructions which have operands for designating which register of which controller is to be accessed. Values fetched from controller registers via the **IN** instruction may be copied into a specified CPU general register. Similarly, the **OUT** instruction might copy data from a general register into the indicated controller register.

Writing values into a control register causes the indicated action of the controller to start. For example, storing a write command value in a control register causes the data currently in the data register to be transmitted to the connected device. Output of data thus requires three actions: fetching the contents of the status register to verify that the device is ready to receive data, storing the data to be transmitted in the data register, and storing a write command in the control register.

A more advanced and easier to understand implementation uses the **IN** and **OUT** instructions for accessing the data registers only. Two additional instructions are provided for changing the control registers and sensing status values. In the MOS computer, commands are sent to controllers and transfers initiated by a start I/O, **SIO,** instruction. Similarly, a test I/O, **TIO,** instruction is used retrieve the controller status value and update the condition code field of the PSW register, which can be examined by other instructions.

4.1.2 Instructions for Direct Input/Output

For direct input operations, three I/O instructions are therefore needed.

```
SIO device,register
```

stores the controller command contained in the specified CPU general register into the control register associated with the device.

```
TIO device
```

fetches the status from the controller register associated with the device and updates the condition code field of the PSW register of the CPU, and

```
IN device,register
```

copies the contents of the data register associated with the device into the specified CPU general register.

Similarly, direct output operations use

```
OUT device,register
```

to copy the contents of the specified CPU general register into the data register of the associated controller. **SIO** and **TIO** perform as indicated previously.

Using these instructions to write a record to device 9 would use the following functional program sequence.

Begin DIRECT_IO

    Load a write command value into general register 5

    For each byte in the record to be output
    Do
        Load the next data atom to output into general register 2
        Do
            Test the status from the control and status register associated
                with device 9, e.g., TIO 9
        Until the device is ready
        EndDo
        Copy the next byte of data from general register 2 into the data
            register for device 9, e.g., OUT 9,2
        Start transmission to the device, e.g., SIO 9,5
    EndDo

End DIRECT_IO

4.1.3 The Memory-Mapped I/O Alternative

A popular alternative to this formal I/O interface is the **memory-mapped I/O** technique [Levy and Eckhouse, 1980; Intel, 1975]. With this approach, each controller register is physically mapped to, or associated with, an address value in the CPU address space. Controller registers therefore appear to be bytes or words in main memory.

The strength of this approach is that the entire processor instruction set is available for input/output programming. Since all instructions that reference memory are available for manipulating the contents of controller registers, there is an advantage of instruction efficiency in dealing with I/O. For example, data no longer need pass through a CPU general register and can even be examined in the controller data register before it is removed. The data, status, and control registers appear to be just other memory elements.

The cost of memory-mapped I/O flexibility is that of reduced real memory address space. Frequently, one half of the address range of the CPU is reserved for I/O controller register use with this technique. For example, a 16-bit address has a range of 0 to 65535 units of memory. However, if memory-mapped I/O is used, the most significant bit may indicate whether real memory is to be accessed or a controller register address is intended. In the latter case, real memory is restricted to the range 0 to 32767 and the range 32768 to 65535 is reserved for I/O controller registers. In this case the instruction

LOAD 30000

would fetch the value from real memory location 30000 while the instruction

LOAD 50000

would fetch the value from the controller register mapped to address 50000.

4.1.4 Characteristics of Direct Input/Output

Regardless of which implementation technique is used, the significant characteristics of direct input and output are that

1. Not much processing power is required in the controllers.
2. Extensive assistance of the CPU is required to accomplish data transmission.

These characteristics are evident when we recall that the transmission mode is only one data atom at a time.

External devices are usually several orders of magnitude slower than the CPU. For example, a high-speed terminal running at 9600 baud still requires about a millisecond to receive or transmit a byte. Most commercial and industrial computers in operation today can execute between several hundred and a few tens of thousands of instructions during this period. With slower devices and faster computers, the speed disparity may approach a million instruction cycles per character transmission time. Large amounts of CPU time are therefore potentially available for other functions between input/output events.

A sample sequence of events performed to output a record is shown in Figure 4-3. Here the CPU is released for executing other instructions during instruction cycles 4 through n, where n is a function of the data atom transmission speed of the device. The sequence shown in the figure is repeated for each data item in the record being output.

As will be seen in the following section, the data transmission rate of some mass storage devices is so great that even the fastest computers can be taxed, just moving data between memory and the controller data registers. Such conditions require alternative methods of communication with I/O controllers.

4.2
Indirect Input and Output

If data are to be transferred in any mode except one atom at a time, more processing power must be placed in the controllers. The most obvious general extension of controller capability is the addition of data record control registers and providing the controllers with direct access to memory. Each controller functionally now has five registers per device, as shown in Figure 4-4. With

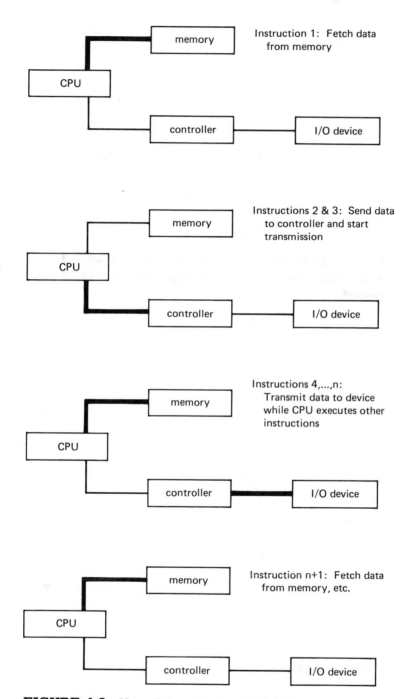

FIGURE 4-3 Use of the CPU for Direct Output

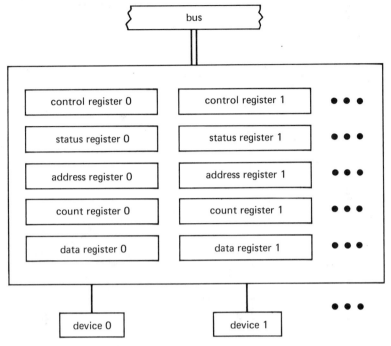

FIGURE 4-4 Functional Register Set of an Indirect Controller

this configuration, the CPU need not have access to the data registers or be involved with the actual moving of the data; therefore, I/O transmissions can be accomplished with only two I/O instructions. As described earlier,

```
TIO device
```

retrieves the device status and updates the condition code field of the PSW. When the device is ready to accept a transmission request, the command, data address, and count are loaded into three consecutive CPU registers. Then the instruction

```
SIO device,registers
```

is used to transmit

1. The read or write command from the specified CPU general register.
2. The memory address of the data area from the next CPU register.
3. The count of the number of items from the third register in the sequence.

4.2.1 Direct Memory Access

IN and **OUT** instructions are not needed in the MOS computer with indirect controllers attached since the CPU does not access the data registers. The controller will move the data items directly between its data registers and the memory locations designated. This approach produces the much more efficient transmission sequence shown in Figure 4-5.

Using indirect I/O controllers, transmissions are initiated by supplying the memory address, the amount of data to transfer, and the direction of the transfer

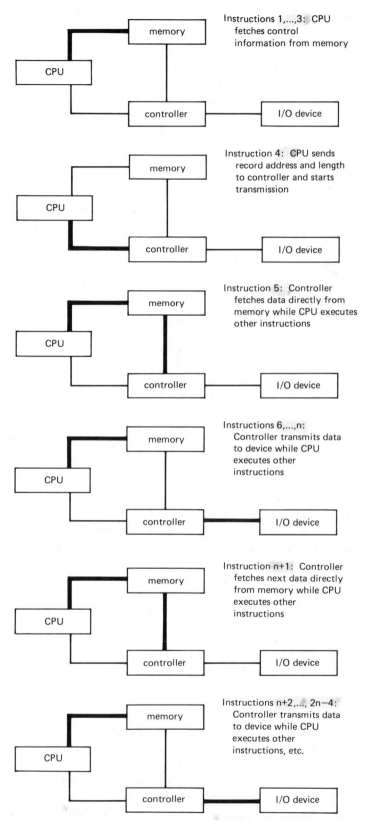

FIGURE 4-5 Use of the CPU to Initiate Indirect Output

to the controller. Communication may be either by explicit I/O instructions or by moving data with the standard instruction set if memory-mapped I/O is available. The mechanism for communicating with the controllers is immaterial. Once the transmission control information is provided to the controllers, they are allowed to fetch or store data as needed, thus eliminating the need to have the CPU explicitly handle each data atom for the controller. The controller is now a primitive processor in its own right, dedicated to I/O operations.

This technique of block data transfer with **direct memory access** (DMA) is indeed used in most minicomputers and many microcomputers today. Functionally, this method proceeds as follows.

1. The status of the device is retrieved from the controller and checked to verify availability, just as with direct I/O.
2. The starting address, amount of data, and command are stored in the control registers appropriate for the selected device, and the transfer is initiated.
3. The CPU is now released for other duties until transmission of the data record is complete.
4. Meanwhile, the controller sets the status bits to busy, copies an atom of data into its internal data register, and provides it to the device at the proper rate. (In the case of input, the completed atom is transferred from the data register directly into memory without the aid of the CPU.)
5. When the device has processed an atom, the controller decrements its data count. If the count is nonzero, the memory address is incremented and transfer of the next atom is initiated as in step 4.
6. The cycle continues until either a data count of zero has been reached or a transmission failure occurs, at which time the status bits of the control and status registers are updated accordingly.

As can be seen, indirect I/O removes a tremendous data handling and status checking load from the central processor. Assuming that just 50 microseconds is required of the CPU to stop what it is doing, service the I/O operation, and resume its original task, the savings shown in Table 4-1 illustrate the improvements possible by using indirect I/O controllers rather than direct controllers. (Fifty microseconds is a very conservative estimate. In a minicomputer multiprogramming environment supported by interrupts, the actual context switch and I/O service execution requires a few milliseconds.) The card reader in the

TABLE 4-1 Performance Improvements Using Indirect I/O with DMA

Device	Block Size (bytes)	Time (sec/block)	Direct I/O (CPU %)*	Indirect I/O (CPU %)*
Card reader	80	0.100	4	0.05
Printer	132	0.060	11	0.08
Magnetic tape	2048	0.007102	1442†	0.70
Disk	256	0.000242	5289†	20.66

*Assuming 50 microseconds per transfer quantum for context switching and I/O data processing and ignoring cycle-stealing effects.

†For data transfer rates associated with these devices, direct I/O methods are obviously not possible.

table is rated at 600 cards per minute. It can provide data from an 80-column card to the controller in 100 milliseconds. During this time, 50 microseconds of CPU time for context switching and data item receipt is required 80 times when direct I/O is used.

$$\frac{80\ (\ 0.000050\ \text{second}\ )}{0.100\ \text{second}} = 4\%$$

of all CPU time is necessary to keep the card reader operating at maximum speed. Ninety-six percent of the processing power could be used for other work not related to reading cards.

As faster devices are considered, the CPU becomes overwhelmed while attempting to maintain rated operating speeds in a multiprogramming environment. There is insufficient time between data atoms to switch back and forth between the I/O service routine and some other processes and to handle the actual memory accesses for the transferred data.

As an example, a typical disk drive can provide a character to the controller approximately each microsecond. Obviously, the CPU cannot spend 50 microseconds preparing to accept each of them. As shown in the last row of Table 4-1, over 5000 percent of the CPU, or a CPU 50 times faster, would be required to support such rates while attempting to provide computational support to processes. Increasing the data register size of the controller to eight bytes still presents an impossible situation in the direct I/O environment, since the input rate of the larger data item is still one atom every 8 microseconds.

Contrast this situation with the demands on the CPU when supporting indirect I/O. The CPU need only be involved with the controller once for each record, rather than once per data item in the record. Therefore,

$$\frac{1\ (\ 0.000050\ \text{second}\ )}{0.100\ \text{second}} = 0.05\%$$

of the CPU is needed to run the card reader at maximum speed and a manageable 20.66% is required for the high-speed disk.

4.2.2 Cycle Stealing

Indirect I/O benefits do not come free, however. To accomplish these improvements, more processing power has been placed in the controllers, which, as expected, are now more expensive. In addition, the controllers have been allowed to access memory which was previously the private domain of the CPU (refer to Figure 4-5). When read or write commands are placed on the bus for data transfer to or from memory, only one such request can be honored per memory cycle. Since high-speed devices are pouring data into the controller data registers based on rates determined by moving electromechanical parts, and since, for efficiency, these data must be accepted when available (the alternative being to stop the tape or wait an entire revolution of the disk), the controllers must vacate their data registers quickly and make room for the next byte or word. In other words, the controllers must have access to the bus on demand.

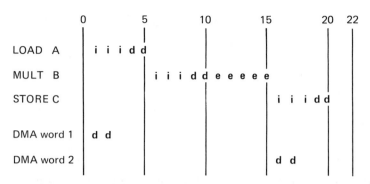

FIGURE 4-6 Independent Use of Memory (**i** and **d**) Times of the CPU and DMA Controller

For this reason, DMA controllers generally have priority over the CPU for memory accesses. This is reflected in Figure 4-1 by the location of the indirect controllers being physically closer to memory than is the CPU. If any processor, either the CPU or an I/O controller, is accessing the bus and another processor requests access, the requester must be delayed until the bus is released. This denial of preemption rights is required to maintain the integrity of data transmissions along the bus and ultimately to maintain the integrity of the entire computer system.

However, if two processors request access simultaneously, the one with higher priority will be recognized while the other is delayed until the bus has been released. In the MOS computer, indirect I/O controllers, which service high-speed devices, are located closer to memory than is the CPU. They thus have a higher priority and will be granted control of the bus whenever their requests are made during the same cycle as a request by the CPU. By precedence, the controller has stolen a cycle from the CPU; thus the term **cycle stealing** is applied to high-priority DMA-type controllers.

Figure 4-6 illustrates the concept of cycle stealing. Suppose that the execution of each memory-referencing instruction requires a time equivalent to three memory cycles to fetch and decode the instruction (i-time), two additional cycles to fetch or store the data (d-time), and a variable length execution time from zero to five which is instruction dependent (e-time). Suppose further that a fast device such as a disk or drum is connected to an indirect controller with a four-byte data register. If the data input rate from the device is 1.07 million bytes per second, and the memory cycle time is 250 nanoseconds, a four-byte value must be fetched from or placed in memory once every 15 cycles. The figure shows the independent demands of the CPU and the DMA controller for a simple instruction sequence.

With the bus structure adopted, the i-time and d-time of an instruction cannot be overlapped with a DMA access to memory (also shown as d-time in Figure 4-6). Therefore, one processor must wait for the other to complete its access. Since it has precedence, the I/O controller is granted access to the bus at time 0. This delays the fetch of the LOAD instruction until time 2, as shown in Figure 4-7.

There is a corresponding delay in the absolute start time of the other instructions in the sequence as well. At time 15, when the next word is ready for accessing by the controller, the bus is not in use since the CPU is still com-

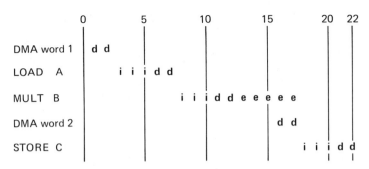

FIGURE 4-7 Interleaved Use of Memory by the CPU and DMA Controller

pleting the execution phase of the multiply instruction. The controller is granted access to the bus, makes its transfer, and releases the bus in time for the CPU to fetch the STORE instruction without additional delay.

In this example the CPU has temporarily slowed to 90% of its maximum instruction execution speed due to the cycle sealing interference from the controller.

4.3
Channels

Larger computers take the distribution of I/O processing power to the controllers one step further. Rather than just including block transfer capabilities in the controllers, stored program input/output processors are provided. Controllers with such extended capability are referred to as **channels** or input/output processors. Their capability varies greatly. Basically, they are programmable processors specifically designed for input/output processing. Like the CPU, they retrieve both their commands and data from the main memory and have their own internal registers and program counter. The operation of input/output using channels is as follows:

1. In memory, construct a program of input/output commands to be executed by the channel.
2. Test the channel status for availability.
3. Send the starting address of the channel program and device identifier to the channel and command it to start executing the program.
4. The CPU is now released for other duties while the entire set of data transfers and other operations specified by the program are being completed by the channel.
5. Using DMA, the channel now sequences through the channel program fetching, decoding and executing commands, and moving data between the device(s) and memory until the end of the program is reached or an error is detected.
6. The channel maintains a status in a channel status word stored in memory so that the CPU may interrogate the status at any time.

Now the CPU need not be involved in data transfer even at the block level. For example, a channel may skip to the top of a print page, print a heading

command code	data address	flags	count

control=eject	λ	continue	λ
write	address of header	continue & repeat command	132
λ	address of line 1	continue & repeat command	132
λ	address of line 2	continue & repeat command	132
λ	address of line 3	continue	132
control=eject	λ	continue	λ
write	address of trailer	stop	132

FIGURE 4-8   Sample IBM-Style Channel Program for a Printer

from one area of memory, cycle copying several discontiguous blocks of data to the printer, skip to the top of the next page, print a trailer, and stop, all without involving the CPU.

Figures 4-8 and 4-9 provide a functional implementation of the example above using the IBM 4341 channel command structure [IBM, 1980, 1984]. Each command in the channel program has a command code, data buffer address, flag field, and data byte count. Some fields are not used in all commands, depending on the command code. The flag field, which is always used, indicates whether this is the last command in the program, whether the next command is a repeat of the current command but with a different buffer address, and so on.

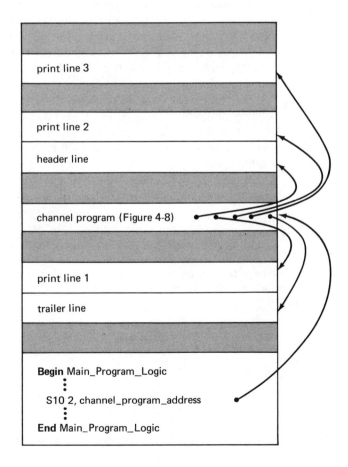

FIGURE 4-9   Program Using an I/O Channel for Concurrent Output

The data to be output are assumed to reside in the five discontiguous buffer areas shown. The program constructs the channel program illustrated in Figure 4-8. (Except for the control operations, the data address field of each command contains the memory address of the appropriate buffer.) The **SIO** instruction is then executed to initiate channel operation. At this point the channel controlling device 2 will begin asynchronous processing of commands from the channel program designated. Meanwhile, the CPU will be available to execute subsequent instructions of the main program. The entire task of producing the three pages of output will be accomplished by the channel without assistance from the CPU.

4.4
Sharing Peripheral Devices Through SPOOLing

4.4.1   The Need for Peripheral Device Management

Now let us turn from the problems of accomplishing input and output operations to the problem of managing the input and output data and the peripheral devices supporting those operations. Suppose that the computer is to execute several programs similar to that of Algorithm 4-1. Each program uses the card reader, computes results based on the input data, and then uses the printer. With a uniprogramming operating system, dedicating the input/output devices to the process as needed presents no problem. Figure 4-10 illustrates the utilization of the CPU, card reader, and printer during an arbitrary sequence of three such jobs in this batch environment. The duration of the read, compute, and print phases of each of the fictitious jobs is illustrated by appropriate groups of letters identifying the job.

A much superior device utilization can be obtained by using the power of multiprogramming as defined in Chapter 3 and illustrated in Figure 4-11. Here the card reader is used to provide data to as many jobs as possible. As soon as its input phase is complete, each job enters its compute phase at the earliest possible time.

Still, the CPU is underutilized due to the slow speeds of the peripheral devices. Additionally, beginning at time 8 both process D and process E need

Begin PROGRAM_MODEL_1

> **Do**
>> Read a data card
> **Until** last card has been read
> **EndDo**
>
> Compute results
>
> **For** each value computed
> **Do**
>> Print result
> **EndDo**

End PROGRAM_MODEL_1

ALGORITHM 4-1   Simple Three-Stage Program

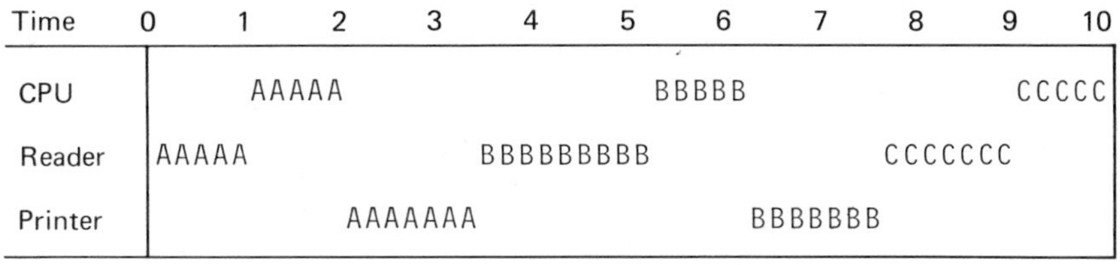

Time	0	1	2	3	4	5	6	7	8	9	10
CPU		AAAAA					BBBBB				CCCCC
Reader	AAAAA				BBBBBBBBB				CCCCCCC		
Printer		AAAAAAA					BBBBBBB				

	CPU*	Reader	Printer
Utilization	30%	42%	28%

*Useful CPU time determined by ignoring small times required to read a card and print a line

FIGURE 4-10   Device Utilization with Uniprogramming

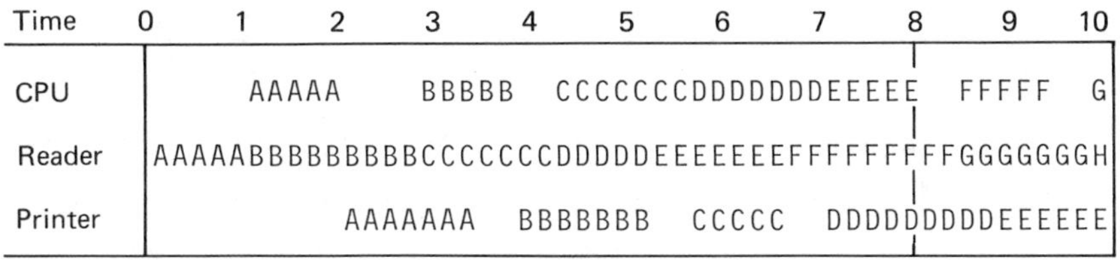

Time	0	1	2	3	4	5	6	7	8	9	10
CPU		AAAAA	BBBBB	CCCCCCCDDDDDDDDEEEEE					FFFFF	G	
Reader	AAAAABBBBBBBBBBCCCCCCCDDDDDEEEEEEEEFFFFFFFFFGGGGGGGGH										
Printer		AAAAAAA	BBBBBBB	CCCCC	DDDDDDDDDEEEEEE						

	CPU*	Reader	Printer
Utilization	68%	100%	68%

*Useful time only

FIGURE 4-11   Device Utilization with Multiprogramming

the printer (in the figure process E waits for D to complete). This contention for the printer also occurs between processes E and F after time 9. A similar access conflict exists for the card reader throughout the time period. (All processes are in need of cards at time 0 so that they can commence computing.)

One method of resolving peripheral contention problems is to allocate the devices exclusively to requesting processes for the duration of their need. (This is the scheme used to obtain the utilizations shown in Figure 4-11.) Suppose, however, that the job model of Algorithm 4-1 is changed to a cyclic one interleaving periods of input, computation, and output as shown in Algorithm 4-2. With exclusive use device allocation, utilizations deteriorate, as shown in

Begin PROGRAM_MODEL_2

   Do

      Read data card(s)
      Compute result(s)
      Print result(s)
   Until last card has been read and processed
   EndDo

End PROGRAM_MODEL_2

ALGORITHM 4-2   More Realistic Cyclic Program

Time	0	1	2	3	4	5	6	7	8	9	10
CPU	A	AAA	A BBB		B	B		CDC C CCCCD			D
Reader	AA	A A	ABB	BBB B	BBBCCCCCCCD						DDEE
Printer	A		A	AAAAA	B		BBBBBBC C C C			CDD	

	CPU*	Reader	Printer
Utilization	40%	52%	42%

*Useful time only

FIGURE 4-12 Device Utilization with a More Realistic Process Model and Exclusive-Use Device Allocation

Time	0	1	2	3	4	5	6	7	8	9	10
CPU	A BBAAAB A			DBCECBCDDEFFFCCCCDDDEFEDEF						G	E
Reader	AABBAACCCCABBBCCCCDBEBBBBDDFFGEGGFFDDFEEFEFFFGGGGEEF										
Printer	A		A	AAAAABCD C	CBBBBBBCDDEECF DDD		DDDEEFF				

	CPU*	Reader	Printer
Utilization	72%	100%	72%

*Useful time only

FIGURE 4-13 Device Utilization with a More Realistic Process Model and No Exclusive-Use Device Allocation

Figure 4-12. Notice that not until one process finishes reading cards does the next process acquire use of the card reader and begin processing. Similar serialization applies to the printer. In spite of lower utilizations than seen with the simpler job model, there is still a significant improvement over that of the uniprogramming system shown in Figure 4-10.

As can be seen from Figure 4-13, relaxing the constraint of allocating peripherals for exclusive use produces higher utilizations. It also results in chaos on the devices! Blocks of cards and print belonging to different processes are now interleaved. What is needed is a mechanism for sharing the devices while prohibiting the data interleaving. Attaching more card readers and printers and allocating each exclusively to a requesting process solves the problem but at great expense and with vastly underutilized equipment.

4.4.2 Virtual Devices and SPOOLing

Recall that when the appearance of more memory was needed to increase the degree of multiprogramming, a virtual memory space was created on secondary storage and the operating system moved programs and program segments between memory and secondary storage. Similarly, the **SPOOL** processes of the operating system create virtual peripheral devices on secondary storage and move data between the real devices and the virtual ones as needed. SPOOL stands for Simultaneous Peripheral Operations On-Line, which is exactly what is provided. Processes are able to access virtual card readers and printers concurrently without the danger of data interleaving. The SPOOL processes are a part of the operating system that is implemented in the process environment. They have exclusive use of the real card readers and printers. As cards are loaded into a card reader, the card reader SPOOL process, CRSPOOL, copies them into disk files, one file per job. As cards are needed by application processes, they are actually transferred from the appropriate disk file to the program's input buffer area rather than coming directly from the card reader as perceived by the application processes.

Print generated by processes is handled in a similar fashion. Output is communicated to a line printer SPOOL process, LPSPOOL, which "owns" the printer. Output from other processes is diverted to disk files, one file per process output unit. As processes terminate, the files are closed and placed in a queue waiting for a printer to become available. When a printer has finished the output for a job, another print file in the output queue is opened by LPSPOOL and its contents copied to the printer. Completed files are deleted. Thus the utilizations of Figure 4-13 can be achieved without data interleaving on the real devices.

As can be seen, the two basic SPOOL functions are managing files representing the virtual devices and transferring data between the files and the real devices. Figure 4-14 illustrates these functions.

Of necessity, the files of the SPOOL processes must be dynamic, since their sizes are not known in advance. Card deck files grow as more cards are copied to disk. Only when the last card of a deck has been transferred is the final size of the corresponding virtual card reader file known. Similarly, the volume of print from a process is not established until the virtual printer file is closed, generally when the process terminates.

Consider a problem that arises with such dynamic SPOOL files. What happens if, for instance, print is being generated by active processes faster than it can be removed by LPSPOOL? Eventually, disk space may become exhausted.

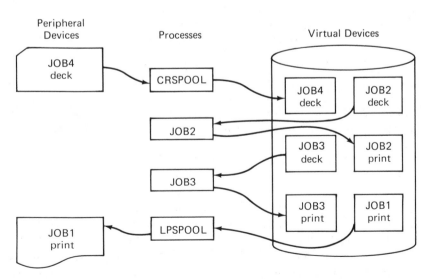

FIGURE 4-14   Concurrent Use of Virtual Peripherals via SPOOLing

In the example of Figure 4-14, print from neither JOB2 nor JOB3 can be started until the corresponding processes close their print files, since starting such print necessitates completing it before the printer can be used for other files. But neither user process can complete because no space remains for storing print on the disk, and space will not become available until a process finishes generating print and LPSPOOL copies the images to the printer. This condition is known as deadlock and will be investigated at length in Chapter 7. Basically, both JOB2 and JOB3 own disk space the other needs and neither will release its space, via LPSPOOL, until it acquires what it needs to finish. Unfortunately, in this example, no more space is available.

4.5
Double Buffering

4.5.1   Buffered Data Transfer

Next consider the details of transferring data between the real peripheral devices and the virtual devices represented by disk files. Algorithm 4-3 presents a simple algorithm for copying blocks of information from a card reader into a disk file. The routine assumes an indirect I/O block transfer capability using DMA controllers as described in the previous sections. The statements dealing with I/O imply testing device status in a loop, initializing the control and status registers to initiate the data transfer, and so on.

To analyze the performance of Algorithm 4-3, assume that the card reader has a maximum rated speed of 1000 cards per minute and that the average disk access time is 30 milliseconds. Except for the time spent in the **TIO** loops waiting for the operation to complete, the total CPU time in each cycle of the algorithm probably would not exceed 100 microseconds on a computer of modest power. Thus the elapsed time in one cycle of transferring a card image to disk would be

Card read time	0.060000 second
Disk write time	0.030000
CPU time	0.000100
Elapsed time	0.090100 second

resulting in utilizations of 0.11 percent for the CPU, 67 percent for the card reader, and 33 percent for the disk. (Notice that the CPU is actually busy 100 percent of the time due to the wait loops; however, 99.89 percent of that time is not productive.)

A box of computer cards contains 2000 cards. Using Algorithm 4-3 our 1000-card-per-minute reader, which should be able to process these cards in 2 minutes, actually requires slightly more than 3 minutes to transfer the cards to a disk that is twice as fast as the reader. This is attributable to the environment created by the algorithm: an environment of totally serialized operation.

With this algorithm, the CPU is used to start the card reader and then loops waiting for input completion. The disk is also waiting during this period. When a complete card image has been acquired, the card reader waits while the disk

Begin CARD_TO_DISK
⎡ Transfer images from a card reader to disk
Input   – Card images from a dedicated card reader
Output   – Card images to disk
              – STATUS of transfer operation
              – COUNT of the number of images
                 successfully copied to disk
Assume – Both the card reader and the disk are
                 dedicated to this program and neither is
                 busy initially
              – Card decks are terminated by an end-of-
                 file (EOF) card which is not transferred
                 to disk
              – Allocation of disk sectors is always
                 successful ⎤

Default STATUS to indicate that the transfer function is in progress
Initialize COUNT to zero

Do [Attempt to transfer a card image from the reader to disk]

Start reading a card image into an internal buffer
Wait until the read completes

If the read was successful
Then [Process an end-of-file or attempt to copy to disk]
     If the card was an EOF
     Then
          Change STATUS to indicate that the function was successful
     Else
          Allocate a sector of disk space to receive the image
          Start writing the image from the buffer to the sector allocated
          Wait until the write completes
          If the write was successful
          Then
               Increment COUNT by one
          Else
               Change STATUS to indicate a disk error
          EndIf
     EndIf

Else
     Change STATUS to indicate a card reader error
EndIf

Until STATUS indicates that the function is no longer in progress, i.e., EOF
          or error
     EndDo

End CARD_TO_DISK

ALGORITHM 4-3   Simple Card-to-Disk Algorithm

accepts the image. The CPU is waiting via another loop. A hardware configuration with indirect I/O controllers is capable of considerable parallel or overlapped operation, but this software is not taking advantage of it.

4.5.2 Data Transfer Using Pairs of Buffers

Now, suppose that the CARD_TO_DISK routine had two buffers available to
it. While one buffer was being filled from the card reader, the other one could
be being emptied to the disk. Then when both operations were complete, the
roles of the buffers could be interchanged (i.e., the full buffer could be emptied
to disk while the other was being refilled). An illustration of the improved
efficiency of such an operation is given in Figure 4-15. The corresponding
algorithm is presented in Algorithm 4-4.

Notice the two major differences in CARD_TO_DISK between Algorithms
4-3 and 4-4.

1. The wait associated with disk writes precedes the start-write logic. Once
   a write has started, the entire algorithm cycle is executed, including the
   read and wait for the next card, prior to delaying for write completion.
   This exchange of position allows the CPU and card reader to operate
   concurrently with the disk.
2. The count of successful image transfers is split into two parts. COUNT
   reflects the actual number of completed images and PENDING indicates
   the number currently being transmitted. PENDING (always zero or 1 in
   this algorithm) is added to COUNT only after successful completion of
   the output operation is detected.

At what speed does the improved algorithm accomplish the transfer? For the
60-millisecond card reader, 30-millisecond disk, and dedicated devices, the
transfer obviously proceeds at the speed of the card reader. But what would
happen if the disk were slower than the card reader? Would Algorithm 4-4
function properly and efficiently? Consider two possibilities: first, where the
card reader is slower than the disk, and second, where the card reader is faster
than the disk (see Figure 4-16). In both cases, a write of the first image will
be started immediately after the first read has completed. If the disk is faster
than the reader, this write will complete while the read of the second card is
in progress such that the wait for the disk to complete is always instantaneous
with no wait effected. Similarly, after the second card has been read, the
corresponding write commences immediately and finishes before the next card
is read. This cycle continues at maximum card reader speed.

Reducing the speed of the disk so that it is slower than the card reader
produces the second case in Figure 4-16. While the first image is being written
to disk, the second card is read completely but must await disk availability
before being written. (As will be seen in Chapter 5, in a more realistic system,
the write itself might only be queued, but the next read could not start since

Time ⟶

Buffer 1	read card 1	write card 1	read card 3 ....
Buffer 2	.... idle	read card 2	write card 2 ....

FIGURE 4-15 Overlapped
Operations Using Double Buffering

Begin CARD_TO_DISK

Transfer images from a card reader to disk
Input   – Card images from a dedicated card reader
Output   – Card images to disk
              – STATUS of transfer operation
              – COUNT of the number of images
                 successfully copied to disk
Assume – Both the card reader and the disk are
              dedicated to this program and neither is
              busy initially
              – Card decks are terminated by an end-of
                 file (EOF) card which is not transferred
                 to disk
              – Allocation of disk sectors is always
                 successful

Default STATUS to indicate that the transfer function is in progress
Initialize COUNT to zero
Initialize the number of images currently in transmission to disk to zero,
      i.e., set the number of PENDING images to zero
SELECT buffer number 1 for the next input operation
Do [Attempt to transfer a card image from the reader to disk]
      Start reading a card image into the SELECTed buffer
      Wait until the read completes
      If the read was successful
      Then [Check for an end-of-file]
            If the card was an EOF
            Then
                  Change STATUS to indicate that the function was successful
            EndIf
      Else
            Change STATUS to indicate a card reader error
      EndIf
      Wait until any previous write of an image to disk completes
      If the previous write, if any, was successful
      Then
            Increment COUNT by the number of PENDING images
      Else
            Change STATUS to indicate a disk error
      EndIf
      If STATUS indicates that the card-to-disk function is still in progress,
            i.e., no EOF or errors detected
      Then [Start transfer of image to disk]
            Allocate a sector of disk space to receive the image
            Start writing the image from the SELECTed buffer to the
                  sector allocated
            Set the number of PENDING images to 1
            SELECT the other buffer for the next read operation
      EndIf
Until STATUS indicates that the function is no longer in progress, i.e.,
      EOF or error
EndDo
End CARD_TO_DISK

ALGORITHM 4-4   Card-to-Disk Algorithm with Double Buffering

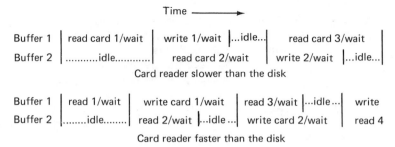

Time ———————➤

Buffer 1 | read card 1/wait | write 1/wait |...idle...| read card 3/wait |
Buffer 2 |..........idle..........| read card 2/wait | write 2/wait |...idle...|

Card reader slower than the disk

Buffer 1 | read 1/wait | write card 1/wait | read 3/wait |...idle...| write |
Buffer 2 |........idle........| read 2/wait |...idle...| write card 2/wait | read 4 |

Card reader faster than the disk

FIGURE 4-16 Operation of Double Buffering as a Function of the Device Speed

the other buffer will not be available until the write completes.) Examination of the algorithm reveals that as soon as the previous write finishes, the next write is started, followed immediately by the reading of another card into the recently vacated buffer.

From this simple analysis it can be seen that the double buffering approach, as presented in Algorithm 4-4, will operate at the speed of the slowest device. As a matter of fact, if the speed of the disk varies between these two cases, due to interference from other processes, the algorithm still functions at the speed of the currently slowest device, thus keeping it busy 100 percent of the time.

Returning to the utilization calculations made earlier, it can be seen that the utilization of all equipment has improved with double buffering. The elapsed time for dedicated devices using double buffering is

Card read time	0.060000	second
Disk write time	(0.030000)	(overlapped with next read)
CPU time	0.000100	
Elapsed time	0.060100	second

This results in 99.83% card reader utilization, 49.92 percent disk utilization, and 0.17 percent utilization of the CPU. Again notice that the CPU is actually 100 percent utilized but mostly in the nonproductive wait loop for the card reader.

PROBLEMS

1. In the MOS computer system, I/O devices have three states: ready, busy, and failed. List the transitions between these states and describe the events or activities that cause each.   [Ana]

2. Add a row to Table 4-1 for a floppy disk rotating at 60 rpm and containing 16 sectors per track with 256 bytes per sector.   [Ana]

3. Write a program containing instructions that store directly into the controller registers of a terminal on your computer system. (If your terminals are connected via a channel, code a channel program within your program.)

The program should prompt you for your name, then echo print your response. If you have a laboratory computer that can be dedicated to your use, test and debug your program.   [OS]

4. In reference to cycle stealing: who steals what cycles from whom, when, and why?   [Ana]

5. Code a fragment of a typical assembler language program to multiply an array of 1000 integers by a constant. Determine the i-time, d-time, and e-time for each instruction in the loop. Assume that this code is executing while a DMA transfer for one sector of data from a disk is being input. Using the disk transfer rate for your computer system, calculate the expected impact of cycle stealing on the execution of the program. Assume that the first DMA transfer begins at the instant the first instruction in the loop is to be executed.   [OS]

6. Work the general case of problem 5, assuming an unknown relationship between the first DMA transfer and instructions in the loop.   [OS]

7. The discussion related to Figure 4-14 presented a scenario for the processes becoming deadlocked due to lack of disk space.

   a. What could be done to detect impending deadlock due to depletion of disk space?
   b. What actions could be taken to attempt to prevent the deadlock once the threat has been detected?
   c. In order, what actions should be taken to remove such a deadlock once it has occurred?   [Ana]

8. Throughput is defined as the amount of useful work done in a given period of time. Discuss the importance of SPOOLing with regard to throughput.
                                                                              [Ana]

9. Discuss the importance of SPOOLing with respect to resource utilization.
                                                                              [Ana]

10. Assume that the allocation of disk sectors in Algorithms 4-3 and 4-4 is valid regardless of the number of processes requesting disk space. Explain the necessity of the first assumption in these algorithms; that is:

    a. Why must the card reader be dedicated to this process?
    b. Why must the disk be dedicated to this process?
    c. Why must neither device be busy initially?   [Ana]

11. Implement and test a program to copy a disk file using the techniques of Algorithm 4-4. (See problem 13 in Chapter 1.)   [OS]

12. Rewrite Algorithm 4-4 to support blocking of the card images three per disk sector. Remove the assumption that sector allocation is always successful and ensure that all I/O is complete before terminating the routine.
                                                                              [OS]

13. Implement and test the program in problem 12. (Refer to problems 7 and 13 in Chapter 1 for interfaces.)   [OS]

14. Design, code, and test a program that will simulate SPOOLer card-to-disk activities. The program is to accomplish its input and output via the MOS simulator. Your program must therefore be compatible with the simulator interfaces defined in Appendix B. GET and FREE service routines from

problem 21 of Chapter 2 should be used to dynamically acquire and release
buffer and status variable space. Aside from these modules, your program
should consist of four additional subprograms as follows.

(1) The main program should be a simple driver that calls the MOSUP
initialization routine, then repeatedly calls CARD_TO_DISK to
transfer entire simulated card decks to the simulated disk, one deck
per call. The main program should display the returned status, job
name, and card count after each call to CARD_TO_DISK and
terminate execution upon detection of any device failure.

(2) CARD_TO_DISK should use double buffering to copy and block
cards, three per sector, as they are written to disk and should ensure
maximum device overlap. Buffer space and status variable space
must be obtained from your GET routine and all acquired space
must be released via your FREE routine before returning to the
main program. Disk sector numbers should be obtained as needed
from the simulator GETDSK service. Finally, all errors should be
detected and returned via the status output parameter. (Note that it
is possible for multiple errors to occur simultaneously; thus some
encoding of the status is in order.) The recommended interface to
CARD_TO_DISK is shown below.

(3) INITIO is a very simple interface routine between the MOS SC
interrupt handler and the simulated SIO instruction. It is called by
CARD_TO_DISK via the simulator SC routine as specified in Appendix B.

(4) WAITIO is a also a simple interface routine. It is called by the SC

Begin CARD_TO_DISK | Copy an entire card deck to disk blocking
three cards per sector. Terminate the copy
function upon detecting the characters "EOF "
in the first four columns of a card. Do not
explicitly copy the EOF card to disk.

Input　　− SC_PARAMETER_INDEX to an array of
　　　　　eight words for communicating calling
　　　　　parameters to service routines
　　　　− Card images from the simulator

Output　− An eight-character JOB_NAME from
　　　　　columns 5–12 of the first card of a
　　　　　deck, provided that the card starts with
　　　　　the characters "JOB "
　　　　− COUNT of the number of non-EOF
　　　　　cards successfully transferred to disk
　　　　− STATUS indicating the termination
　　　　　state of CARD_TO_DISK, e.g., success,
　　　　　failure due to missing JOB card,
　　　　　memory allocation error, card reader
　　　　　failure, disk failure, combinations
　　　　　of the above, etc.
　　　　− Supplied images to the simulated disk

interrupt handler and implements a busy-waiting loop calling the simulated **TIO** instruction routine until a nonbusy device state is detected. [MOS]

15. Provide the DISK_TO_PRINTER version of Algorithm 4-4. It should copy a specified number, COUNT, of print lines from consecutive sectors of disk beginning with a specified sector, START. COUNT may be either odd or even. The algorithm should execute with maximum device overlap regardless of which device is slower. [Alg]

16. a. Extend the algorithm of problem 15 to deblock print lines that have been packed two per disk sector. You may read only whole sectors. Simplify the algorithm by ignoring all types of errors.
    b. Provide an analysis of your algorithm similar to that associated with Figure 4-16. If it does not execute at the speed of the slowest device, fix your algorithm. [Alg]

17. Extend the algorithm of problem 16 to include handling all possible error conditions. [Alg]

18. Implement and test the program in problem 17. (Refer to problems 7 and 13 in Chapter 1 for interfaces.) [OS]

19. Design, code, and test a program that will simulate SPOOLer disk-to-printer activities. The program is to accomplish its input and output via the MOS simulator. Your program must therefore be compatible with the simulator interfaces defined in Appendix B. GET and FREE from problem 21 of Chapter 2 should be used to dynamically acquire and release buffer and status variable space. Aside from these modules, your program should consist of four additional subprograms as follows.

    (1) The main program should be a simple driver that calls the MOSUP initialization routine, then repeatedly calls the simulator GETJOB routine and DISK_TO_PRINTER to transfer entire simulated print jobs from SPOOL files to the simulated printer. The main program should display the returned status, starting sector number, and job line count after each call to GETJOB, print the status and count of successful line transfers after each call to DISK_TO_PRINTER, and terminate execution upon detection of any device failure or when GETJOB indicates that no more jobs are waiting for the printer.

    (2) DISK_TO_PRINTER should use double buffering to copy and deblock pairs of print lines from each sector and copy them to the printer. It should also ensure maximum device overlap. Buffer space and status variable space must be obtained from your GET routine and all acquired space must be released via your FREE routine before returning to the main program. Blocks of print lines for each job are stored in consecutive sectors beginning with the sector specified by GETJOB. Finally, all errors should be detected and returned via the status output parameter. (Note that it is possible for multiple errors to occur simultaneously; thus some encoding of the status is in order.) The recommended interface to DISK_TO_PRINTER is shown below.

(3) INITIO is a very simple interface routine between the MOS SC interrupt handler and the simulated **SIO** instruction. It is called by DISK_TO_PRINTER via the simulator SC routine as specified in Appendix B.

(4) WAITIO is a also a simple interface routine. It is called by the SC interrupt handler and provides a busy-waiting loop calling the simulated **TIO** instruction routine until a nonbusy device state is detected.   [MOS]

Begin DISK_TO_PRINTER

> Copy all lines of a single print job from disk to printer deblocking pairs of lines from each sector
>
> Input   – STARTING_SECTOR_NUMBER for the job
> – NUMBER_OF_LINES in the job
> – SC_PARAMETER_INDEX to an array of eight words for communicating calling parameters to service routines
> – Images from the simulated disk
>
> Output   – COUNT of the number of lines successfully transferred to the printer
> – STATUS indicating the termination state of DISK_TO_PRINTER, e.g., successful, memory allocation error, printer failure, disk failure, combinations of the above, etc.
> – Supplied images to the simulated printer

20. Consider the Algorithm 4-4 extended to use three buffers.

   a. What modifications are necessary?
   b. What are the advantages, if any, of using three buffers? Explain your answer.
   c. What are the advantages, if any, of using $n > 3$ buffers?   [Ana]

21. Design an algorithm to accept characters as they are typed on the keyboard of a terminal, store them in a supplied buffer, and echo them to the associated CRT. Consider the terminal as two devices, each connected via a byte (character)-oriented direct controller. You have **SIO, TIO, IN,** and **OUT** instructions, as they apply to direct controllers. Simplify your algorithm by ignoring all hardware error possibilities. Use the following interface.   [Alg]

Begin TERMINAL_IN

Input – INPUT device address
        – ECHO device address
        – ADDRESS of the output BUFFER
        – MAX size of the buffer

Output – STATUS
        – BUFFER containing user input
        – COUNT of the number of characters in BUFFER

Notes – Backspace character erases the previous character in the BUFFER, if any
        – Carriage return character signals the end of the input line but is not stored in the BUFFER
        – Carriage return is sent to the ECHO device followed by a line feed character
        – Control-X character deletes all previous characters in the BUFFER, if any

22. Work problem 21 considering all error possibilities.   [Alg]

CHAPTER 5

Interrupts and Input/Output

The extensive amounts of CPU time needed in the I/O wait loops of Chapter 4 may be acceptable in a uniprogramming environment, but definitely are not acceptable in a multiprogramming system. Other processes are awaiting their turns for the CPU and such unproductive expenditures of the CPU resource are in opposition to the objectives of multiprogramming. A mechanism is needed whereby a process performing I/O can temporarily relinquish control of the processor, then regain its services when the I/O operation is complete. Such a capability is provided by the combined actions of the hardware interrupt facility and the software interrupt subsystem.

5.1
Interrupts

5.1.1 The Concept of Interruption

An **interrupt** is a signal to the central processor indicating that a special event has occurred and that at the earliest convenient time, the system should temporarily suspend its current activity and respond to the needs of the event. Frequently, interrupts are triggered by asynchronous, unscheduled, or unexpected external events. The ringing of a telephone, doorbell, or kitchen timer is the analogous condition for the human processor. When these interrupts, or signals, are detected, the person normally suspends the present activity in a timely but orderly manner and responds to the external stimulus.

Human experience encompasses several different classes of interrupts with an implied hierarchy or priority. For example, if one is reading a book, this current process may be interrupted by an event of virtually any importance. One such interruption, of low priority, might be another person entering the room and asking a question. In polite company, this interruption is itself normally not interrupted by other events of the same class, such as a comment from yet another person. Hearing a telephone at this time will, however, normally result in the processor, the original person, suspending the conversation temporarily to respond to the higher-priority event, the telephone call. The suspension is again accomplished in an orderly fashion. Conversations are normally suspended in an orderly manner at the end of a sentence and with mutual agreement. Should a fire alarm now sound, processing of the telephone interrupt would itself be suspended, perhaps indefinitely, in favor of the relatively more important event.

The human processor informally identifies several classes of interrupts, each of which has a unique position within the hierarchy and each of which may include several elements. The door bell and telephone may share a class that is of lower priority than the class containing the fire alarm and the needs of an injured child.

5.1.2 Computer Interrupts

Similarly, computer systems have classes of interrupts ordered by priority. Table 5-1 contains a list of typical interrupt classes and a representative hierarchical structure. Actual supported interrupts and their priorities depend on the computer manufacturer, model of computer, and the operating system configuration of the particular installation.

Although most interrupts originate external to the environment of a process, some are not externally caused. A process voluntarily relinquishes control of the CPU to the operating system by requesting a class of interrupts referred to as executive, supervisor, or **system call** (SC) interrupts. This interrupt is the mechanism for accessing an operating system service that would otherwise be outside the addressable memory area of the process. For example, processes are not allowed to execute calls directly to dynamic memory management or I/O controller interface software. Such access could constitute unacceptable compromises of system integrity. Therefore, access to the services of the operating system is obtained by executing a special instruction that triggers an

TABLE 5-1 Typical Interrupt Classes and Relative Priorities

Class (Increasing Priority)	Description
System call	Request to the operating system for a standard service
Program error	Invalid instruction, invalid access to protected memory, division by zero, etc.
Input/output	Input/output device needs attention
Timer	Designated time of day is reached or an interval of time has elapsed
Machine malfunction	Memory parity error, invalid CPU state, etc.
Power fail	Loss of electrical power

interrupt. The SC interrupt handler of the operating system is thus given control, in a regulated manner. It checks the validity of the caller's request, then transfers control to the requested service on behalf of the calling program.

The second class of interrupts in Table 5-1 is that of program exceptions. They are also triggered by the executing process but are normally involuntary relinquishings of control. Typically, the operating system will determine that further execution of the process is inappropriate and will abort it.

All other interrupt events are asynchronous and external to the CPU. Relative to the currently executing process, the instant and nature of I/O and timer interrupts are unknown, but their occurrence is as normal as the telephone ringing, and the operating system handles them in an orderly and routine manner. As in the human experience example, when servicing of the interrupt is complete, normal processing will resume. When a telephone conversation has ended, the previously suspended discussion with another person may be resumed. After the conversation is in turn complete, the reading of the book will be continued at its point of suspension.

This orderly suspension and resumption is not followed by machine-malfunction and power-failure interruptions. These are considered catastrophic events requiring a "drop everything" approach in order to save hardware and information from severe damage. They are events analogous to the building being on fire and necessitate immediate action to protect equipment by shutting down the computer. For example, when a power failure occurs, disk and drum read/write heads must be retracted since failure to do so will result in the heads settling to the surfaces with velocities of several tens to a few hundreds of miles per hour. Such crash landings invariably result in loss of extensive amounts of recorded data and expensive physical damage to the equipment.

5.2
Process- and Device-State Changes

5.2.1 The Three Basic States

Before addressing the mechanics of interrupt processing, let us refine the concept of process states and state transitions. In general, a process is always in one of three basic states: running, ready, or blocked. The relationships between these states are illustrated in Figure 5-1.

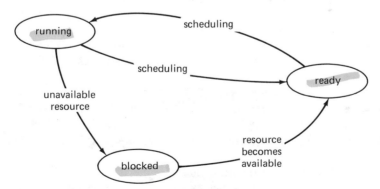

FIGURE 5-1 Basic Process State Transitions

The **running state** is defined by a process PCB being addressed by the contents of the current PCB pointer field of the SCB. Generally, an instruction for the running process is being executed by the CPU. (The exceptions to executing the running process exist when the CPU is executing an instruction within the interrupt subsystem or service subsystem software.) In a uniprocessor system, only one PCB can be in the running state at any given time.

In MOS, the **ready state** is defined as a condition in which all resources necessary for execution are available except for the CPU and possibly memory. The list of PCBs in such a state may be maintained in any of several orders, depending on how process scheduling policies are to be implemented. The ready-state list is, however, generally referred to as the ready queue, as indeed it frequently is.

Transitions between ready and running are governed by the scheduling policies of the system. This is the private domain of the dispatcher, and therefore no process can take explicit action to cause itself to move from the running state to the ready state or from ready to running.

The third basic state, **blocked,** applies to processes that are ineligible for execution consideration. They are blocked from being ready due to missing resources other than the CPU and memory. If a process reads a card, and if the read operation must complete prior to continuing execution, the process transitions from the running state to the blocked state to await completion of the read. A process remains in the blocked state until the missing resource is available. When its blocking obstruction is removed, it becomes ready to run again.

5.2.2 State Transitions

It is precisely this sequence of transitions that is needed in the CARD_TO_DISK module (Algorithm 4-4) of CRSPOOL, the card reader SPOOL process. Rather than remain in the running state executing a "wait until I/O completes" loop, CRSPOOL should become blocked, allowing other processes to execute. When the MOS interrupt subsystem determines that the I/O operation has been completed, it can cause CRSPOOL to move back to the ready queue. Eventually, the dispatcher will reschedule the process, allowing it to continue executing productive logic.

In practice there are many substates within the blocked state. Processes can be blocked while waiting for an I/O operation to complete, waiting for a tape to be mounted, until 8:00 A.M., until a signal is received from another process, and so on. As the study of MOS proceeds, many different reasons for process blocking will be introduced. (A more complete state transition diagram can be found in Chapter 9 in conjunction with the presentation of SCB list management and process scheduling.)

As seen in Chapter 4, I/O devices have states and transitions similar to those of processes. In simplest terms, the state of a device can be represented by one of three controller status register values: ready, busy, or failed. In the ready state the device is operational but not actively performing input or output operations. It is ready to accept work on command.

When the controller successfully initiates the transfer of information, the device is switched from the ready to the busy state, where it remains until the transmission is complete. During this time the controller maintains a value of

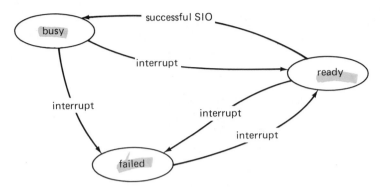

FIGURE 5-2 I/O Device State Transitions

busy in the corresponding status register. The ready-to-busy state transition is one of the five possible transitions shown in Figure 5-2. When the device completes a transmission, the controller changes the status register value to either ready or failed, depending on whether the transmission ended successfully or in failure. In either case an interrupt signal will be sent to the CPU.

The final two transitions in Figure 5-2 do not involve I/O operations. Devices are perfectly capable of entering a failed state while not actually transmitting data. For example, a terminal that is not in use can be switched off, placing it in a failed state. Similarly, a failed device can be repaired or reactivated, thus transitioning from the failed state back to the ready state.

5.3
Data Structures and Processing for Input and Output

A step-by-step analysis of the primary actions necessary to accomplish input/output in an interruptible environment will serve to identify the major logic and data components of the task. First, recall that the existence of a MOS dispatcher, which will implement the process scheduling policy, has already been declared. Also, there exists a system control block, SCB, containing pointers to the various lists within MOS. So far, the nodes of these lists are process control blocks (PCBs) and free space blocks (FSBs). The particular list on which a PCB resides indicates the state of the process and, thus far, the PCB contains information that indicates where the process swap file is located on disk and what portion of memory, if any, is currently occupied by the corresponding program. Figure 5-3 provides a review of these structural relationships.

Now suppose that the double-buffered CARD_TO_DISK routine of Algorithm 4-4 is executing as part of the CRSPOOL process in a multiprogramming environment. What are the I/O related elements of its job? Examination of the algorithm indicates three basic interfaces to the I/O services: (1) operations must be initiated to read a card and write a disk sector, (2) CRSPOOL must wait for operations to complete and relinquish control of the CPU to other processes during this period (i.e., it must block itself when no productive use can be made of the CPU), and (3) the status of completed I/O operations must be ascertained. Recall that these functions must apply to a multiuser system in

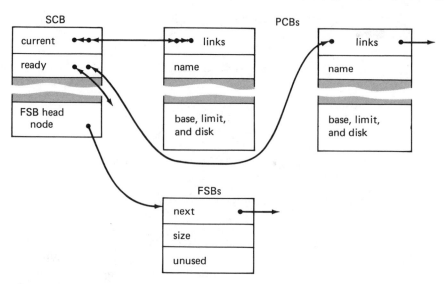

FIGURE 5-3   Review of Previous MOS Data Structures

which the use of some devices, such as the card reader, are dedicated, while others are concurrently shared among many processes. (Disks are obviously shared devices, a characteristic of which is that they may already be in use at the time a process wishes to initiate an activity to them.) Let us now investigate these three elements of I/O in more detail and derive the MOS system data structures necessary for their support.

5.3.1 Initiating Input/Output Transfer

Device-State Dependence

Recall from Chapter 4 that **initiating an I/O transfer** involves examining the state of the associated device and, when found ready, issuing the start command. From Figure 5-2 it may be seen that there are three possibilities for the device state:

1. The device has failed.
2. It is ready to accept work.
3. It is currently busy.

Appropriate action for the first device state is rather straightforward. In the case of device failure, it is not possible to proceed; thus a status variable supplied by the caller should be set to indicate the failure. CARD_TO_DISK will then abort its mission.

When the device is found in a ready state, logic is executed to load the appropriate controller registers and initiate the data transfer. But more is needed. We must think ahead to the time the operation is completed and anticipate the needs of software that must process the completion. When the transfer completes, an I/O interrupt will result in the temporary suspension of whatever activity is currently being executed by the CPU, and the I/O interrupt portion of the MOS interrupt subsystem will execute. This software must be able to decide to which process the just completed I/O transfer belongs. Thus some mechanism must be used to designate the process associated with currently active I/O operations. Such designation must apply on a device-by-device basis. If there are four disks in the system, all four could be busy at one time for up to four different processes. Disk interrupt-handling logic must know with whom each operation is associated in order to remove the correct process from the blocked state when its I/O is complete. If each I/O operation is managed by its own control block, a field in this block can point to the associated process and thus identify the originator of each operation.

In summary, when a device is found to be ready, it is not sufficient merely to send the start information to its controller. Since a requesting process will frequently not be in the running state when the operation completes, some mechanism for identifying the requesting process must be available to the interrupt subsystem modules.

The third possibility in initiating a transfer is that the device is found to be in the busy state. As we have seen, it is unacceptable to expect a process to loop or spin waiting for a device to become available. That is, we do not wish to have I/O start logic in CARD_TO_DISK similar to

> **Do**
>> Test the state of the device
> **Until** the device is not busy
> **EndDo**
>
> **If** the state is ready
> **Then**
>> Start the next data transfer
>> .
>> .
>> .

A common solution to this problem is to form the new request into a node and place it in a queue of pending operations for the specified device. The node must contain all information necessary to initiate the transfer operation when the device becomes available. Availability will occur when an I/O interrupt from the controller is processed and the device is found to have transitioned from the busy state to the ready state. The software that handles the interrupt for that device can therefore perform the start function. From this analysis, we see that the task of the interrupt handler is to gain control when an interrupt is detected, cause the process associated with the completed operation to become unblocked, and start the next I/O operation in the queue, if any.

The Elements of I/O Data Transfer

From this analysis, one data structure and two standard service modules are indicated directly. First, a **queue of I/O operations** associated with each device is needed. The queue nodes must contain all information necessary to start the operation and to identify the requesting process.

A service module, INITIATE_IO, is needed to construct the queue node and start the transfer if the device is available. This module must also return the status of the start function.

The second I/O service module, WAIT_IO, should provide the function of **waiting for an operation to complete.** (It is important to note that the wait is for an I/O operation to complete, but not for the device itself to finish all current and pending operations.) WAIT_IO must address the question of how to know when to wait and how to do so efficiently. Consider the case of the shared disk. Is it adequate to test the current state of the device to determine whether or not a write from CRSPOOL is complete? Specifically, if the disk is busy, can the CARD_TO_DISK routine conclude that its write is still pending? No, it cannot.

Suppose that CARD_TO_DISK initially finds the disk ready and starts an operation, as described in the preceding paragraphs. Execution then continues in parallel with an overlapping card-reading operation. During this period, some other process attempts to start a transfer to the disk. By the time CARD_TO_DISK reaches its disk-wait logic, the original write may have long since completed, but the subsequent transfer for the other process might still be in progress. Indeed, there may be many transfer operations queued to the device. It certainly is not appropriate to force the CRSPOOL process to remain blocked waiting for unrelated disk operations to finish just so the condition of a ready disk can indicate success for the original operation.

A reasonably clean solution to the problem of relating completion of I/O operations to the correct process is for the MOS service WAIT_IO to function as follows:

1. If the device is busy, examine the queue of pending operations. If a node associated with the current process is located, block the current process pending completion of all such requests. Should no such operation be found in the queue, any and all previous requests have cleared the queue. In this case, there is no reason to block the process; therefore, it can be allowed to continue executing.
2. If the device is ready, all operations for all processes have apparently completed and again the current (requesting) process can continue executing.
3. A failed device indicates that no further transfers are appropriate; however, the question of whether or not the subject operation completed prior to failure must be answered. Since all previous operations will have either completed successfully prior to the failure or will, by definition, have failed at the time the device failed, no additional information can be gained from the WAIT_IO function, so no specific action is needed.

The queue of I/O requests and the INITIATE_IO and WAIT_IO services address the obvious requirements of CARD_TO_DISK, but in doing so raise the issue of how to block a process. Adding an I/O wait list to the system control block and causing the PCB of the running process to be moved to this list from the current list will satisfy the blocking requirement.

Thus far we have analyzed process support activities for initiating I/O operations and waiting for them to complete. The final activity which requires MOS support is that of **determining the status** of completed operations. As can be seen from the analysis of the wait problem, the current state of the device tells us nothing about the status of an operation completed previously. If the device has failed, did it fail after or prior to completion of the operation? Similarly, if it is ready, might it not have failed during the subject transfer and subsequently become restored? These questions produce the requirement that, upon completion, the interrupt subsystem must return the correct status of the operation to the associated process. This requirement applies both to successful operations and to operations in progress or pending at the time of a failure.

With this analysis we have completed the requirements for program interface to the I/O portion of the service subsystem. If the interface were now to be explicitly designed and algorithms developed, one would see, however, that there is a key component still missing. I/O operations are performed in an asynchronous fashion. The completion times do not correspond to the execution of any of the identified interface functions. When I/O completes, the controller generates an interrupt to the CPU, notifying it of the event. But the defined interface routines all execute on behalf of some calling program. When an I/O interrupt occurs, MOS does not know immediately which device, let alone which process operation, is associated with the interrupt. Identifying these elements and acting appropriately will be the function of the MOS interrupt-handling software, which executes not on behalf of a process, but rather, on behalf of a device. The remainder of this section will define data structures that permit the MOS I/O software to support process I/O in a multiprogramming environment.

Interrupts are hardware signals to the CPU. Interrupt handlers are software. A method must exists to bridge from a hardware event to a software module execution. Each interrupt can be viewed as an asynchronous call by the hardware to a software interrupt-handling routine. A common way to accomplish this call is via an interrupt vector. The **interrupt vector** is a sequentially allocated linear list located at a fixed location in memory. Through this list the interrupt facility invokes the appropriate software handler and communicates fundamental information about the source of the interrupt to the handler. Typically, the interrupt vector contains the starting address of the interrupt handler module and provides a place to store the cause of the interrupt and the current state of the CPU.

Summary of Basic I/O Elements

This section has now identified five additions to the MOS computer system.

1. The INITIATE_IO service either starts or queues an I/O request.
2. The WAIT_IO service determines if all previous I/O requests by the calling process have been completed and blocks the caller if not.
3. A queue of active and pending requests exists for each I/O device.
4. An I/O wait list provides a place to keep track of PCBs for processes blocked due to incomplete I/O operations.
5. The interrupt vector is used by the hardware to initiate interrupt processing by the software.

5.3.2 MOS Data Structures Supporting I/O

An expanded and more detailed view of the MOS data structures, including all of those necessary for controlling input and output, is given in Figure 5-4. This is a very important summary, and thorough knowledge of it is essential for understanding the I/O algorithms and techniques presented in the remainder of this chapter.

Device Control Block

One of the new structures shown in Figure 5-4 is the **device control block** (DCB). This is a central structure in the MOS I/O philosophy. There is a single unique DCB for each I/O device connected to the computer. It is to the device

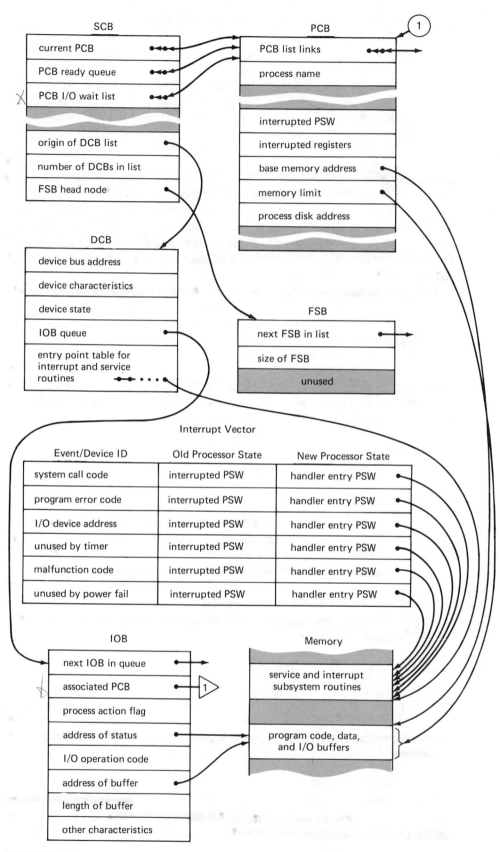

FIGURE 5-4 Data Structure for Accommodating I/O

Device address
>   3

Device characteristics
>   Serial access
>   Nonsharable
>   Indirect I/O controller
>   Block size of 80 bytes
>   etc.

Device status
>   Ready, busy, or failed

IOB queue
>   Null or pointer to last node of a circular queue of pending
>   I/O operations

Entry point table
>   Address of the interrupt subsystem module for handling
>   interrupts for this type of device, e.g., DEVICE_IH (see the
>   next section)
>   Address of the service routine for reading the device, e.g.,
>   INITIATE_IO
>   Address of the service routine for writing the device (null
>   for card readers)
>   Address of the service routine for rewinding the device
>   (null for card readers)

>   .
>   .
>   .

>   Address of the service routine for nonstandard operations
>   (null for card readers)

FIGURE 5-5 Functional Contents of a Card Reader DCB

as a PCB is to a process. Each DCB describes the characteristics and state of one device in a standard format. For example, a card reader having a physical address of 3 might have a DCB containing the data shown in Figure 5-5.

The device address in the DCB is determined by where the controller is connected to the bus and to which port of the controller the device is assigned. This is the physical address of the device and is the identifier stored in the first field of the I/O row of the interrupt vector by the interrupt generation hardware (see Figure 5-4). The device characteristics, which follow the identifier in the DCB, are very dependent on the type of device and are not of major concern in the general discussion of I/O.

As indicated in Figures 5-4 and 5-5, a copy of the current device status is maintained by MOS in the DCB associated with each device. When an interrupt occurs, the interrupt subsystem software must be able to determine which transition the device has taken. Knowing the old state from the DCB and the new state from the controller status register determines the transition. Obviously, different interrupt-handling actions are appropriate depending on whether the transition is from busy to ready, busy to failed, failed to ready, or ready to failed.

The fourth area of the DCB is the queue of I/O operations control data. The nodes of this queue are called input/output blocks and are maintained in a simple circular queue, the rear node of which is addressed by the pointer in the DCB. The front of the queue is addressed by the link field of the rear IOB; thus, both add and remove operations may occur without traversing the list and only a single pointer is needed to access the list. Adding a new node to the rear of the queue simply involves inserting a node between the rear and front nodes and advancing the IOB queue pointer in the DCB to the new rear node. If an I/O operation is in progress (i.e., the device is busy), its operation is specified by the IOB at the front of the queue.

The last area of the DCB provides linkage to the many software modules needed to support a particular device. The function of these modules varies with each device type. The fixed-length table of entry-point addresses contains a value for each standard function. Those services not appropriate (e.g., rewind the card reader) are indicated by null addresses; those routines available are indicated by nonnull addresses. The only entry point not programmatically accessible via SC instructions is that of the second-phase interrupt handler. This module handles the details of interrupt processing for the particular device once the initial phase I/O interrupt handler has determined which device needs attention. It will be covered in more detail in the algorithms in Section 5.4.

In summary, the DCB structure is a sequentially allocated, ordered linear list with a unique node for each device in the system. The correct DCB for a device is identified by the device physical address stored in the first field of the DCB. Many devices of the same type, e.g., terminals with similar characteristics, may share common service and interrupt code by addressing the same modules in their entry-point tables. The DCB list is located by a pointer in the SCB.

Input/Output Blocks

Input/output blocks (IOBs) completely describe an individual I/O operation. All IOBs for a device are linked together in a queue, pointed to by the DCB for the device. The structure of IOB nodes is also shown in Figure 5-4.

The associated PCB field of the IOB indicates the PCB of the process for which the operation is being, or is to be, performed. This pointer is used by WAIT_IO in determining whether or not I/O operations are pending for the current process. A flag in the IOB also indicates whether or not the process should be unblocked when this I/O operation completes. Together the PCB and flag field allow the proper process to be identified when the operation is completed and to be unblocked when appropriate.

The status field of the IOB is an address indicating a memory location within the associated process. The variable at this address will be updated to reflect the results of the operation when it completes.

The last four fields in the IOB are dependent on the type of controller to which the device is connected. Figure 5-4, and the remainder of this text, assume that indirect controllers are used, as defined in Chapter 4. For them, the important information is the type of operation and the address and length of the data buffer. If either direct I/O controllers or channels were used, other fields would be defined. For example, an IOB for a device connected via a channel would need an address field to locate the beginning of the channel program, but would not need the operation and buffer information fields.

Interrupt Vector

The last new MOS data structure is associated directly with interrupt handling. The **interrupt vector,** which is located at a fixed address in memory, is updated by the interrupt hardware as part of the activity of changing the state of the CPU for interrupt processing. For each class of interrupt, the vector contains a row of three fields.

1. A **code** or identifier indicating the cause of the interrupt is stored in the first field of the vector element. For example, if the I/O device at physical address 3 causes an interrupt, the value 3 will be stored in this field of the third row of the vector.

2. The current contents of the processor status word, PSW, are saved in the **old PSW** field for the class of interrupt being signaled. (Recall that the PSW contains the program counter, condition code, interrupt mask, and other fields which, when considered with the general registers and memory address mapping registers, specify the state of the CPU and the currently executing activity.)

3. The final action in changing to an interrupt processing mode is the reloading of the PSW from the **new PSW** field of the element for the interrupt class. The contents of the new PSW should be such that loading the PSW makes four significant changes to the state of the CPU:

    a. Memory address mapping is disabled, thus allowing absolute addresses to be used rather than process relative addresses.

    b. The CPU is placed in the system state, where privileged instructions can be executed.

    c. The interrupt mask is changed to reflect the new state of interrupt disabling appropriate to the type of processing that is to follow. (In the MOS computer the interrupt mask is a logical template that describes which interrupt classes are to be allowed and which are to be ignored or blocked. Interrupt classes that are still allowed can interrupt the current processing. Those which are disabled will be queued by the hardware for later processing.) An interrupt is thus able to issue a call to a MOS software module to handle the event and to guarantee that other similar events will be delayed just as telephone hardware triggers processing by a human and blocks further telephone interruptions during processing of the first call.

    d. The program counter is changed to the address of the first instruction in the initial phase interrupt handler (e.g. IO_IH).

The activity just described is actually a unit operation accomplished by the interrupt hardware. The occurrence of an interrupt stores the identifying code and the contents of the PSW register into the vector and loads new contents of the PSW from the vector. All of this is accomplished as a single action.

5.4
Program Logic for Multiprogrammed Input/Output

In Section 5.3 we developed a set of requirements and defined an architecture for accomplishing input and output in a MOS uniprocessor, multiprogramming environment. The structure may seem complex, but actually it has been simplified several times over from the complexity of contemporary operating systems. The MOS structure is nonetheless both instructional and representative.

5.4.1   An Example of Input/Output Within MOS

As a prelude to examining detailed I/O software logic, consider a functional example of performing disk I/O within this framework. A simple read to a shared disk is carried from initiation through completion with emphasis on data structure manipulation. Algorithm design will then proceed to formalize the function.

Initially, assume that a high-priority process, JOB1, is running and that the disk is busy servicing a request from a medium-priority process, OTHER1. There is also a third process of lower priority, OTHER2, in the computer system. Figure 5-6 provides a graphical representation of the initial conditions. As can be seen, OTHER1 is blocked as indicated by its presence in the I/O wait list and the flag field of the IOB for its write request. The DCB indicates that the disk and controller are processing the write operation.

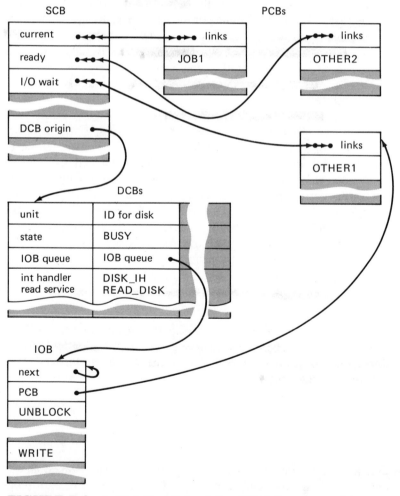

FIGURE 5-6   Initial Conditions for JOB1 Starting a Disk Read

Now assume that JOB1 executes an SC instruction to invoke the disk read service, READ_DISK (a specialized version of INITIATE_IO). READ_DISK is a privileged service subsystem module accessible only by a system call interrupt to MOS. The first-phase SC interrupt handler, SC_IH, is therefore given control by the PSW swapping action of the interrupt hardware. By examining the SC identification code stored in the interrupt vector by the hardware, SC_IH can determine that a disk read service is needed. Because this is an I/O-device-dependent function, SC_IH will locate the DCB for the disk and use the entry-point table therein to invoke READ_DISK on behalf of JOB1.

Since all I/O operations are managed by IOBs, READ_DISK must construct an IOB for the read operation requested. IOB space is allocated by a call to the GET_MEMORY service. Next READ_DISK completes the various fields of the IOB node and adds it to the rear of the queue for the disk. (Note that a second SC interrupt is not generated by the call to GET_MEMORY, since READ_DISK, running in the system state with memory address mapping disabled, has direct access to all other MOS services.)

Examination of the device-state field of the DCB by READ_DISK reveals that another operation, the write for OTHER1, is already in progress; thus the read initiation action is left to the second-phase interrupt handler for the disk, DISK_IH. (The DISK_IH version of DEVICE_IH will execute when the interrupt signaling completion of the current write operation is detected.) Through the actions of the MOS dispatcher, READ_DISK returns to the original calling routine of JOB1. As seen in Figure 5-7, JOB1 is still in the running state since it has not yet executed WAIT_IO. Its read request is pending. (Notice that in the figure the DCB points to the last IOB in the queue.)

Suppose that the next action by JOB1 is to wait for the disk read to complete. Again a MOS service is invoked via a system call. This time SC_IH executes the WAIT_IO service on JOB1's behalf. Examination of the DCB state field and the disk IOB queue reveal that JOB1 still has a request pending and that the device is working on its backlog. (The device is busy, IOBs are in the queue, and one IOB points to JOB1.) The IOB for JOB1 is therefore marked to indicate that the process is being blocked pending completion of the operation. The PCB for JOB1 is moved to the I/O wait list with the point of resumption being with the instruction following the WAIT_IO SC instruction. The JOB1 execution environment (PSW and general registers) will have been saved in the PCB for JOB1 as part of the SC_IH activity.

Later, when the current disk transfer for OTHER1 completes, the interrupt handler software will find the configuration shown in Figure 5-8. The interrupt hardware will save the current PSW in the interrupt vector element for I/O interrupts and call IO_IH, the first-phase interrupt handler for I/O interrupts. This routine is pointed to by the program counter of the new PSW field of the interrupt vector element, as shown in Figure 5-4. The interrupt mask in the new PSW indicates that additional I/O interrupts are disabled (as well as those of all lower-priority interrupts, such as system calls and program errors). The disabling of interrupts prevents the DCB and IOBs from being externally modified while the interrupt subsystem is updating them.

IO_IH first saves the CPU general registers in local storage, then examines the system/process state bit of the old PSW, stored in the I/O interrupt vector element, to determine whether the activity interrupted was a process or another interrupt handler. In the example, the activity interrupted is process OTHER2.

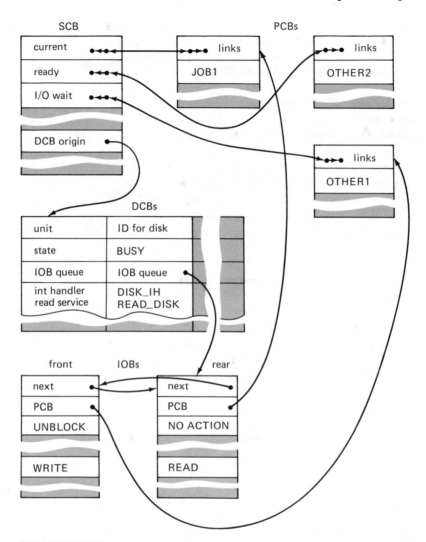

FIGURE 5-7   JOB1 Disk Read Has Been Queued to a Busy Device

IO_IH will therefore copy the old PSW contents and the saved general register contents into the designated save areas of the PCB for OTHER2. This action ensures that OTHER2 can be resumed properly at a later time.

Finally, the DCB list is examined by IO_IH to locate the control block for the device corresponding to the identifier stored in the interrupt vector. Having located the DCB for the disk, IO_IH calls the second-phase handler, DISK_IH, pointed to by the DCB. DISK_IH is provided with the address of the disk DCB.

Summarizing to this point, OTHER2 was running when an interrupt for the disk occurred. The interrupt hardware called the first-phase I/O interrupt software, IO_IH, and provided it with the physical address of the disk. This was all accomplished via the interrupt vector. IO_IH, in turn, saved the state of the OTHER2 process and then used the device address to find the DCB from which it obtained the entry-point address and called DISK_IH.

Examination of the status register of the appropriate controller by DISK_IH

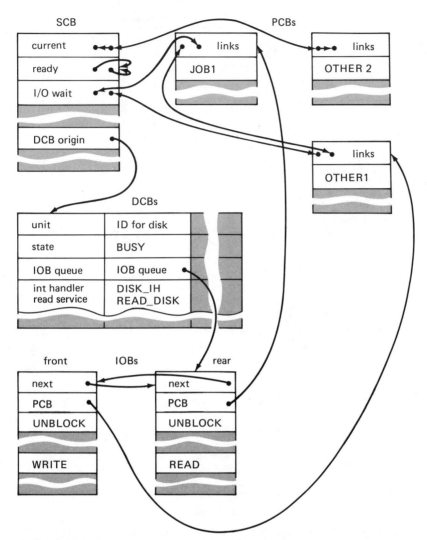

FIGURE 5-8 Conditions at the Time of the First Disk Interrupt

reveals that the disk has made the transition from busy, the state indicated in the DCB, to ready, the state from the controller. Its I/O being complete, the waiting process OTHER1 is now ready to resume. The pointer to the status variable in the program for OTHER1 and the memory base address from OTHER1's PCB are used to locate and update the program status variable. Through the status variable, DISK_IH communicates successful completion of the write operation. Next, a request is formed for the MOS dispatcher to remove OTHER1 from the blocked state and place it in the ready queue. Finally, the first IOB is removed from the queue and discarded via the FREE_MEMORY service.

With the processing of the operation associated with the original IOB complete, the IOB for JOB1 migrates to the front of the queue. DISK_IH extracts the transfer control information (e.g., the read command, buffer address, and size) and sends them to the appropriate controller to start the transfer of the data from disk into the JOB1 buffer area.

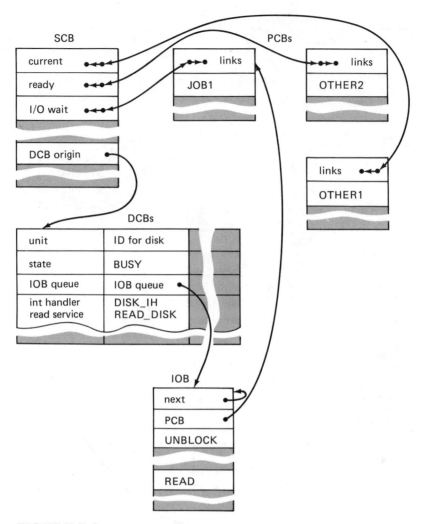

FIGURE 5-9   After Completion of the First Disk Transfer

Assuming that all of the foregoing activities proceed without error, DISK_IH returns to IO_IH. Since changes to process states and scheduling activities may be in order, as indeed they are, IO_IH does not resume the OTHER2 process suspended by the interrupt but rather transfers to the dispatcher. The dispatcher performs PCB list management and scheduling appropriately. These activities will have precipitated changes to the data structure such that the resulting state is as shown in Figure 5-9.

Finally, when the transfer for JOB1 completes, another interrupt will be generated and the same sequence will repeat, this time for the JOB1 read operation. In summary, the interrupt handling for successful I/O completion of the last transfer is as follows.

1. The interrupt facility saves the device code and old PSW and executes IO_IH.
2. IO_IH saves the processor general registers, locates the correct DCB, and calls the second-phase interrupt handler designated therein.

3. The second-phase handler ascertains status, updates the DCB and program status variable value, notifies the dispatcher (if the process is to become unblocked), discards the old IOB, and starts any next transfer operation.

4. Returning to IO_IH, and thence to the dispatcher, causes all requested PCB lists changes to be implemented and some process to be selected for execution.

5.4.2 The Five Basic I/O Modules

The example described above, and the requirements preceding it, have referenced five new MOS modules: SC_IH, INITIATE_IO, WAIT_IO, IO_IH, and DEVICE_IH. In the example, a specific implementation of INITIATE_IO, READ_DISK, existed for initiating read operations to the disk. Similarly, a disk-specific second-phase interrupt handler, DISK_IH, represented an instance of the more general routine DEVICE_IH. SC_IH and IO_IH are initial-phase interrupt handlers, callable by the interrupt hardware. They are members of the MOS interrupt subsystem. DEVICE_IH is a second-phase interrupt handler

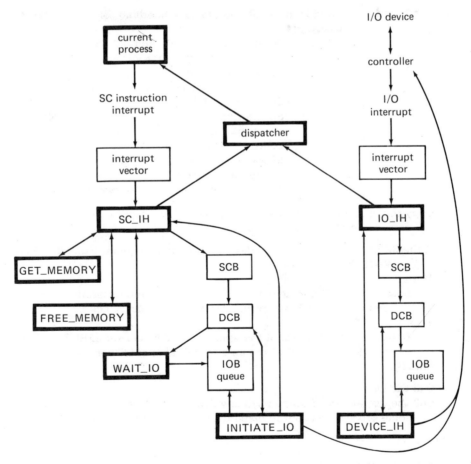

FIGURE 5-10 Functional Linkeage of Components Through SC and I/O Interrupts

also residing in the interrupt subsystem. All three of these modules run on behalf of MOS to help manage resources and/or protect system integrity.

As with the GET_MEMORY and FREE_MEMORY services of Chapter 2, INITIATE_IO and WAIT_IO execute on behalf of the calling program and for its specific benefit. They are therefore classified as service subsystem modules. (Technically, most service subsystem routines are second-phase interrupt handlers for system call interrupts.)

Figure 5-10 summarizes the access to the new modules and data structures through the use of interrupts. Software modules are shown as heavy boxes in the figure. The basic logic for the five routines is presented in Algorithms 5-1 through 5-5. The logic shown is for general service routines and I/O interrupt handlers representative of all modules of similar function. The logic is typical, but simplified, in that device-dependent features and secondary function logic are not included. Some of the capability omitted is addressed in the problems for this chapter. Indirect I/O controllers with direct memory access capability are assumed throughout the presentation.

Begin SC_IH

> Provide initial-phase interrupt handling for system call interrupts
> Input   – SC identification code and old PSW from the SC
>   element of the interrupt vector
>   – SCB and associated lists
> Output – SCB and associated lists
> Assume – SC code is valid
>   – SC interrupts are the lowest priority of all
>   interrupts; therefore, SC_IH always transfers
>   control to the MOS dispatcher
>   – Memory address mapping has been disabled by the
>   loading of the new PSW
>   – The CPU is operating in the system state

Copy the old PSW and all general register values into the appropriate
    save areas of the current PCB

If the SC code indicates an I/O-device-dependent request, e.g., INITIATE_IO
    or WAIT_IO
Then
    Locate the DCB for the device in the DCB list and determine the appropriate
        second-phase interrupt handler for the input SC code
Else
    Determine the address of the appropriate service, e.g., FREE_MEMORY
        or GET_MEMORY, from an internal table of SC services
EndIf

Call the located module
Call the dispatcher to accomplish any PCB list updates and to schedule
    some process to run (the dispatcher will not return to SC_IH)

End SC_IH

ALGORITHM 5-1   System Call Interrupt Handler

Begin INITIATE_IO

> Initiate, or queue the initiation of, an I/O operation. Note that this could easily be a less general routine for reading, writing, or otherwise manipulating a specific device, thus requiring fewer input parameters
>
> Input — DCB and IOB queue for the associated device provided by SC_IH
> — Command code for the I/O OPERATION to be started
> — BUFFER address and SIZE of the transfer
> — Address of the operation STATUS variable
> — SCB and associated lists
> Output — Program STATUS variable value
> — SCB and associated lists
> Assume — All inputs are valid
> — I/O interrupts are enabled
> — Memory address mapping is disabled
> — The CPU is operating in the system state

Disable I/O interrupts to prevent DCB and IOB queue updates
If the DCB device state is nonfailed, i.e., the device is operational
Then [Build an IOB, queue it, and start the operation if the device is ready]

Call **GET_MEMORY** to allocate space for a new IOB
If allocation was successful
Then

Complete the fields of the IOB, i.e., copy the addresses of the current PCB, STATUS, and BUFFER and the values of OPERATION and SIZE into the IOB and clear the process action flag
Add the IOB to the rear of the queue for the input DCB
Initialize the STATUS variable in the program to busy
If the DCB device state is ready
Then [The new IOB must be first, so start the operation]
Set the DCB status field to assume a busy device state
Command the controller to start the OPERATION

> Note that a device transition to failure will generate an interrupt to IO_IH after I/O interrupts are enabled and thus need not be handled here

Else [The operation is queued to start later and no further action is required at this time]

EndIf
Else
Set the STATUS variable to indicate IOB space is not available
EndIf
Else
Set the STATUS variable to indicate a failed device
EndIf
Enable I/O interrupts

End INITIATE_IO

ALGORITHM 5-2 Typical I/O Initiation Service Module

Begin WAIT_IO

> Ensure that all I/O requests from the current process to the
> specified device have completed
> Input   – DCB and IOB queue for the associated device
>   provided by SC_IH
>   – SCB and associated lists
> Output – SCB and associated lists
>   – Process state via the dispatcher
> Assume – I/O interrupts are enabled
>   – Memory address mapping is disabled
>   – The CPU is operating in the system state

Disable I/O interrupts to prevent DCB and IOB queue updates

If the DCB device state is busy
Then [Suspend the current process for any outstanding I/O]
       Examine the IOB queue for IOBs associated with the current PCB

       If any IOBs for the current process were located
       Then [Force the process to wait for the last such I/O operation
                to complete]
           Change the action flag in the last located IOB to indicate that
                the process is to be unblocked when this IOB is removed
         Notify the dispatcher that the current process is to be blocked,
            placing it in the I/O wait list
           [The dispatcher will be called from SC_IH upon completion of
           WAIT_IO]
       EndIf

Else [Any previous IOBs for this process have been cleared by
         DEVICE_IH; therefore, execution is allowed to continue]
EndIf

Enable I/O interrupts

End WAIT_IO

ALGORITHM 5-3   I/O Wait Service Module

5.5
A Final Look at Buffering

The concept of blocking processes was developed for the purpose of improved
resource utilization and sharing. If a process is not able to make meaningful
use of the CPU while an interactive user formulates a response, it is appropriate
and desirable for that process to issue a WAIT_IO call and move into a suspended state until the response is forthcoming. The techniques of this chapter
allow processes operating under MOS to do just that. However, when these
capabilities are merged with those of memory management covered in Chapter 3, a conflict arises. When the competition for memory is intense, memory
management algorithms will attempt to swap suspended processes to secondary
storage to make room for processes that are ready to run except for lack of
memory space. But a problem exists with the swapping activity. Consider the
following scenario.

Begin IO_IH

Provide initial-phase interrupt handling for I/O
interrupts
Input — DEVICE identifier and old PSW from the I/O
element of the interrupt vector
— SCB and associated lists
Output — SCB and associated lists
— Process states via the dispatcher
Assume — DEVICE identifier is valid, i.e., interrupts
generated due to hardware errors are not
considered
— I/O and lower-priority interrupts were disabled
by the loading of the new PSW
— Memory address mapping is disabled by the
loading of the new PSW
— The CPU is operating in the system state

Save all general register values in a local save area
Locate the DCB for the interrupting DEVICE

If the interrupted activity was a process (determined by examining the
old PSW system/process-state bit)
Then

Copy the old PSW and saved register values into the appropriate save
areas in the current PCB
Call the second-phase interrupt handler indicated by the DCB, e.g.,
DEVICE_IH
Enable I/O interrupts and call the dispatcher to accomplish any PCB
list updates and to schedule some process to run (the dispatcher
will not return to the interrupt handler)

Else [Some other interrupt handler was active]

Call the second-phase interrupt handler indicated by the DCB, e.g.,
DEVICE_IH
Return to the interrupted activity in the appropriate interrupt state
by restoring the general register values from the local save area
and the PSW from the old PSW field of the interrupt vector

EndIf
End IO_IH

ALGORITHM 5-4 Initial-Phase I/O Interrupt Handler

JOB1 issues a read to a terminal providing a buffer area at relative location
1000 in its address space (1000 bytes from its partition origin). The call to the
terminal version of INITIATE_IO is followed by a call to WAIT_IO to await
the user's response. JOB1 is now blocked until the user responds, the completion interrupt is generated, and the second-phase interrupt handler has updated
the status variable and requested the dispatcher to transition JOB1 back to the
ready state.

In the meantime, other processes are started, while still others, which have
been swapped to secondary storage, become ready to return to memory. Memory
management determines that JOB1 is not eligible to compute and therefore is

Begin DEVICE_IH ⎡   Complete interrupt processing for an I/O device
Input   – DCB and IOB queue for the device
         – Actual device STATE from the controller
         – SCB and associated lists
Output   – Associated program STATUS variable as
            addressed in the front IOB
         – DCB status and IOB queue
         – Process state via the dispatcher
         – Initiation of pending I/O operations
         – SCB and associated lists
Assume – I/O interrupts are disabled
         – Memory address mapping is disabled
         – The CPU is operating in the system state ⎤

Retrieve the CURRENT_STATE of the device from the controller [TIO]
If the previous device state, from the DCB, was busy
Then [Perform queue management based on the CURRENT_STATE]
    If the CURRENT_STATE of the device is ready
    Then ⎡ An operation just completed successfully. Update STATUS
        ⎣ variable and start any next pending operation ⎤
        Remove the front IOB from the queue
        Indicate success in the STATUS variable addressed by IOB
        If the IOB is marked to unblock a waiting process
        Then
            Notify the dispatcher that the associated process is to be removed
                from the I/O wait state
        EndIf
        Call FREE_MEMORY to release the IOB space
        If the queue is not empty
        Then [Initiate the next operation in the queue]
            Command the controller to start the operation contained in the
                front IOB [SIO]
            Reset the CURRENT_STATE to assume a busy device state
        EndIf
    Else [An operation failed. Clear the IOB queue reporting failure]
        While the IOB queue is not empty
        Do [Notify the associated process of failure and remove the IOB]
            Remove the front IOB from the queue
            Indicate failure in STATUS variable addressed by IOB
            If the removed IOB is marked to unblock a waiting process
            Then
                Notify the dispatcher that the associated process is to be
                    removed from the I/O wait state
            EndIf
            Call FREE_MEMORY to release the IOB space
        EndDo
    EndIf
Else ⎡ Failed-to-ready and ready-to-failed transitions require no
     ⎣ processing ⎤
EndIf
Set the DCB status field to the CURRENT_STATE of the device
End DEVICE_IH

ALGORITHM 5-5   Typical Second Phase I/O Interrupt Handler

a candidate to be swapped out, thereby making room for other processes to be swapped into memory. But JOB1, and other processes in a similar condition, cannot be removed from memory due to the I/O techniques described previously. Why not?

If the I/O operations have already started, data are being moved between the I/O device and the program area of memory. If memory is vacated and assigned to use by other processes, either the new program will be overlaid by extraneous data incoming from the read operations or garbage will be transferred via ongoing write operations!

On the other hand, if the transfers are not yet started, and if the interrupt software and the IOB contents were extended to check for swapped processes prior to initiating new transfers, the erroneous events just presented could be avoided. But now another undesirable condition has emerged: JOB1 would be swapped until the read completes, but the read is blocked until JOB1 returns to memory. Therefore, JOB1 is permanently swapped to secondary storage. It is in the computer equivalent of a permanent coma: the process exists but can never accomplish its intended function. A single-process deadlock condition has developed.

There are two common solutions to this problem. The most obvious is not to allow the swapping of processes that are in the I/O wait state. This is not a particularly desirable solution for an interactive time-sharing system, since most of memory could be occupied by such blocked processes. The second solution is to provide **staging buffers** within the operating system area of memory, as shown in Figure 5-11.

This second level of buffering involves extending the INITIATE_IO-type modules to include the allocation of a second buffer area which is transparent to the calling program. When data are being transmitted to a device, they are first copied from the user-supplied buffer into the staging buffer, from which they will ultimately be written. The calling program is now free to continue or to be swapped as necessary.

Conversely, when data are being input, they are first accumulated in a staging buffer. Once the read is complete, the receiving process is swapped into memory as necessary, the input data copied into a local buffer within the process, and execution is resumed. This technique requires more complex logic in both the I/O service and interrupt software, consideration in the SWAP_IN module, and appropriate handling of the program status variables pointed to by IOBs.

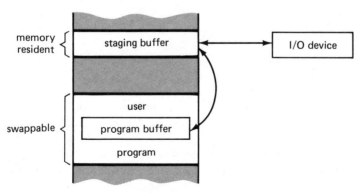

FIGURE 5-11 I/O Using a Nonswappable Staging Buffer

Further consideration will reveal that in terms of program swapping, not all I/O operations are equal. If a process is waiting for a disk write to complete, it hardly makes sense to queue other disk writes to the same device for the purpose of swapping the process to disk. This attempt to swap the program and release memory will itself not complete until after the initial write finishes, at which time swapping the process to disk may no longer be appropriate.

If, however, the blocking operation is a read from a terminal, the completion of which is dependent on comparatively slow human reflexes, swapping the process might be entirely appropriate. Unfortunately, the added complexity required to distinguish between such cases occurs all too frequently in systems programming problems.

5.6
Alternative Input/Output Queuing Strategies

There are many facets and intricacies of input/output programming which have not been addressed here. Entire books have been written on the subject. Much of the missing detail is, however, frequently involved in minimizing the duration of disabled processing periods or handling the complex details of communication with specific types of devices.

As a final note providing some insight into processing options available to the systems programmer, consider the problem of obtaining the "best" I/O performance from a disk. Performance is not a problem in a lightly loaded system in which the disk is ready almost every time a data transfer request is made. It is not doing anything anyway, so let it perform the requested transfer immediately.

But what if the disk is busy and several requests are already pending for it? How should the IOB queue be ordered? The INITIATE_IO routine maintained strict first-in, first-out (FIFO) order, which is generally the fairest ordering. But is it the best? The answer is one that can be addressed only by considering computing facility objectives and policy; however, there are several options commonly available, namely: FIFO queuing, priority queuing, and scan queuing by disk address.

If the system is supporting on-line or real-time operations, **priority queuing** may be mandated to meet foreground performance requirements. (Real time is discussed in Section 8.5. Basically, it refers to the operation of computer programs in such a way as to allow interaction with external events at a pace consistent with the ongoing demands of those events.) In this scheme each IOB is assigned the priority of the associated process and the queue is kept functionally ordered by priority. IOBs of equal priority are ordered FIFO. The relative importance of the process thus governs serving order.

But is system performance actually improved by ordering the IOB queues by priority? In a light I/O environment, queue waiting time is probably not a contributor to poor performance. Changing queue ordering schemes would therefore not relieve a performance problem. In a moderate-to-heavy I/O period, priority ordering of the queues alone may have little or no impact on I/O performance problems. By moving the high-priority work to the front of the queue, the disk seek arm is forced to the position of the data needed by those processes, regardless of the arm's previous position. After satisfying the high-priority requests, the arm is then allowed to return to the original cylinders, assuming that low-priority work was queued. Now, when the next high-priority request is initiated, the arm must again move to the region of the disk containing data for that process and the cycle repeats. Such cyclic arm movement could contribute heavily to poor system performance. In this particular example, priority queuing could actually result in worse performance than FIFO queuing, which might allow a block of low-priority work to be performed without moving the arm at all, followed by a single movement to the area containing data for the high-priority processes, and so on.

As can be seen, the position of data on the disk may have a greater effect on performance than does IOB queue order. Generally, it is important to allocate high-frequency data near the center of the disk recording area with low-frequency access data near the extremes (independent of process priority). The objective of such placement is to reduce greatly the expected seek distance during periods of heavy activity. (This is the reason most disk file directories are located on the central cylinders of the disk packs.) In a real-time system, it is generally appropriate to combine this data organization with IOB priority queuing.

For the computing facility that is concerned primarily with throughput, as opposed to real-time response or fairness, very attractive alternatives exist which order the IOB queues according to disk address. (Several variations of address ordering are examined in the problem section.) As an example of their value, consider the simple **scan** ordering technique. Here the IOBs are ordered in such a way as to allow the seek arm to sweep from the edge of the disk to the center, then back. During each leg of the cycle, the arm stops at each intermediate cylinder requested. Only when no addresses are pending in the direction of motion does the arm reverse direction and begin the reverse leg of the sweep. See Table 5-2 for an example.

With this strategy an attempt is made to keep the arm sweeping back and forth across the disk rather than allowing totally unpredictable movement. This is accomplished by inserting new IOBs into the queue based on whether the requested position can be reached by continuing the current direction of movement or whether it should be accessed on the return sweep.

Table 5-2   Comparison of FIFO Ordering to Scan Address Ordering

FIFO Order of Requests		Scan Order of Requests	
Cylinder	Relative Movement	Cylinder	Relative Movement
300		300	
10		380	
150		150	
380		70	
70		10	

seek distance = 1170 cylinders   seek distance = 550 cylinders

where the seek distance is computed assuming that the arm is initially at cylinder 200

Scan ordering has the advantage of reducing seek distance at the expense of fairness. However, minimizing the seek distance contributes to a general improvement in performance that benefits all users. Therefore, short-term inequities may be more than offset by superior service to the general user community.

PROBLEMS

1. a. Describe the condition of each process and device shown in Figure 5-12.
   b. Describe the condition of each process and device shown in Figure 5-13.
   c. Describe the events that occurred between the state of Figure 5-12 and the state of Figure 5-13.   [DS]

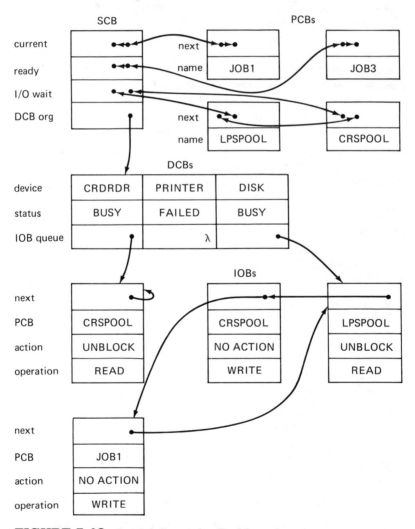

FIGURE 5-12   Initial State for Problem 1

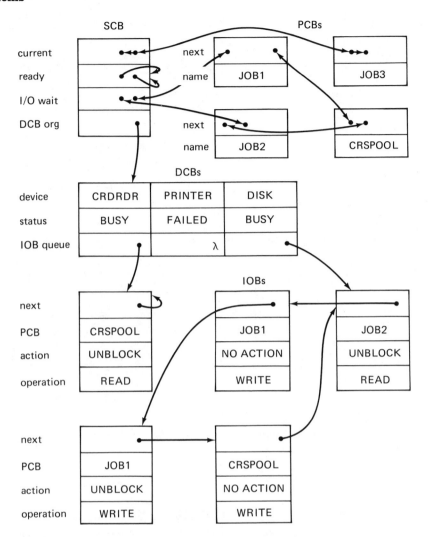

FIGURE 5-13   Second State for Problem 1

2. Illustrate the state of the MOS system at each of the times indicated. Process scheduling is on a priority basis and the relative priorities of the processes from highest to lowest are LPSPOOL, CRSPOOL, JOB1, JOB2, and JOB3. All events are to be taken in sequence.

Time = 0:
(1) Only CRSPOOL exists, and it is copying cards to disk using double buffering, as shown in Figure 5-14.

Time = 1:
(1) CRSPOOL continues cycling cards to disk.
(2) JOB3 starts and is reading from disk. Continued execution is dependent on the input data.
(3) JOB1 starts and begins reading from disk.

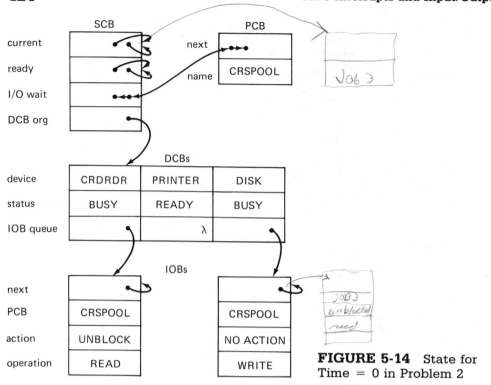

FIGURE 5-14   State for Time = 0 in Problem 2

Time = 2:
(1) CRSPOOL continues cycling cards to disk.
(2) JOB3 read completes.
(3) JOB1 read completes and it begins writing to disk.

Time = 3:
(1) CRSPOOL continues cycling cards to disk.
(2) JOB1 write completes and the process terminates.
(3) LPSPOOL starts and begins copying images from the disk to the printer using double buffering.
(4) JOB3 begins reading from disk.

Time = 4:
(1) The card reader jams and CRSPOOL begins the write of the last successful card image to disk.
(2) LPSPOOL continues cycling lines to the printer.
(3) JOB3 read completes and it starts a write to disk. Continued execution is dependent on the operation completing.
(4) JOB2 starts and enters a compute phase.

Time = 5:
(1) CRSPOOL write completes.
(2) LPSPOOL has read the last print line but it has not completed transfer to the printer.
(3) JOB3 write completes.   [DS]

3. Explain the general I/O data structure of your computer system by comparison to the MOS data structures, such as DCBs and IOBs. Discuss the

major differences from MOS. What capabilities are provided by these differences? How is the address of the interrupting device communicated?

[OS]

4. Modify your program from problem 13 of Chapter 4 to call the system I/O wait service rather than using busy-waiting loops. [OS]

5. Rewrite the DISK_TO_PRINTER algorithm from problem 16 in Chapter 4 to take full advantage of IOB queuing in achieving concurrency in device operation. (*Hint:* Reconsider the number of calls to WAIT_IO.) [Alg]

6. Discuss the importance of the following fields of the PSW to interrupt processing.

a. Interrupt mask.
b. System/process state bit.
c. Memory address mapping bit.
d. Program counter. [Ana]

7. Discuss the importance of interrupts to a multiprogramming system. [Ana]

8. Explain how the relative priorities of interrupts are established and how pending interrupts are queued in MOS. [Ana]

9. Why do SC_IH and IO_IH not return control of the CPU back to the interrupted process directly? [Ana]

10. Assuming that other MOS modules are coded correctly, what modifications are necessary to SC_IH and INITIATE_IO if the validity of input values from the calling process cannot be assumed? [Ana]

11. Extend your program from problem 14 of Chapter 4 to include I/O interrupt handling in a simulated multiprogramming environment provided by the MOS simulator. You should replace your INITIO and WAITIO service modules with subprograms based on the INITIATE_IO and WAIT_IO algorithms provided in this chapter. In addition, you must provide two levels of I/O interrupt-handling modules similar to IO_IH and DEVICE_IH. The first-phase handler must be named IOIH and exactly meet the interface requirements as specified in Appendix B. The following module guidelines should be used.

(1) The main program should be modified to call the MOS data structure dump routine MOSDMP after the call to CARD_TO_DISK. You may find MOSDMP a useful debug tool in other modules as well.

(2) Assuming that CARD_TO_DISK is functioning properly, the only change necessary to support this new program is the removal of the status variable from the parameter packet used to call the WAITIO service.

(3) The modified INITIO and WAITIO as well as the new IOIH and DEVICE_IH should be written considering all facets of the simulated I/O interrupt environment as specified in Section B.4 of Appendix B. [MOS]

12. Extend your program from problem 19 of Chapter 4 to include I/O interrupt handling in a simulated multiprogramming environment provided by the MOS simulator. You should replace your INITIO and WAITIO service modules with subprograms based on the INITIATE_IO and WAIT_IO algorithms provided in this chapter. In addition, you must provide two

levels of I/O interrupt-handling modules similar to IO_IH and DE-VICE_IH. The first-phase handler must be named IOIH and meet exactly the interface requirements as specified in Appendix B. The following module guidelines should be used.

(1) The main program should be modified to call the MOS data structure dump routine MOSDMP after the call to DISK_TO_PRINTER. You may find MOSDMP a useful debug tool in other modules as well.

(2) Assuming that DISK_TO_PRINTER is functioning properly, the only change necessary to support this new program is the removal of the status variable from the parameter packet used to call the WAITIO service.

(3) The modified INITIO and WAITIO as well as the new IOIH and DEVICE_IH should be written considering all facets of the simulated I/O interrupt environment as specified in Section B.4 of Appendix B.   [MOS]

13. Redesign the TERMINAL_IN algorithm from problem 21 of Chapter 4 to operate in an interrupt environment. Provide any lower-level system modules necessary for a terminal-type device.   [Alg]

14. a. Analyze the problem of implementing the staging buffer technique in MOS, thus allowing swapping of processes blocked awaiting I/O completion. Which algorithms should be changed and in what ways?

b. Provide modified I/O algorithms for supporting the staging buffer technique.   [Alg]

15. Shortest-seek-time-first queuing of disk requests uses a "greedy" approach to maximizing disk throughput. The queue is always maintained such that the next access will be to the disk address closest to the current position.

C-scan (circular scan) queuing of disk requests is a modification of the scan technique that views the disk addresses as a circular structure. The highest address and lowest address are considered to be logically adjacent. From such a perspective there is never a need to logically reverse the direction of seek arm movement. The arm can move from the low addresses to the high addresses, then jump back to the low addresses and start the next cycle in the same direction as the first.

Compare the FIFO, shortest-seek-time-first, scan, and C-scan queuing strategies by using the same sequence of 20 disk addresses. Produce the sequence of approximately uniformly distributed addresses by the following technique.

(1) Roll two six-sided dice.
(2) Double the value of the top face of the first die to produce a preliminary disk address.
(3) If the second die has an odd value on its top face, subtract 1 from the preliminary address; otherwise, use the preliminary number as the final address.

Use the first five values to initialize the IOB queue appropriately for each of the queuing strategies in turn. Now step through 15 accesses using the address at the front of the queue. Replenish the queue such that it always contains five addresses ordered appropriately for the current strategy.

  a. Which method produces the best throughput for the disk? What causes this result?

  b. Which method produces the best average service time? What causes this result?

  c. Which method is the most unfair? Explain why. [Ana]

16. Work problem 15 using approximately normally distributed disk addresses derived by summing the top faces of the two dice. [Ana]

17. Write an ADD_TO_IOB_QUEUE algorithm for use by INITIATE_IO in implementing shortest-seek-time-first queuing for improved disk performance (see problem 15 for the definition of shortest-seek-time-first queuing). [Alg]

18. Work problem 17 using scan queuing. [Alg]

19. Work problem 17 using C-scan queuing (see problem 15 for the definition of C-scan). [Alg]

20. N-scan (new scan) queuing of disk requests eliminates the possibility of indefinite postponement by batching requests in one of the scan methods. The destinations of the seek arm are fixed at the beginning of a scan cycle. All future requests are batched in the appropriate order for service during the next cycle. Work problem 15 using combined N-scan and C-scan queuing. [Alg]

21. What are the implications for the logic of WAIT_IO and/or DEVICE_IH if one of the non-FIFO queuing methods for ordering the disk IOB queue is used? [Ana]

22. A proposal is made to control an elevator using either the FIFO, scan, C-scan, shortest-travel-distance, or N-scan queuing method (see problems 15 and 20 for definitions). Each rider makes two requests: one to cause the elevator to come to the starting floor and one to go to the destination floor. Evaluate the options considering

  (1) Elevator system throughput.
  (2) Mean customer service time, which is the sum of the time waiting to be picked up and the time spent in the elevator.
  (3) Fairness.

What are the significant differences between this problem and that of disk-seek scheduling? [Ana]

CHAPTER 6

Cooperating and Communicating Concurrent Processes

6.1
Processes, Subprocesses, and Process Relationships

In non-real-time systems[1] most processes are not permanent elements within the computer system. They come and go as tasks for them to perform arise and are subsequently completed. When work is identified, processes are created to perform that work. When the work is finished, the processes are disposed of by the operating system.

6.1.1 Command Interpreter Programs

How does an operating system determine that there is work available to do? In MOS a technique is followed which is superficially similar to that used by the UNIX[2] operating system [Ritchie, 1978]. As part of starting the computer system, an operating system process is created to manage each device from which work can be defined. For the MOS system, this is the card reader and each interactive terminal. The purpose of these processes is to read requests from the associated device, interpret the requests, determine the appropriate program to execute to accomplish the work, and initiate another process to execute that program. The programs that read and interpret work requests (commands) are called **command interpreter** (CI) programs.

Since the card reader is a SPOOLed device, the SPOOLer process CRSPOOL is started in addition to a command interpreter program. Each time a card deck is placed in the reader, CRSPOOL copies it to a disk file, then adds the file to

---

[1]Real time is discussed in Section 8.5. Basically, it refers to the operation of computer programs in such a way as to allow interaction with external events at a pace consistent with the ongoing demands of those events.

[2]UNIX is a trademark of Bell Laboratories.

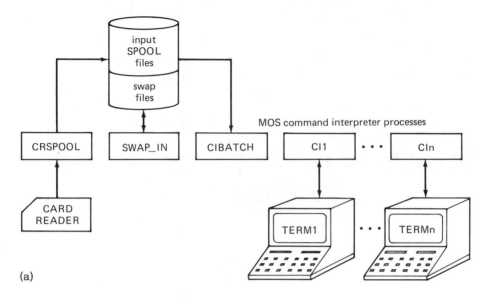

(a)

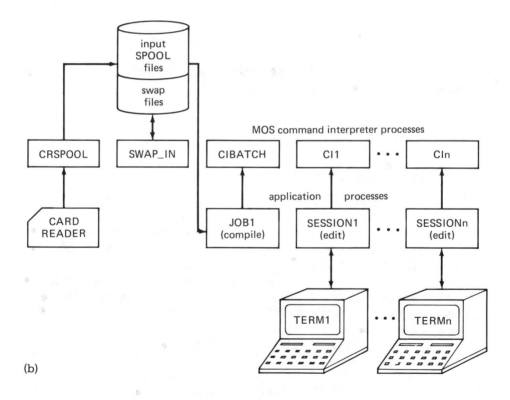

(b)

FIGURE 6-1 Process Configuration (a) at Startup and (b) After Work Has Been Submitted

a queue of pending batch work. Another system process, known as the batch job manager (a command interpreter for batch jobs), removes a job from the front of the queue, scans the cards for commands, and initiates other processes to execute the programs that implement those commands.

MOS also starts a command interpreter process for each terminal. These processes read user commands and determine which programs should be executed to accomplish the requests. Each valid command entered by a user names a program to implement the command. When a valid command program name is entered, the command interpreter creates another process to execute that program. The command interpreter process then waits for the new process to terminate. When this happens, a prompt for the next user command is issued to the terminal and the cycle repeats.

A process hierarchy of creating processes (parents) and created subprocesses (children) is thus established. Figure 6-1(a) shows the MOS process configuration immediately after system startup and before any work has been submitted. The SPOOLer and command interpreter parent processes have been started and these programs have initiated read operations to the devices. (SWAP_IN is also started to help manage program memory.)

In Figure 6-1(b) a batch job stream has been copied from the card reader to disk, from where it is being processed by the batch manager, CIBATCH. In the figure, the manager has read and recognized a command to compile a program and has initiated another process, JOB1, for that purpose. CIBATCH is awaiting completion of JOB1. When that termination occurs, the CIBATCH process will read its next command from the SPOOL file, and the next program in the job sequence will be executed as a new creation of the JOB1 process. (Depending on facility policy and system configuration options, CIBATCH might start multiple JOBi processes, thus allowing many SPOOLed card streams to run concurrently.)

The interactive command interpreters, CI1, CI2, ... CIn operate similar to CIBATCH except that their commands come directly from users via terminal devices. As each valid command is recognized, the corresponding program is executed as a subprocess, SESSIONi, of the creating CIi parent process (i = 1, . . . , n).

6.1.2 Partitioning Application Processes

The hierarchy of processes might be extended further if some of the SESSIONi and JOBi processes became parents themselves. This can happen when an application process requests initiation of its own subprocess. For example, suppose that the user at device TERMi has an application which has been partitioned such that two or more parts of the problem can be solved independently, then combined for calculation and display of the results. Such a main program might request the creation of several subprocesses, each executing its own program or copy of a program, and running more or less independently of, but concurrently with the initiating process.

Such a problem might involve determining three intermediate values, B, C, and D, from input data and initial calculations. (B, C, and D can be calculated independently.) A sequence of computer instructions could be written to determine B, C, and D in any order. One such sequence is shown in Algorithm

Begin SERIAL_SOLUTION
    Read INPUT1
    Determine A = f(INPUT1)

    Read INPUT2
    Determine B = f(A, INPUT2)

    Read INPUT3
    Determine C = f(A, INPUT3)

    Read INPUT4
    Determine D = f(A, INPUT4)

    Determine RESULT = f(B, C, D)
    Display RESULT

End SERIAL_SOLUTION

ALGORITHM 6-1 Serial Formulation of a Partitionable Problem

6-1. This problem can be partitioned for concurrent solution of B, C, and D. Such partitioning might be expeditious if determining each intermediate value is sufficiently complex and mixes computation with input/output operations such as queries to a data base. Algorithm 6-2 shows the reformulation of the problem to include requests of MOS to start two subprocesses. Each of the subprocesses solves a part of the problem and the main process solves the remaining part. The main program then combines the intermediate values into a final result.

Begin CONCURRENT_SOLUTION

    Read INPUT1
    Determine A = f(INPUT1)

    Start SUBSOLUTION_1 to determine B = f(A, INPUT2)
    Start SUBSOLUTION_2 to determine C = f(A, INPUT3)

    Read INPUT4
    Determine D = f(A, INPUT4)

    Wait for a subprocess to complete and return its result
    Wait for the other subprocess to complete and return its result

    Determine RESULT = f(B, C, D)
    Display RESULT
End CONCURRENT_SOLUTION

Begin SUBSOLUTION_1 (SUBSOLUTION_2 is similar)
    Retrieve A from the parent process
    Read INPUT2
    Determine B = f(A, INPUT2)

    Return B to the parent process

End SUBSOLUTION_1

ALGORITHM 6-2 Concurrent Formulation of a Partitionable Problem

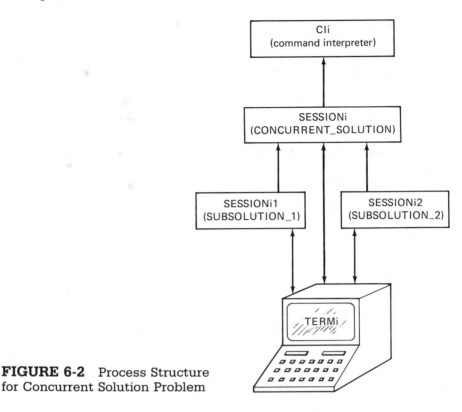

FIGURE 6-2 Process Structure
for Concurrent Solution Problem

As shown in Figure 6-2, three processes of SESSIONi will exist simultaneously and will execute concurrently. When the two subprocesses have returned their results to the main process, SESSIONi, they will terminate. Since
SESSIONi is a creating process, it becomes a parent process itself. Being a
parent process, it is allowed to wait for actions of its subprocesses to occur.
In the example, the program for SESSIONi, CONCURRENT_SOLUTION,
requests suspension (becomes blocked) pending termination of both subprocesses. As these events occur, MOS will unblock the main process. SESSIONi
will then compute and display the final results of the solution.

The concepts of parent processes and subprocesses have defined a need for
three additional MOS service subsystem modules: initiating a subprocess, communicating with other processes, and waiting for interprocess events to occur.
The remainder of this chapter discusses MOS functions that fulfill these and
related needs. Since communicating between processes is necessary as part of
both starting and stopping processes, a communication technique is presented
first. As with most elements of MOS, the services defined are primitive compared to those of full-function operating systems.

6.2
Messages

In MOS the basic task of communicating between processes is accomplished
through an interprocess message service facility. A **message** is a single package
of data communicated from the memory domain of a sending process into the

memory space of a receiving process. It is similar to communication between processes using input/output operations but with direct buffer-to-buffer transfers rather than actually moving data through secondary storage. As with input and output, the data contents and meaning of the message are independent of MOS and left to the processes to define and interpret. Implementation of a simple message facility requires only a pair of service subsystem modules for transmitting and receiving messages and a data structure to accommodate them.

To send a message, the originating process only needs to indicate the recipient of the message, the length of the message text, and then supply the data. The SEND service will acquire buffer space for the message, form the message packet, and transmit it to the designated process.

Communication requires the cooperation of both parties. How is process cooperation accomplished? The receiving process may or may not be ready to receive a message, or it may have messages arriving from many processes during the same period. Transmission of a message therefore includes adding the message to a queue of messages associated with the recipient process. This parallels the use of the IOB queues to serialize input/output operations for a particular device.

When ready, the target process can retrieve the contents of a message via the second message service module, RECEIVE, which will remove the message node from the queue and copy the text data into the program's data area. Figure 6-3 defines the contents of message nodes and establishes the linkage between the message blocks and the PCB. Algorithms 6-3 and 6-4 present functional logic for basic SEND and RECEIVE message services.

The SEND service is thus similar to a deviceless output function which identifies the output destination, acquires a control block and staging buffer area, and queues the request to the recipient. RECEIVE, on the other hand, functions somewhat like a deviceless input function without a corresponding wait if the data are not instantly available. The STATUS indicates whether or not data are returned. If data are available, the control block and staging buffer

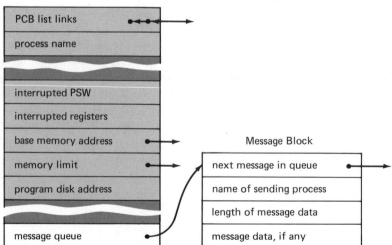

FIGURE 6-3 Data Structure for Interprocess Message Communication

Begin SEND

Transmit a message to another process
Input — NAME of the process to which DATA are to be sent
  or the PCB_ADDRESS of the process
  — LENGTH of the message DATA
  — DATA to be transmitted
  — SCB and associated lists
Output — STATUS of the SEND operation
  — Message queue of the receiving process
Assume — SEND and RECEIVE are invoked only via SC
  instructions or calls from other modules
  processing an SC interrupt; this ensures that
  only one use of the message facility will be
  active at a time
  — No PCB list changes occur while SC interrupts are
  being processed
  — Memory address mapping is disabled

If the PCB_ADDRESS of the receiver is not provided
Then [Locate the receiver's PCB]
  Examine all PCB lists for the target process NAME
EndIf

If the PCB_ADDRESS is now known
Then [Acquire buffer space and transmit the message]

  Call GET_MEMORY to allocate space for the message block
  If allocation was successful
  Then
    Copy the name of the current (sending) process into the message
      block
    Copy the LENGTH of the message text and any DATA into the message
      block
    Add the new message block to the rear of the message queue of the
      target process
    Set STATUS to indicate successful transmission
  Else
    Set STATUS to indicate that space is not available
  EndIf

Else
  Set STATUS to indicate that process NAME does not exist

EndIf

End SEND

ALGORITHM 6-3   Message Transmission Service Module

area are released and the transmission is complete. With this technique, the
text of a message actually exists in three different places at one time or another
in the communication sequence. First the text is formed in the sender's space
by the executing program. When the SEND service is executed, a message
block, or buffer, is acquired in system space and the text is duplicated into this
space, external to both processes.

When the target process executes the RECEIVE service, it designates an
area within the process address space to receive the text. Again this is similar

Begin RECEIVE

Retrieve a message

Input — MAXIMUM allowable length of the message
— PCB of the current process

Output — NAME of the process sending the message
— Actual LENGTH of the message data
— DATA transmitted, if any
— STATUS of the RECEIVE operation
— Message queue of the current process

Assume — SEND and RECEIVE are invoked only via SC
instructions or calls from other modules
processing an SC interrupt; this ensures
that only one use of the message facility will
be active at a time
— Memory address mapping is disabled

If the message queue of the current process is not empty
Then

Index to the front message block in the message queue
Copy the NAME of the sending process from the message block
Copy the LENGTH of the message data from the message block
Copy the minimum of MAXIMUM and LENGTH units of DATA from the
message block
Remove the message block from the front of the message queue
Call FREE_MEMORY to release the message block space
Set STATUS to indicate that a message was successfully received

Else

Set STATUS to indicate that no messages currently exist

EndIf

End RECEIVE

ALGORITHM 6-4   Message Reception Service Module

to input/output. (A read requires the caller to provide an area for receipt of the
incoming data, even if the system has already performed the physical input/
output using an intermediate staging buffer.) The final action of copying the
text from the message block into the buffer provided by the process creates the
third instance of the message text.

Figure 6-4 illustrates the general activity just described. Note, however, that
the message text does not necessarily exist in all three areas simultaneously.
As soon as the SEND service has returned to the caller, the sender's local
buffer area may be reused for other purposes since its contents have already
been replicated in the acquired message block. RECEIVE will similarly release
the message block as soon as a copy of the contents has been placed in the
area provided by the receiver.

The communications capability defined so far requires repeated polling of
the RECEIVE service by the target process to determine if other processes have
transmitted information to it. As was seen in Chapter 4 with noninterrupt-based
I/O, this is both a program-inefficient and CPU-expensive approach. Operating
systems normally provide an additional service (e.g., WAIT_MESSAGE) which
allows a process to enter a wait state and remain blocked pending receipt of a

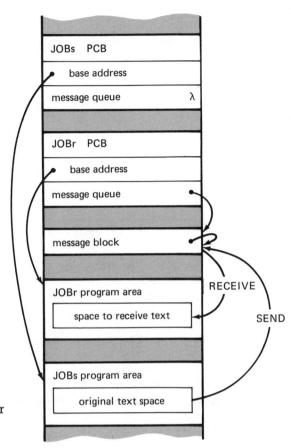

FIGURE 6-4 Actions for
Interprocess Message
Communication

message from another process. The logic of such a service is quite simple. If the message queue is empty, the process is blocked until a message is added to the queue, at which time the process resumes and presumably issues a RECEIVE call. When the queue is not empty, execution is continued and any subsequent RECEIVE call is processed immediately.

This approach requires modification of SEND to include logic for examining a new SCB wait list. If the PCB of the target process is in the appropriate wait state, the dispatcher is notified to resume the process. All other functions of SEND and RECEIVE remain as defined previously.

The rational for WAIT_MESSAGE is similar to that for having separate INITIATE_IO and WAIT_IO services, although some operating systems provide automatic waiting when both SEND and RECEIVE calls are made. The significance of forced blocking of processes at both the SEND and RECEIVE steps is that two-way communications and synchronization are always established during message transmission. When the SEND service returns to a caller, that program knows that the receiver of the message has already obtained the text transmitted.

Such synchronization can be accomplished voluntarily using the MOS message services already defined. If each call to SEND is followed by a WAIT_MESSAGE call and a subsequent RECEIVE call, the sender is blocked until the receiver has transmitted an acknowledgment message. As shown in

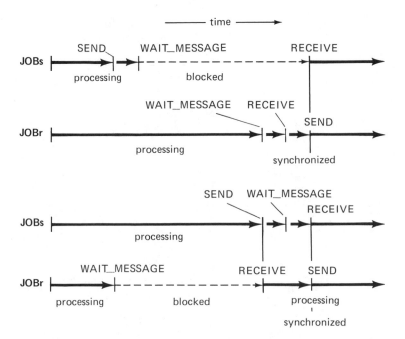

FIGURE 6-5   Process Synchronization via Message Exchange

Figure 6-5, a receiver should follow each RECEIVE call with a call to SEND to complete synchronization with the other process. In the top illustration, JOBs reaches the point of synchronization before JOBr does. JOBs sends the synchronization request message and blocks itself via WAIT_MESSAGE pending acknowledgment from JOBr. When JOBr reaches the synchronization point in its logic, its WAIT_MESSAGE call is satisfied immediately (its message queue is not empty) and it receives the message sent by JOBs. JOBr completes the synchronization procedure by responding with the acknowledgment message, thus awakening JOBs. The lower part of Figure 6-5 depicts events in the other scenario. Here JOBr reaches the synchronization point ahead of JOBs. Now it must wait for JOBs to initiate the message exchange in order to synchronize execution.

To illustrate the need and utility of interprocess messages, consider a more complete picture of operations within a computer system. Most activities are carried out not by the operating system in privileged modules of the nucleus or kernel, but in system processes that communicate via messages. CIi, CIBATCH, CRSPOOL, and LPSPOOL are examples of such communicating, concurrent system processes.

Suppose that some user program is executing as process JOB1 and that the printer is being managed by the LPSPOOL process. The computer operator interacts via his or her version of the command interpreter, CIOP. Let LPSPOOL be copying images to the line printer while JOB1 executes generating more print to a file on disk.

When JOB1 completes, a termination function will execute as the last phase of its process. This activity will ensure that all input/output transfers have finished, all resources have been released, and so on. One of the final actions performed on behalf of JOB1 is the notification of LPSPOOL that the new

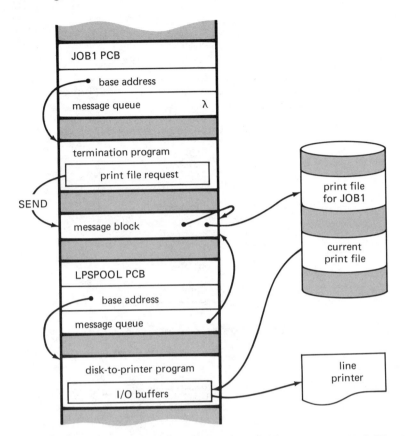

FIGURE 6-6 Termination Program Notifying the SPOOLer of Availability of Another File to Print

print file is now complete and available for printing. This is accomplished by sending a message to the LPSPOOL process. Figure 6-6 is a representation of the events at this point.

When LPSPOOL completes the printing of its current file, it will issue WAIT_MESSAGE and RECEIVE service calls to identify any next print file ready to copy to the printer. Finding the message from JOB1 allows LPSPOOL to start printing the file for the recently completed process.

Now suppose that the printer runs out of paper. LPSPOOL will receive a device failure status, indicating that error recovery is possible with help from the operator. The appropriate action is therefore to notify the operator to add more paper. Just as any other process cannot write to the printer, LPSPOOL cannot just call INITIATE_IO to write to the system console. The console is not one of its devices. Only CIOP, and its subprocesses, can read from or write to the operator's terminal. LPSPOOL must therefore use the SEND service to request that CIOP notify the operator that the printer needs attention. This action is followed by a call to WAIT_MESSAGE, since LPSPOOL has nothing productive to do until the printer is fixed and a message to that effect is available. When the printer is again ready, the operator will tell CIOP to notify LPSPOOL to continue processing and all will be back to normal. Figure 6-7 illustrates this scenario.

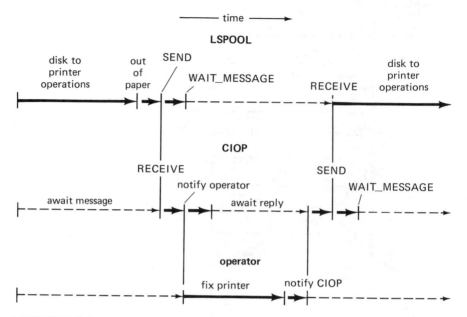

FIGURE 6-7 Communication of Printer Failure and Subsequent
Repair

Unfortunately, by providing a mechanism to wait for communications from other processes, we have introduced another mechanism for potentially causing deadlock. This occurrence of deadlock is perhaps impossible to detect or prevent. Regardless of whether an explicit WAIT_MESSAGE is used or an implicit wait version of RECEIVE exists, nothing is to prevent a process from blocking itself pending receipt of a message that will never be sent (i.e., some process calls WAIT_MESSAGE and no process exists that will ever SEND a message to the waiting process).

This deadlock condition develops completely independently of the resources managed by the operating system. No CPU, input/output devices, or other resources are involved. Interprocess communication is strictly within the domain of the program developers. MOS simply supplies a mechanism to facilitate the communication. When a process chooses to wait for a message, there is no way MOS can know whether or not valid design criteria have been followed. Therefore, there is no way of knowing whether or not the message expected will ever be forthcoming.

6.3
Process Creation

Sufficient support services now exist to discuss process initiation. As a minimum, spawning a new process requires that the program to be executed be identified and that the process be given a name. In addition, data relevant to process startup may be communicated. For example, in Figure 6-1, the CI1 process received a command to invoke the editor program. Perhaps the user entered the character string "EDIT MYFILE." CI1 then examined this input string for syntax errors and to determine the command program name, EDIT. Next a system call to the CREATE service was issued requesting that MOS locate program EDIT, create a process called SESSION1 to execute it, and pass the text "MYFILE" to the process.

To fulfill its function, CREATE must

1. Locate the load module file for EDIT.
2. Allocate memory for a PCB.
3. Allocate a swap file for the new process and copy the program image into it.
4. Complete the various fields of the PCB, storing the name (SESSION1), program size, disk swap file address, null base register value (the process is initially swapped out), saved PSW pointing to the first instruction of the program, and so on.
5. Send a message containing the initialization text "MYFILE."
6. Notify the dispatcher that a new process is to be initiated and its PCB placed in the ready queue.

The process now has the appearance of any other process that has been swapped to secondary storage and that has a message pending. Figure 6-8 illustrates the example starting of the editor after CI1 has completed these steps for SESSION1. Algorithm 6-5 formalizes the procedure.

When the program begins executing, one of its first actions will be to issue a RECEIVE system call to fetch the initialization data from the creating process. In the previous example, the editor program will receive the name of its input file, "MYFILE," from the message provided by the CI1 command interpreter.

With the capabilities of the CREATE, SEND, RECEIVE, and WAIT_MESSAGE services, the scenario for the CONCUR-RENT_SOLUTION program of Algorithm 6-2 could be clearly and concisely

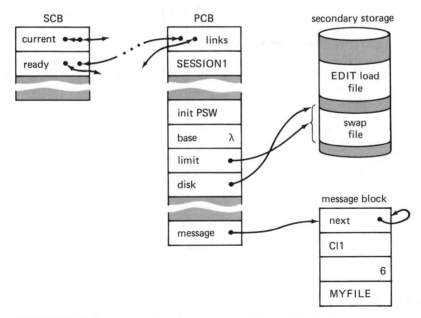

FIGURE 6-8   Initial Configuration of New SESSION1 Process

Begin CREATE
> Establish a new process and supply it with any available initial data
> Input — PROCESS_NAME for the new process
> — PROGRAM_NAME of the load module file
> — LENGTH of any initial message data
> — DATA to be transmitted if LENGTH > 0
> Output — STATUS of the CREATE operation
> — PCB and swap file for the new process
> Assume — CREATE is invoked only via SC instructions or calls from other modules processing an SC interrupt; this ensures that only one process will be in the creation phase at a time
> — Allocation of the swap file is successful
> — Memory address mapping is disabled

Locate the load module file for PROGRAM_NAME
If the program exists
Then
> Determine the size (LIMIT) of the memory partition needed and the initial PSW contents from the load module file
> Call GET_MEMORY to allocate memory for a NEW_PCB and set STATUS
> **If** NEW_PCB allocation was successful
> **Then**
>> Allocate a swap file for the process
>> Copy the program image into the swap file
>> Copy the PROCESS_NAME, initial PSW, swap file address, and LIMIT into the NEW_PCB
>> Clear the base memory address to indicate a swapped state
>> Complete other fields of the NEW_PCB appropriately
>> **If** the LENGTH of the initial message data > 0
>> **Then**
>>> Call SEND with the address of the NEW_PCB to transmit the initialization message and set STATUS
>>> **If** the SEND operation was successful
>>> **Then**
>>>> Notify the dispatcher that the NEW_PCB is to be placed in the ready queue
>>> **Else**
>>>> Call FREE_MEMORY to release the NEW_PCB
>>>> Release the swap file space
>>> **EndIf**
>> **Else**
>>> Notify the dispatcher that the NEW_PCB is to be placed in the ready queue
>> **EndIf**
> **EndIf**
Else
> Set STATUS to indicate that PROGRAM_NAME is invalid
EndIf

End CREATE

ALGORITHM 6-5   Creating a New Process

Begin CONCURRENT_SOLUTION

Read INPUT1
Determine A = f(INPUT1)

Call CREATE to start SUBSOLUTION_1 executing as a new process,
   SESSIONi1, with initial data A
Call CREATE to start SUBSOLUTION_2 executing as a new process,
   SESSIONi2, with initial data A

Read INPUT4
Determine D = f(A, INPUT4)

Call WAIT_MESSAGE to await a subprocess completion
Call RECEIVE to retrieve the intermediate result (either B or C)
Call WAIT_MESSAGE to await completion of the other subprocess
Call RECEIVE to retrieve the other intermediate result

Determine RESULT = f(B, C, D)
Display RESULT

End CONCURRENT_SOLUTION

Begin SUBSOLUTION_1 (SUBSOLUTION_2 is similar)

Call RECEIVE to retrieve A from the parent process
Read INPUT2
Determine B = f(A, INPUT2)

Call SEND to return B to the parent process

End SUBSOLUTION_1

ALGORITHM 6-6   Concurrent Formulation Using MOS Services

implemented. Algorithm 6-6 presents a more detailed version of this solution
using the new services.

6.4
Process Traps

Many application processes, as well as system processes, require the capability
to process certain events in an asynchronous manner. Within MOS, the CIOP
process, used for communications with the operator, needs the ability to receive
commands from the system console and messages from other processes, such
as the SPOOLer. The time of occurrence of these events is unknown.

Another example of process response to asynchronous events is program
handling of arithmetic faults, rather than accepting system default actions.
Similarly, on-line systems, such as data base applications, may require orderly
quiescing of transactions before termination due to device failures is allowed.
Since data integrity is at stake, orderly handling of program errors by the
application is necessary, even when such severe errors as memory protection
and invalid instructions occur.

6.4.1   The Use of Process Traps

All of these problems requiring asynchronous processing can be solved by a feature call a **process trap.** The definition and capability of traps varies considerably from one type of computer to the next and from one operating system to the next. For MOS a process trap is defined as an event that causes an asynchronous and unconditional transfer of control to a prespecified routine or procedure within the address space of a process. Such designated routines will be called **process-trap handlers.** Their function is to handle the asynchronous events. Upon completion of trap handling, the process may return to its previous state or it may take other action as established by the trap handler. This definition and function should sound familiar. Within the context of a single process, trap handlers provide a capability very similar to that provided by MOS interrupt handlers.

Consider the case of a programmer wishing to have a program maintain control, for debugging purposes, when an arithmetic fault occurs. Under the default provisions of the assembler, compiler, and linker, a division by zero, for instance, will cause a program error interruption. In the absence of special provisions by the programmer, the program error interrupt handler of the operating system will handle the interrupt and typically terminate process execution. With the existence of a process-trap capability, this need not be the case. The programmer can request alternative processing by providing a service routine within the program itself. Such a routine is to be given control in arithmetic-fault situations during which it might allow interactive debugging of the error. In this case, the trap-handler routine might display the relative location of the instruction just executed and the contents of key registers and variables. Next, it might prompt the user for succeeding action: terminate, correct some calculated value and continue, or continue as if nothing had happened.

6.4.2   MOS Data Structure Supporting Traps

Consider a MOS structure for implementing a process-trap capability. Paralleling the interrupt structure of the operating system, there must be structures for

1. Storing the cause of the trap.
2. Saving the state of the affected process at the time of the trap.
3. Inhibiting additional traps of the same type until the current trap condition is cleared.
4. Obtaining the entry-point address of the process-trap-handling routine.

This is a very close parallel to the requirements for handling hardware interrupts as defined in Chapter 5. Figure 6-9 contains the additions to the MOS data structure satisfying these requirements. First, a new wait list is provided for those processes with nothing to do until a trap event occurs. Since receiving a message from another process may be an asynchronous event, a call to the WAIT_MESSAGE service, suggested in Section 6.3, will actually be a request to enter a trap-wait state. When WAIT_MESSAGE determines that no trap event has been signaled (no message is pending), the PCB for the process will be added to the trap-wait list of the SCB.

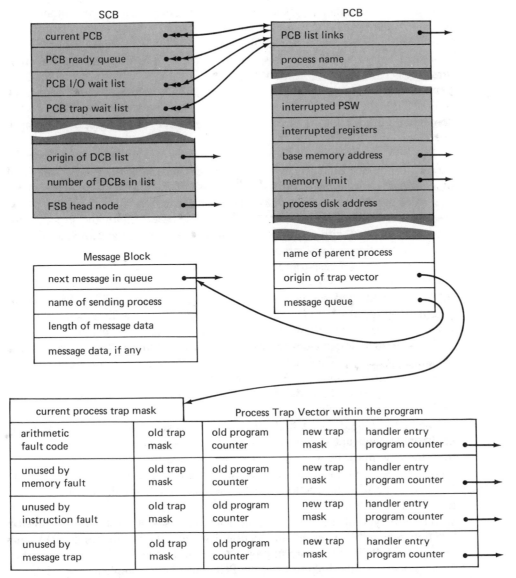

FIGURE 6-9 MOS Data Structure for Implementing Process Traps

Except for this new PCB list, the remaining structural elements associated with enabling, signaling, and handling traps are process dependent and are, therefore, provided either directly or indirectly by the PCB of the target process. First, observe that when subprocesses such as SUBSOLUTION_1 terminate, it may be necessary to notify the parent processes that created them (e.g., CONCURRENT_SOLUTION). Thus it is necessary to be able to identify the parent of each process. This is the purpose of the parent process name field which has been added to the PCB definition in Figure 6-9. Each time a process terminates, this field is used to locate its parent process, if it still exists. When such a process is found, and is expecting subprocess termination messages, such notices will be posted to it.

Since most parameters associated with trap processing are potentially significant to the process, these data are stored in the program area of memory. They are organized into a single table which is a logical extension of the PCB contained within the address space of the process. The trap data are therefore directly accessible by application programs. This table, which we shall call the **process-trap vector** (PTV), is normally a statically allocated block of storage provided by the program. The program is free to examine and update the contents of the PTV to control the associated environment while servicing a trap.

The PTV contains the functional counterpart of a PSW and an interrupt vector. It provides each process with its own extension of the PSW in the form of a **current process-trap mask.** The purpose of the mask is to indicate which classes of traps, if any, the process is currently capable of handling and which are to receive standard MOS default handling. Each bit of the process-trap mask is associated with a specific class of trap: arithmetic fault, memory fault, invalid instruction, or interprocess message receipt.

Following the process-trap mask are 20 fields, equally divided among four classes of traps. As shown in Figure 6-9, each element is composed of five fields. The first field contains the condition code value from the PSW at the time the trap occurred. This value is meaningful only for arithmetic-fault traps, where it indicates the specific type of arithmetic error (e.g., division by zero).

The second field provides an area for saving the current process-trap mask when a trap occurs. The next field provides a storage place for a copy of the program counter from the PSW at the time the event causing the trap was detected. Together, these two fields function in the same way as do the old PSW fields of the system interrupt vector.

The last two fields in each element of the trap vector parallel the new PSW fields of the interrupt vector. When a trap occurs, a new trap mask is fetched from the new mask field of the vector element and the program counter in the PSW is loaded with the address of the next program instruction to be executed. Normally, the next instruction will be the entry point for the handler routine for this class of trap.

With this type of trap structure, the operating system must supply a service function, accessible by an SC instruction that formally establishes the PTV and links it to the PCB of the current process. (Recall that the PCB is not accessible by its process, so the linking from the PCB must be accomplished by MOS on behalf of the process.) The MOS service DEFINE_TRAPS accomplishes such a function. To use it the programmer first provides an area of sufficient size (21 fields) to accommodate the PTV. Figure 6-10 provides a functional example of the PTV definition portion of an assembler language program. The table itself is defined in lines 5 through 12 using various constants and addresses established in the first three lines. Line 13 is an SC instruction to call the DEFINE_TRAPS service. This call will notify MOS of the address of the trap vector area. At any time after this instruction is executed, if a trap occurs for the process, MOS will examine the process-trap mask field and if that class of trap is enabled in the current trap mask, copy the current mask and the appropriate PSW fields into the save areas of the vector, place the new mask in the current process-trap mask field, then branch to the starting address of the corresponding trap-handler routine.

```
    * Begin EXAMPLE_PROGRAM_WITH_TRAP_PROCESSING
    *
    * Define external references and constants
    *
 1              EXTERNAL  ARITHMETIC_FAULT_TRAP_HANDLER,
 2                        MESSAGE_TRAP_HANDLER
 3  TRAP_MASK   EQUATE    "9"HEX     Binary 1001 enables
    *                                arithmetic-fault and message
    *                                traps
 4  DEFINE_PTV  EQUATE    xxx        xxx = SC code for
    *                                DEFINE_TRAPS
    *
    * Allocate Process-Trap Vector
    *
 5  VECTOR      CONSTANT  TRAP_MASK  Initial trap mask value
 6              SPACE     3          Area to save arithmetic fault
    *                                code, mask, and program
    *                                counter
 7              CONSTANT  "0"HEX     No traps allowed during
    *                                arithmetic-fault trap
    *                                handling
 8              CONSTANT  ARITHMETIC_FAULT_TRAP_HANDLER address
    *                                of arithmetic-fault trap
    *                                handler
 9              SPACE     2*5        Memory protection and
    *                                invalid-instruction faults
    *                                not handled
10              SPACE     3          Area for message condition
    *                                code, mask, and program
    *                                counter
11              CONSTANT  "8"HEX     Arithmetic-fault traps
    *                                allowed during message trap
    *                                handling
12              CONSTANT  MESSAGE_TRAP_HANDLER Address of message
    *                                trap handler
                   ⋮

    *
    * Define Process-Trap Vector to MOS via DEFINE_TRAPS SC
    *
13              SC        DEFINE_PTV,VECTOR
    *
    * Traps are now enabled and any arithmetic-fault or message-
    * receipt event will cause the appropriate handler routine
    * of this program to be invoked by MOS
    *
                   ⋮

    *
    * End EXAMPLE_PROGRAM_WITH_TRAP_PROCESSING
14              END
```

FIGURE 6-10   Generic Assembler Language Program Defining a PTV

How does MOS know when a process is equipped to handle traps? The PCB contains a field for the address of the process-trap vector. This address is initially null; however, when DEFINE_TRAPS is called, it stores the address of the vector provided in this field of the PCB. Thus, when a nonnull value is found by MOS, the trap can potentially be handled by the process. Examining the process-trap mask allows the final determination to be made based on the type of trap. If the mask bit corresponding to the class of the trap event that is occurring is enabled, MOS will pass control to the appropriate trap handler. Otherwise, standard handling by MOS will be provided.

Returning from a trap handler to the interrupted activity of the process involves restoring the previous value of the current trap mask and changing the program counter field of the PSW to specify the point of resumption. The two values to be restored are contained in the old trap mask and old program counter fields of the appropriate PTV element. From the perspective of the process, restoring these values must be accomplished as a unit operation. Why?

To facilitate the necessary unit operation of returning from a trap handler, a second system trap service is supplied by MOS, TRAP_RETURN. This service allows restoration of the state existing prior to initiation of the trap, subject to whatever changes are accomplished by the trap handler. It is the equivalent to restoring the old PSW at the end of a first-phase interrupt handler.

6.4.3   Arithmetic-Fault Trap Handling

Before stepping though an example of the MOS actions to initiate and terminate trap processing, let us examine the hypothetical actions of a process-trap handler for arithmetic-fault traps. Algorithm 6-7 outlines a typical handler. Many actions are possible in such routines. This algorithm illustrates how an interactive debugging facility could be included within the logic of a process. By running as part of an application program, it is able to display the type and the location of the error from the PTV condition code and program counter fields and the contents of the general registers from its local save area. If the user changes the contents of the registers, execution will resume at the location indicated in the old program counter field of the PTV with the new (and presumably corrected) general register values.

Now let us turn to the operating system processing for trap events in general, and to the processing of arithmetic-fault traps in particular. Recall that any fault initially results in a program error interrupt to the CPU. All interrupts transfer control to a system interrupt handler as indicated by the new PSW field of the MOS interrupt vector. It is the program error interrupt handler that must determine the potential for relinquishing responsibility to a trap handler routine of the faulting process.

From the perspective of MOS, there are three cases to consider when faults occur in processes. First the process causing the error may not have requested handling of arithmetic-fault traps, or other similar faults. This is the normal case. Most programs are written to accept the default actions provided by the operating system. (These actions vary from computer to computer but usually call for either ignoring the problem, assigning some predefined result such as zero or the largest magnitude number that can be represented by the host computer, or aborting the process.) Invoking the default action is indicated either when the process has failed to establish a trap vector, thus leaving the

Begin ARITHMETIC_FAULT_TRAP_HANDLER

> Handle arithmetic-fault traps for a process allowing user control of the activity
>
> Input — Type of error via the saved condition code in the PTV
>
> — Address of the instruction being executed when the fault occurred via the saved program counter in the PTV
>
> — Contents of the general registers at the time of the fault
>
> — Desired action as specified by input from the interactive user
>
> Output — Messages and prompt to user
>
> — User modifications to the general registers
>
> Assume — A PTV is defined and traps are enabled as shown in the example of Figure 6-10
>
> — Arithmetic-fault traps are disabled by the current process-trap mask in the PTV

Save all general registers in a local save area

Retrieve the condition code and program counter from the arithmetic-fault element of the PTV

Display a message indicating the type and location of the arithmetic fault

Display the contents of the general registers from the local save area

Prompt the user for the trap-handling action

Read and wait for the user's response

If the response is to correct an erroneous result
Then
    Modify the contents of the specified register in the local save area
Else
    If process termination is requested by the user
    Then
        Terminate program execution
    Else [Assume that the user wishes to continue without modifying the computational results. This requires no action.]
    EndIf
EndIf

Restore the contents of the general registers from the local save area

Call TRAP_RETURN to enable arithmetic-fault traps and request MOS to resume the process activity that was suspended for trap processing

End ARITHMETIC_FAULT_TRAP_HANDLER

ALGORITHM 6-7 Typical Arithmetic-Fault Trap Handler for Program Debugging

PCB trap vector address field null, or when a PTV has been established but the process trap mask indicates that arithmetic-fault traps, for example, are disabled.

    The second case encountered by the MOS interrupt handler for program errors is that of relinquishing responsibility for error handling to the faulting process (e.g., initiating processing of an arithmetic-fault trap by some program

Begin PROGRAM_ERROR_IH | Provide initial-phase interrupt handling for
all types of program error interrupts
Input — Program ERROR code and old PSW from
the program error element of the
interrupt vector
— SCB and associated lists
Output — SCB and associated lists
— Process state via the dispatcher
Assume — ERROR code is valid
— Program error interrupts were
disabled by loading the new PSW
— Memory address mapping is disabled
— The CPU is operating in system state

Save all general register values in a local save area
Determine the type of error from the program error element of the interrupt
vector

If the activity causing the error was a process (determined by examining
the old PSW system or process state bit)
Then

Copy the old PSW and saved register values into the appropriate save
areas of the current PCB
Call the appropriate second-phase interrupt handler for program errors,
i.e., ARITHMETIC_FAULT_IH, MEMORY_FAULT_IH,
or INSTRUCTION_FAULT_IH
Enable program error interrupts and call the dispatcher to accomplish
any list updates and to schedule some process to run (the dispatcher
will not return to the interrupt handler)

Else [MOS was active when the fault occurred, so crash the system]

Display a system crash code to the operator
Place the system in a wait state with all interrupts disabled (This
will preserve the contents of all registers and memory locations.
The state can be changed only by reloading the operating system.
Frequently, the reload is with a system dump program.)

EndIf

End PROGRAM_ERROR_IH

ALGORITHM 6-8   Initial-Phase Program Error Interrupt Handler

module as specified in the PTV). This case occurs when a PTV exists and the
contents of the current process-trap mask show that this class of trap is enabled.

Finally, there is the related case of disposing of a fault when the trap handler
of previous case causes an error itself. The latter case occurs when the process-
trap handler causes a second arithmetic fault while arithmetic traps are disabled.

All three cases are covered in the sample logic for the initial- and second-
phase program error interrupt handlers presented in Algorithm 6-8 and Algorithm 6-9. If the process has arithmetic-fault traps enabled, it is allowed to
handle them and continue execution; otherwise, it is terminated and an error
message is issued. The termination case covers both the first and third cases

Begin ARITHMETIC_FAULT_IH | Complete interrupt processing for an
arithmetic-fault program error interrupt
Input   − Condition code from the saved PSW
              − PCB of the current process
              − PTV of the current process
Output − PTV of the current process or
              messages to the standard output
              file of the process
Assume − Program error interrupts are
              disabled
              − Memory address mapping is disabled
              − The CPU is operating in system
              state

If arithmetic-fault trap processing is enabled for the current process,
i.e., a PTV has been defined and linked to the PCB and the current
process-trap mask in the PTV has arithmetic-fault traps enabled

Then | Allow the process to handle the fault via a routine
       | similar to that shown in Algorithm 6-7

Copy the condition code and program counter fields of the old PSW into
the arithmetic-fault element of the PTV
Copy the current process trap mask into the old mask field of the arithmetic-
fault element of the PTV
Copy the new mask field from the arithmetic-fault element of the PTV
into the current process trap mask field
Change the program counter field of the PSW, saved in the PCB, to the
starting address specified by the handler entry program counter
field of the arithmetic-fault element of the PTV (the dispatcher
will restore the general register values and the PSW when called
by PROGRAM_ERROR_IH)

Else [Perform standard program error processing, e.g.,]

Generate an error message to the standard process output file. The
message will contain the type of error and address of the instruction
causing the error.
Call the process termination service to abort the current process

EndIf

End ARITHMETIC_FAULT_IH

ALGORITHM 6-9   Second-Phase Program Error Interrupt Handler
for Arithmetic Faults

described above since it makes no difference whether the process has never
had program-error traps enabled or whether it caused a second fault while
processing a previous error.

6.4.4 SPOOL Process Use of Traps

Let us return to the processing of messages and to the traps associated with
their receipt. The WAIT_MESSAGE service logic, to place the calling process
on the trap-wait list when appropriate, is left as an exercise, as is the task of

extending SEND to cause a waiting receiver to resume execution. Assuming, however, that these functions are available, consider their application in the LPSPOOL process.

The scenario of Figure 6-6 is incomplete: LPSPOOL must receive messages of two entirely different types and urgency. As shown in the figure, terminating processes communicate with LPSPOOL via messages to add their print files to the queue of pending work. However, LPSPOOL must also receive messages from the operator interfacing via CIOP, as shown in Figure 6-7. From time to time, operator messages will be received to suspend printing temporarily, cancel the current print job, display the queue of pending work, change the position of work within the queue, and so on. Obviously, receipt of and response to such messages is more urgent than handling of normal process termination messages. LPSPOOL cannot, therefore, just allow incoming messages to be added to its message queue and await sequential processing. To be responsive to operator requests, LPSPOOL must do more than simply handle the front message in the queue each time the printing of a job is completed. A program structure to service all messages appropriately uses message traps as follows:

1. The LPSPOOL main program initially clears its pending work queue (separate from the process message queue), then establishes a PTV enabling message traps and pointing to a message trap handler (see item 3 below).
2. While the work queue is not empty, LPSPOOL cycles, processing jobs. When no work is pending, it enters a message trap-wait state.
3. The message trap handler is executed to receive each message at the time it is sent to LPSPOOL, regardless of the source of the message. Operator commands are executed immediately by the trap handler while new print jobs are added to the work queue for processing by the main program.

The single LPSPOOL process executes in two parts. The first removes work from the print job queue and copies the corresponding files to the printer. The second part gains control and executes asynchronously to implement operator commands and add new work to the queue.

There are many types of process traps supported by operating systems. The discussions in this chapter have centered on two major capabilities. First, the handling of unexpected, or at least unscheduled, events such as program errors. Second is the use of traps for communication and synchronization among the processes. The case of CIOP receipt of messages from system processes requiring support was considered, as was the case of LPSPOOL message handling. Understanding of these activities provides a basis for learning to use the trap service facilities of real operating systems.

6.5
Implementing System Functions as Processes

With the capabilities provided by interprocess message transmission and process trap handling, the means exist for a more flexible operating system architecture: a **kernel**-style architecture as introduced in Section 1.5. With this approach MOS could be partitioned such that more than just the SPOOLer and command interpreters would execute in the process environment. A MOS kernel could exist containing only the dispatcher, first-phase interrupt handlers, and basic memory allocation and message transmission services. All other functions could execute as processes. Most of the programs implemented as processes would, however, retain many privileges normally accorded operating system functions. System processes still need access to privileged instructions and to all of memory through the disabling of memory address mapping.

In Chapter 2 reference was made to a performance improvement that could be realized by implementing the FREE_MEMORY service as a process. With messages and traps, MOS now has the capability to support such an implementation. When memory is to be released, the only action necessary in the SC module would be to send a message to the FREE_MEMORY process describing the area to be released. Execution of the calling process could then resume immediately.

FREE_MEMORY, normally in a trap-wait state, would then be awakened to accomplish the actual releasing of the memory area. If other requests were queued in the meantime, FREE_MEMORY could systematically remove the message blocks and process these new requests as well. Only after finding the message queue empty would FREE_MEMORY place itself back into a trap-wait state.

The only other adjustment necessary to implement this approach is to have the SC routine form the message block from the actual area being released rather than acquiring additional space for a new message block. This approach is necessary to avoid the potential of a deadlock condition which would arise if insufficient space were available to form a request. (A deadlock could be created when memory space was exhausted and no areas can be released to replenish the FSB list until an area of sufficient size for a message is found. Such an area would obviously never be forthcoming.)

Forming a message block for FREE_MEMORY requires only that all allocated and released areas be of sufficient size to contain the release message. A size limit of perhaps 16 bytes would be adequate for such use.

The SWAP_IN module defined in Chapter 3 could have a similar implementation. Recall that the function of SWAP_IN was to attempt to bring a process into memory for execution from its swap file on secondary storage. This action should occur when the PCB for a nonresident process nears the front of the PCB ready queue, thus becoming a candidate for execution in the near future. If SWAP_IN were a process, the dispatcher could scan the first few PCBs in the queue, form messages to SWAP_IN to restore any processes that were swapped out, then schedule SWAP_IN to run. Each time SWAP_IN entered an I/O wait state while moving program segments between memory and disk, the dispatcher could allow other processes to execute. Thus SWAP_IN could operate concurrently with application processes, but at a higher priority.

As a final example of shifting MOS functions into the process environment, consider the restructuring of the I/O service and interrupt handlers into a separate process for each device. This would produce a one-to-one correspondence between DCBs and device-oriented processes. The process for each device would provide three basic functions exclusively for its associated device: initiating input/output operations, blocking processes pending completion of operations, and handling interrupts. Most of INITIATE_IO, WAIT_IO, and DEVICE_IH could therefore execute as privileged processes.

When other processes executed SC instructions to initiate I/O transfers, the initial phase interrupt handler for SC interrupts, SC_IH, would simply send messages to the appropriate device-related process and return to the caller. If the device management process were in a trap-wait state, it would be awakened to handle the request using logic similar to the INITIATE_IO service of Algorithm 5-2. When the device process was busy (not in a trap-wait state) the request would simply remain in the queue until it could be processed. WAIT_IO requests and second-phase interrupt handling would be accomplished in a similar manner, all within the same process.

What, if anything, is gained by placing major elements of the operating system in processes? Improved resource utilization and throughput should be realized. With a monolithic system structure, as initially defined for MOS, a tremendous amount of unnecessary serialization occurs, just as it does in a uniprogramming environment. For example, when the FREE_MEMORY service routine executes, everything in the service subsystem and process environments is prohibited from executing and thus prohibited from initiating any new non-computational requests such as input or output operations. Similarly, if SWAP_IN executes as part of the MOS dispatcher program, no productive execution can occur while it moves processes between memory and secondary storage.

Equally important is the realization that when any input/output service or interrupt handler is active, execution of all other I/O modules is inhibited since I/O interrupts are disabled. Disabling interrupts ensures DCB and IOB queue stability by serializing I/O-related activities. But this solution to I/O data structure integrity is an overkill. All I/O does not need to be serialized. Only operations for one DCB and IOB queue are of concern.

Placing all functions supporting a single device into a process for that device serializes the required operations by the serial nature of the process message queue while it leaves support for all other devices in an uninhibited condition. Processing associated with multiple devices can thus occur concurrently and on a priority basis.

The net effect of more system processes is reduced intervals of interrupt-disabled processing. This reduces serialization and therefore tends to increase throughput.

PROBLEMS

1. Illustrate the process-related MOS data structures at an instant that encompasses the following set of conditions. Note that command interpreter processes are generally either waiting for a subprocess to terminate or for a user to enter a command, whichever is appropriate. Use pure priority dispatching and state any additional necessary assumptions or conditions.

   (1) In decreasing order of priority, system processes exist for LPSPOOL, CIOP, CI1, CI2, and CI3. LPSPOOL is printing jobs.

   (2) CI1 has created SESSION1 to execute program CONCURRENT_SOLUTION (Algorithm 6-6) at a priority below that of all CI processes. The process for CONCURRENT_SOLUTION has in turn already created SUBSOLUTION_1, which has not started to execute, then invoked CREATE to initiate a lower-priority process

for the SUBSOLUTION_2 program. CREATE has completed its work, but the calling process has not yet been dispatched.

(3) The user at terminal 2 is executing the EDIT program.

(4) The the user at terminal 3 has sent a message to the user at terminal 2.

(5) The printer has just run out of paper and LPSPOOL is sending an appropriate message to the operator.   [DS]

2. Design a WAIT_MESSAGE service routine to operate in a process-trap environment. Your routine should support the final version of the CONCURRENT_SOLUTION program.   [Alg]

3. Rewrite the SEND service to support a process-trap environment compatible with the WAIT_MESSAGE routine of problem 2.   [Alg]

4. Assume that the WAIT_MESSAGE service of problem 2 has been supplemented by a general WAIT_TRAP routine. (WAIT_MESSAGE allows execution to resume with the instruction following the SC instruction, while WAIT_TRAP allows control to pass to a trap handler when a message is received.) Discuss the actions relative to the PTV to support both services. Is there a conflict in data structure definition if both WAIT_TRAP and WAIT_MESSAGE are to be used within the same program? Define any changes necessary to accommodate this capability.   [Ana]

5. Assume that the MOS termination procedure, which executes on behalf of a terminating process, sends an end-of-process message to the parent of any process that terminates abnormally. Provide a detailed design for the CONCURRENT_SOLUTION program to operate under all conditions. You should consider the cases of either subprocess terminating first and both normal and abnormal terminations.   [Alg]

6. CIOP has no way of determining whether its next communication will arrive from a process or from the operator's terminal. Since it is inappropriate for CIOP to use a busy-waiting loop, testing alternately for read completion and message receipt, it must become blocked waiting for both events. MOS does not provide for processes to wait for more than one type of event. A solution to this CIOP problem is to partition the program into two processes, one that receives commands from the operator and one that receives messages from other processes. Discuss the general organization of such a concurrent program and the allocation of CIOP functions between the processes. Consider the requirements to display relevant messages to the operator at any time and to receive commands from the operator and route them to other processes appropriately.   [Ana]

7. Provide the design for both programs of CIOP as described in problem 6.
                                                                                                           [Alg]

8. Illustrate the functional linkage from main program logic to application trap-handler modules for error conditions such as memory protection violations and arithmetic faults. Produce a diagram similar to that for SC interrupts as shown in Figure 5-10.   [DS]

9. Explain how your computer system supports the general capability for processes to await communication or the occurrence of other significant subprocess events.   [OS]

pascal

10. Explain how your computer system supports the handling of program errors by faulting processes. [OS]

11. Study your computer system and explain how processes are allowed to retain control when memory protection faults and invalid instruction faults occur but are prevented from overriding the faults; for example, execution continues when an attempt to access protected memory is made but the access is denied. [OS]

12. Write a program to demonstrate the handling of an arithmetic fault by an application program. Use Algorithm 6-7 as a model. [OS]

13. Provide the design for TRAP_RETURN. Include all interface and assumption information. Be sure to consider the case of a message arriving while the message trap handler is already active processing an earlier message. What should TRAP_RETURN do to ensure orderly processing of this new message? [Alg]

14. Explain the use of services in your computer system to create processes and communicate messages between them. [OS]

15. Write a program to demonstrate the use of the subprocess creation and communication features of your computer system using CONCUR-RENT_SOLUTION and its subprocesses as a model. [OS]

16. Redesign FREE_MEMORY as two programs: a second-phase SC interrupt handler to transmit a message and a system process to manage the FSB list. It is not necessary to reproduce the actual list management logic.

[Alg]

17. Redesign CARD_TO_DISK, Algorithm 4-4, as a concurrent program. One process should perform the card-reading subfunction while the other one writes the images to disk. The programs must, of course, communicate error conditions but should not be unnecessarily synchronized. [Alg]

18. Redesign CARD_TO_DISK from problem 17 to perform blocking of the card records as defined in problem 12 in Chapter 4. [Alg]

19. Rewrite the DISK_TO_PRINTER program of problem 16 in Chapter 4 to be a concurrent program similar to the CARD_TO_DISK solution of problem 18. [Alg]

20. Illustrate the functional linkage from application program logic to device processes and from I/O devices to device processes in a kernel version of MOS. Produce a diagram similar to that in Figure 5-10. [DS]

21. Redesign the SC_IH, INITIATE_IO, and WAIT_IO modules of Chapter 5 to run in a kernel architecture. Be sure to state all assumptions relative to data structure, process privileges, and so on. [Alg]

22. Work problem 21 for IO_IH and DEVICE_IH. [Alg]

CHAPTER 7

Competing Concurrent Processes

concurrent *adj* . . . operating or occurring at the same time . . . exercised over the same matter or area by two different authorities
(*Webster's Ninth New Collegiate Dictionary*)

Considering the definitions of concurrent and process, let us begin this chapter with a reexamination and extension of the definition of a multiprogramming system as presented in Chapter 1. A **multiprogramming system** is a set of sequential processes that operate almost independently of each other, cooperate by sending messages and synchronization signals to each other, and compete for resources. In the previous chapters, some aspects of resource competition and synchronization were examined. Specifically, the competition for main memory was discussed and the process swapping feature of MOS was the manifestation of this contest. In Chapter 5 we used IOB queues to govern the competition for the I/O resources of shared devices, and Chapter 6 dealt with communication and synchronization between processes cooperating to provide solutions and services.

The theme of this chapter is the other key phrases in the multiprogramming system definition, namely: "operate almost independently" and "cooperate by sending . . . synchronization signals." In this chapter the synchronization will be between processes not necessarily related to one another and will be in the interest of serializing the use of various resources.

7.1
Critical Sections and Race Conditions

Before examining the mechanisms of synchronization, let us review the operations involved in reading data from a sector of disk into a process buffer. Part of this procedure involves the INITIATE_IO service allocating space for an

Begin GET_MEMORY

    Default STATUS to failure
    Initialize PREVIOUS pointer to ROVER
    Do
        Set CURRENT to link(PREVIOUS)
        If the current block is adequate
        Then
            Set LOCATION to CURRENT + size(CURRENT) - SIZE

Ⓐ →

            If LOCATION = CURRENT
            Then
                Set link(PREVIOUS) to link(CURRENT)
                  ⋮

End GET_MEMORY

FIGURE 7-1   Portion of Memory Allocation Service

IOB. If the allocation is accomplished by a call to the GET_MEMORY memory management service defined in Algorithm 2-1, the program fragment shown in Figure 7-1 might be executed.

Assume that the initial FSB list is as shown on the left in Figure 7-2, with the size of FSB 3 being exactly that needed for an IOB. When execution has reached the point marked Ⓐ in the GET_MEMORY service, the state shown on the right in Figure 7-2 will exist.

Now assume that just as execution reaches point Ⓐ in the GET_MEMORY service, a timer interrupt occurs and is processed by the timer-interrupt-handling software. (It is entirely feasible that such an event could happen since in MOS, even though all I/O interrupts are disabled, timer interrupts have a higher priority, as indicated in Table 5-1, and would be enabled at the time.) Handling a timer interrupt will, on occasion, require release of time block memory space via the FREE_MEMORY routine. Suppose that while GET_MEMORY is

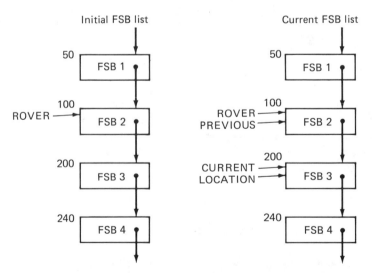

FIGURE 7-2   First Step in the Allocation of Memory Block FSB 3 for an IOB

suspended, FREE_MEMORY is called to release an area immediately preceding FSB 2 in Figure 7-2. Such an activity will modify the FSB list slightly (see the left side of Figure 7-3), so that when GET_MEMORY execution resumes, the logic following point Ⓐ in the GET_MEMORY routine leaves the list structured as shown on the right side of Figure 7-3.

Observe that three totally unacceptable conditions now exist.

1. An area allocated to INITIATE_IO for use as an IOB is still linked into the free-space list and is therefore a candidate for reallocation to some requesting process in the future.
2. INITIATE_IO will add this IOB/FSB to the queue of some DCB. If another execution of GET_MEMORY occurs while this IOB exists, GET_MEMORY would actually jump from the FSB list at FSB 2' to the IOB queue and either appropriate other space or loop endlessly through the circular IOB queue! (All IOBs on the queue of this DCB have been linked into the FSB list.)
3. All valid free space beginning with FSB 4 has been disconnected from the list and lost irrecoverably.

There are several other scenarios that lead to similar FSB list failures and ultimately result in a system crash. For example, the original process could have issued an SC to dynamically request space (perhaps stack space for recursive call executions). While the SC was being processed, an I/O interrupt could occur, resulting in the release of an IOB. Or perhaps while the space was being allocated, some interrupt-handling software requiring additional space issued its own call to GET_MEMORY. This sequence could result in a failure in which both activities are assigned the same block of free space for their individual and exclusive use.

Potential problems similar to those just presented are very common in concurrent programming applications. In general, they are referred to as race con-

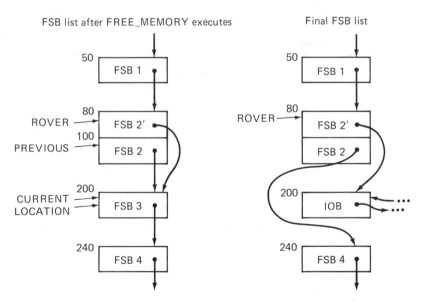

FIGURE 7-3 Results of an Erroneous Allocation of Memory for an IOB

ditions. A **race condition** exists when two or more activities (e.g., processes or interrupt handlers) are vying for exclusive use of some serially reusable resource. [A **serially reusable resource** is a resource that is repeatedly reusable as long as two or more uses are not concurrent (i.e., do not overlap in time).] In the previous example, the serially reusable resource was the FSB list. This list can be used any number of times, but as has been demonstrated, it may not undergo concurrent use. In human experience a narrow doorway is, in general, serially reusable by adults.

Central to the control of race conditions is the identification of **critical sections** of computer programs as those program segments that access serially reusable resources and the serialization of critical section executions. The execution of one critical section must not be interleaved with those of other critical sections accessing the same serially reusable resources. Now the importance of the phrase ". . . operate almost independently of each other, cooperate by sending . . . synchronization signals to each other . . ." is recognized in terms of required actions. Even apparently independent processes must coordinate their use of serially reusable global resources, such as FSB lists, controller registers, printers, and shared disk files.

An analogy to race conditions exists within the railroad industry. Figure 7-4 illustrates the race condition equivalent to those discussed relative to the FSB list. Imagine that the user programs are passengers riding on the trains that serve the function of processes. The locomotives and engineers are services and the rails are computer resources. Railroads solve race condition problems without involving the users (i.e., the passengers). Indeed, it is desirable, even mandatory, to solve these problems without affecting the users. (The integrity of a multiuser computer system must not depend on the applications programs that use it!) If signals or semaphores are installed where they are visible to the railroad engineers prior to the entrances to serially reusable segments of track, and if these service personnel are instructed to recognize and obey them, then the process, or train, which arrives at the resource second can take action to block (stop) itself until the resource becomes available. In this analogy, the engineer must recognize the signal governing a serially reusable resource and proceed only if the semaphore indicates resource availability.

Each program critical section must take action to change the semaphore so that use of the associated resource can be detected by other activities. Similarly, the code in each critical section must change the semaphore again once execution is complete and the resource becomes available for use. In the FSB list example, the destruction of the FSB list could have been avoided had GET_MEMORY signaled its use of the list and FREE_MEMORY recognized that signal and delayed its execution until GET_MEMORY had finished.

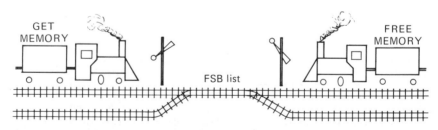

FIGURE 7-4   The Railroad Race Condition

7.2
Lock and Semaphore Operations and Options

7.2.1 LOCK and UNLOCK Functions

What does the need to synchronize the use of serially reusable resources mean to the structure of MOS? A solution to the race condition for the FSB list could easily be implemented if two additional service modules were provided. By functionally defining LOCK and UNLOCK modules to manipulate semaphores at the entrances to and exits from critical sections of code, the GET_MEMORY service could be modified as follows:

> **Begin** GET_MEMORY
>
>> Call LOCK to ensure exclusive use of the FSB list resource
>> Default STATUS to failure
>>
>> ⋮
>>
>> Call UNLOCK to release the FSB list resource
>
> **End** GET_MEMORY

and, similarly, FREE_MEMORY could become

> **Begin** FREE_MEMORY
>
>> Call LOCK to ensure exclusive use of the FSB list resource
>> Initialize a NEW index to the node at LOCATION
>>
>> ⋮
>>
>> Call UNLOCK to release the FSB list resource
>
> **End** FREE_MEMORY .

In these references, the function of LOCK is to examine a semaphore indicating the status of the resource, the FSB list, and if the semaphore indicates availability, change its state status to busy and allow the calling program to continue execution. Otherwise, the caller should be delayed until the resource becomes available. Conversely, UNLOCK should make the resource available by clearing the semaphore controlling use of the FSB list, and permit some other process to have access to the list.

With the addition of these functions, if a process calls GET_MEMORY and some other activity is not currently updating the FSB list, the process will signal its use of the resource and proceed. During this time if interrupts and dispatching conspire to allow a process of higher priority to execute, and if that process also requests exclusive use of the FSB list, its call to LOCK will not complete until the first process releases control by calling UNLOCK.

A simple approach implementing the LOCK function defined might be the following functional assembler code.

```
TEST_LABEL     Test the appropriate semaphore
               Branch to TEST_LABEL if the resource is not
                 available
               Change the semaphore to indicate an
                 unavailable resource
               ⋮
```

Notice, however, that this code has a flaw, a window through which the first stone of a system crash will eventually be thrown. Consider the following sequence.

1. Initially, the semaphore indicates resource availability.
2. Low-priority process JOB2 tests the semaphore and finds it clear and therefore proceeds through the branch instruction.
3. An interrupt occurs and high-priority process JOB1 is resumed from an I/O wait state.
4. JOB1 attempts to lock the same resource just tested by JOB2 but not yet locked by the instruction following the branch. Since the resource is at this instant still shown to be available, JOB1 also proceeds through the branch and now locks the resource.
5. Next JOB1 becomes blocked for some other reason and JOB2 is resumed at the instruction that changes the semaphore.
6. Both JOB1 and JOB2 have been granted exclusive use of a serially reusable resource. This ultimately leads to a system failure.

What is the flaw? The semaphore itself is a serially reusable resource and the three instruction sequence to test, branch, and change the semaphore is a critical section. In this example, both jobs executed critical sections concurrently. This approach would require that LOCK itself use a LOCK service to serialize use of the semaphore; however, this would lead to a potentially never-ending cycle of recursive calls.

The operation of examining and adjusting the semaphore must therefore be an indivisible operation. A process must be able to test a condition, then change it, without losing control of the CPU, thereby preventing any other activity from acquiring control in between instructions of the lock sequence.

7.2.2 Test-and-Set Instructions

Many computers have instructions that are adequate for this task, the most common being a test-and-set instruction. Test-and-set instructions function as single, noninterruptible, instructions that copy the current value of a bit into a register, then set the bit. With such a tool, the lock sequence can be recoded as

```
TEST_LABEL    Test-and-set the appropriate semaphore (bit)
              Branch to TEST_LABEL If the original value
              (now in a register) was a 1
              ⋮
```

The complete design for a bit-string-oriented LOCK and UNLOCK pair is shown in Algorithms 7-1. (Each bit in the string serves as the semaphore for a particular resource.) This simple solution has closed the window but introduced another problem just as serious. The system now has the potential for a deadlock or stalemate condition. Again, consider an example based on pure priority scheduling.

Begin LOCK

> Ensure exclusive use of a specified resource before allowing the calling process to continue
> Input   – Resource (bit) NUMBER within a bit STRING
>   – STRING of lock bits
> Output – Bit NUMBER of STRING is set

   Do
       Test-and-set bit NUMBER of STRING
   Until the bit was originally clear
   EndDo

End LOCK

Begin UNLOCK

> Release a specified resource for other use
> Input   – Resource (bit) NUMBER within a bit STRING
>   – STRING of lock bits
> Output – Bit NUMBER is cleared

   Clear bit NUMBER of STRING

End UNLOCK

ALGORITHMS 7-1   Simple, and Inadequate, LOCK and UNLOCK Services

1. Initially, the semaphore indicates resource availability.
2. Low-priority process JOB2 calls LOCK, acquires use of the resource, and continues processing.
3. An interrupt occurs and high priority process JOB1 is resumed from an I/O wait state.
4. JOB1 calls LOCK and attempts to lock the resource just acquired by JOB2. The bit is set so that LOCK spins in a two-instruction loop waiting for the bit to be cleared (i.e., JOB1 is in a CPU loop).
5. The system has now failed, since JOB1 is looping waiting for a resource to become available; however, the resource will never be released by JOB2 because it is a lower-priority process than JOB1 and can never gain control of the CPU. Gaining control of the CPU by JOB2 is necessary to complete its use of the locked resource and release it to JOB1.

Deadlocks normally involve resources other than the CPU, but the preceding scenario is an elementary form of deadlock that can easily be prevented. Each process has a resource needed by the other, and neither can release its resource until it acquires the other one that it needs. JOB1 had the CPU and needed the locked resource, while JOB2 had the resource and required the CPU in order to release it. The activity of waiting for an event to occur by repeatedly executing a loop that tests for occurrence of the event is referred to as the **busy-waiting** approach. Busy-waiting with test-and-set type instructions is powerful and has many applications in serialization functions but not within operating system lock services in a single-processor environment.

Notice, however, that the busy-waiting activity is not so objectionable if the lock bit is being used to synchronize resource use in a multiprocessor environment. A deadlock condition need not result from this case. Consider a multiprocessor computer system in which each processor executes its own copy of the operating system and references processes (work to be done) in a shared memory. Obviously, simultaneous update of the ready queue could cause a system failure. The individual processors, and their associated operating systems, therefore synchronize PCB list updates by use of a lock bit also located in the shared memory. A busy-waiting loop containing a test-and-set instruction is executed to gain exclusive use of the list. On those rare occasions when two processors simultaneously execute code to access the lists, and a locked state is found by one processor, that processor spins, waiting for the resource to be released by the other processor. Unlike the previous uniprocessor case, however, deadlock does not occur since the processor in the busy-waiting state does not monopolize the only CPU.

7.2.3 Avoiding the Busy-Waiting Condition in a Uniprocessor System

The requirements for guaranteeing mutually exclusive use of a serially reusable resource, without using busy-waiting logic, are similar to those listed by Holt [1983] for the procedures Mutexbegin and Mutexend.

1. LOCK must
   a. Determine if any other process is in a critical section involving the requested resource (i.e., if another process is maintaining a lock on the input resource).
   b. Block the calling process if the determination in step 1a is affirmative.
   c. When the resource is found to be available, allow the current process to proceed and set an indicator so that any other requests to lock the resource will be delayed.
2. UNLOCK must
   a. Determine if any other process is waiting to enter a critical section involving the released resource (i.e., if another process has been blocked by LOCK pending availability of the resource).
   b. Allow some other process to enter its critical section if the determination in step 2a is affirmative.
   c. Clear the indicator when no process needs exclusive use of the resource.

Several alternatives exist for mechanizing these services. First, as in the test-and-set example, the semaphores can be individual binary flags indicating either availability or in-use status. This technique, which will be adopted for MOS, utilizes a bit string. If the bit assigned to a particular resource is 1, that resource is in use and not available for access. Conversely, a zero value indicates that the resource has not been committed to a process for exclusive use. The length of the bit string depends on the maximum number of serially reusable resources whose access is controlled by the LOCK and UNLOCK services.

7.2.4 Dijkstra's Counting Semaphores

A more general technique of using integer values to implement software semaphores was defined by Dijkstra in 1968. He specified two primitive functions to operate on semaphores in general, without regard to whether the variables were restricted to two-state binary values. Nonbinary semaphores are frequently referred to as **counting semaphores** and the functions that use them to implement the LOCK and UNLOCK services were referred to by Dijkstra as the **P-operation** and the **V-operation**, respectively.

The value of the counting semaphore for a resource indicates not only the availability state of the resource but also the number of unallocated concurrent accesses possible for that resource. Requests to lock a resource cause decrementing of the semaphore value, while UNLOCK calls result in incrementing the value. As long as a counter value is positive, allocation can occur. A positive value indicates the number of times the resource can be allocated before a requester must be blocked.

The maximum value for the FSB list resource is 1, since that resource must never be shared. However, if three printers were attached to the computer and viewed as a pool of print capability, rather than just three independent resources, the single semaphore for printer resource management would indicate, by the appropriate positive number, the number of printers available for use. Each time a printer is assigned and removed from the pool, the counter is decremented. When it reaches zero, no additional allocations can be made. Additionally, a zero counter value indicates that no processes are waiting for release of the resource.

Negative semaphore values not only indicate unavailability of the corresponding resource but also the number of processes waiting to use it. If five requests for allocation of printers from a pool of three were made, a counting semaphore value of -2 would result, indicating that the last two requesters were blocked awaiting release of previously allocated devices.

Initially, when all three printers are available, the controlling semaphore would have a value of 3. When some process entered the printer allocation procedure, a positive value would be detected, a printer would be assigned to the caller, and the semaphore would be decremented to 2, indicating that only two resources remained in the pool. This scenario would be repeated for allocation of the next two device requests as well, leaving a semaphore value of 0, indicating that no printers remained for allocation but that no processes were blocked awaiting resources. The next process to attempt to enter the allocation procedure would be blocked, since a nonpositive count would exist. The semaphore would still be decremented and the -1 would indicate that a single process was waiting for a printer to be returned to the pool.

Conversely, each time UNLOCK was invoked, corresponding to the return of a printer to the pool, the counting semaphore would be incremented. When a nonpositive semaphore value results, one of the waiting processes is resumed with exclusive use of the recently returned printer. Incrementation resulting in positive semaphore values causes no additional action since all requests that were delayed, if any, have previously been satisfied.

7.2.5 MOS Approach to LOCK and UNLOCK

In the uniprocessor environment of MOS, we do not, as yet, have an acceptable approach to implementing LOCK and UNLOCK. When Dijkstra defined the P and V operations, they were required to provide more than the simple acquisition and releasing of resources by test-and-decrement and increment operations on counting semaphores. The P-operation had to provide a means of blocking a process when requested resources were unavailable other than by use of the busy-waiting method. Similarly, the V-operation was required to test for waiting processes and resume one if one was found. This function is roughly similar to that of the INITIATE_IO and DEVICE_IH modules of Chapter 5. INITIATE_IO allows a process to request an I/O operation to a serially reusable device, queuing the request if the device is already in use. The DEVICE_IH module processes completion interrupts and starts the next operation in the IOB queue, if any.

As with the I/O operations, a place is needed to maintain pending requests when a resource is busy. In keeping with the data structure philosophy of MOS, it is appropriate that the SCB contain a pointer to a queue of processes waiting for unavailable resources. Since multiple allocations of resources will not generally be needed in MOS, simple binary values will control resources rather than counting semphores. The bit string used to maintain the status of the managed resources can be placed in the SCB. Finally, indications of which resources have been acquired and which requested are needed for each process. Addition of these elements produces expanded SCB and PCB structures, as shown in Figure 7-5.

As with other PCB lists, the resource wait queue is a doubly linked list. It contains the PCBs of processes waiting for unavailable resources. As will be seen in the final logic of the LOCK service, processes will be added in the order in which the requests were made. (There are several other feasible queue structures which are addressed in the problems at the end of the chapter.)

There are two types of bit strings used to control the locking of the resources. The system lock bit string is a global structure that reflects the actual state of all managed serially reusable resources. This string is an array of binary semaphores in one-to-one correspondence with the managed resources. A process

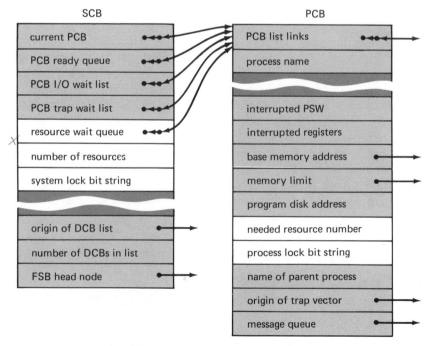

FIGURE 7-5   Data Structure for Accommodating Locks

lock bit string in the PCB indicates all resources currently owned by the associated process. The PCB needed (requested) resource number field indicates the request that resulted in the process becoming blocked.

There are several alternatives to the bit string and single resource wait queue of Figure 7-5. First, a separate wait queue could be maintained for each bit or resource in the string. The principal advantages of these additional queues would be shorter searches when looking for a process to resume once a resource has been released and the ease of implementing different queuing strategies for the resources. Major disadvantages are SCB space for queue head pointers and the need to provide logic for the examination of multiple queues when searching for the PCB of a process that is being terminated.

If counting semaphores are used rather than a bit string, a linear list of counters would replace the bit string in the SCB. Again, the wait queue may be implemented as either a single combined queue or a unique queue for each resource counter with the trade-offs stated above. The counting semaphores provide more information and flexibility than is available with the bit string structure, at the expense of higher memory requirements. In deciding which approach to adopt, the systems programmer must consider the number of instances, if any, in which the maximum value of counting semaphores would be greater than 1, the total number of lock control counters or indicators needed, and the additional space and logic needed for a particular implementation.

7.3
LOCK and UNLOCK Algorithms

Algorithms 7-2 and 7-3 implement resource allocation and release capabilities using the bit strings and queue defined in Figure 7-5. Notice that the LOCK module has no test-and-set operation. There are two reasons for this. The first reason for not using a test-and-set instruction is the avoidance of the deadlock caused by the current process entering a busy-waiting loop, thereby denying use of the CPU to the owner of the needed resource. Second, test-and-set, and its test-and-decrement semaphore counterpart, are indivisible for the duration of a single compound operation. As specified previously, LOCK must accomplish much more than these single instructions provide. There is an entire sequence of instructions necessary to examine the resource lock and, if it is set, save the request and add the PCB to the resource wait queue. The entire LOCK function must be an indivisible operation in its manipulation of the related data structures.

Since only processes can be placed in the resource wait queue, LOCK and UNLOCK may be invoked only by processes. Specifically, only the current process can execute LOCK and UNLOCK, which it does by means of an SC instruction interrupt. Recalling that the MOS interrupt structure guarantees that the lowest-priority interrupt processing is complete before control is passed to the dispatcher, we see that other processes cannot gain control of the CPU until LOCK or UNLOCK returns to its caller, SC_IH, and process scheduling has been completed by the dispatcher. Since nonprocess activities such as interrupt handlers cannot use LOCK and UNLOCK, the required serialized use of the lock bit strings and queue are assured.

Begin LOCK

Ensure exclusive use of a specified resource before
allowing the calling process to continue
Input   – Resource bit NUMBER to be locked
          – PCB of the current process
          – SCB and associated lists
Output – PCB of the current process
          – SCB and associated lists
Assume – The current process does not already have the
          requested resource locked
          – Memory address mapping is disabled
          – LOCK and UNLOCK are invoked only on behalf of
          processes, i.e., interrupt handlers do not call
          them

If the resource is available, i.e., the corresponding bit of the system
     lock bit string in the SCB is clear
Then [Allocate the resource and continue the process]

Set the bit for the specified resource in the system lock bit string
     of the SCB
Set the bit for the specified resource in the process lock bit string
     of the current PCB

Else [Queue the process pending resource availability]

Save NUMBER in the needed-resource-number field of the current PCB
Notify the dispatcher that the current process is to be placed at the
     rear of the resource wait queue (the dispatcher will be called
     from SC_IH upon completion of LOCK module execution)

EndIf

End LOCK

ALGORITHM 7-2   Bit String Lock and Queue Version of the P-operation

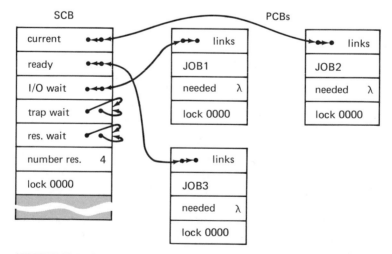

FIGURE 7-6   Initial Conditions for JOB2 Locking Resource 1

Begin UNLOCK Release a specified resource for other use or resume the
first process on the resource wait queue that is
waiting for the resource
Input — Resource bit NUMBER to be released
— PCB of the current process
— SCB and associated lists
Output — PCB of the current process
— PCB of any resumed process
— SCB and associated lists
Assume — The current process has resource NUMBER
locked
— Memory address mapping is disabled
— LOCK and UNLOCK are invoked only on behalf of
processes, i.e., interrupt handlers do not call
them

Clear the bit for the specified resource in the process lock bit string
of the current PCB
Index to the first PCB on the resource wait queue, if any

While the end of the queue is not reached and the indexed PCB is not waiting
for the specified resource
Do
Index to the next PCB in the queue, if any
EndDo

If a process was found that is waiting for the specified resource
Then [Relinquish control of the resource to that process]

Set bit NUMBER in the lock bit string of the located PCB
Notify the dispatcher that the located PCB is to be removed from the
resource wait queue

Else [Return the resource to the available state]

Clear the bit for the specified resource in the system lock bit string
of the SCB

EndIf

End UNLOCK

ALGORITHM 7-3 Bit String Unlock and Queue Removal Version of
the V-operation

To illustrate LOCK and UNLOCK service module operation, assume pure
priority process scheduling and three processes of decreasing priority: JOB1,
JOB2, and JOB3. Initially, JOB1 is in an I/O wait state and JOB2 and JOB3
are attempting to compute. Figure 7-6 illustrates the significant portions of the
initial MOS data structure.

Given this state, let JOB2 issue a call to the LOCK service for resource
number 1. LOCK determines that the resource is available, sets the bit in the
system lock bit string and in the process lock bit string, and allows JOB2 to
continue as shown in Figure 7-7. Now when the I/O operation for JOB1 completes and JOB1 becomes current and attempts to lock resource number 1, it
is blocked and placed on the resource wait queue. The action saves a value of
1 in the needed-resource-number field of the JOB1 PCB.

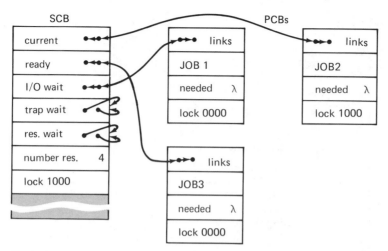

FIGURE 7-7 After JOB2 Has Locked Resource 1

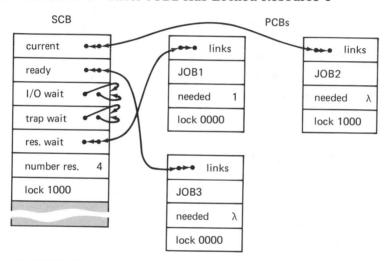

FIGURE 7-8 JOB1 Is Blocked due to the Unavailability of Resource 1

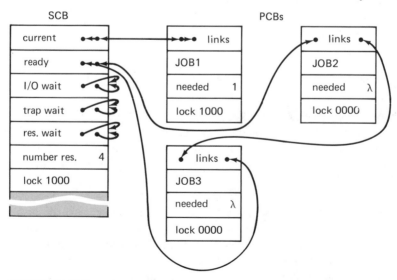

FIGURE 7-9 JOB1 Is Resumed with Exclusive Use of Resource 1

Figure 7-8 indicates that the process is waiting for that resource to be released. Since JOB1 is blocked, JOB2 again becomes the current process. If JOB2 now releases resource 1 via the UNLOCK service, bit 1 in its PCB will be cleared, but the corresponding bit will remain set in the SCB, as shown in Figure 7-9. This is because UNLOCK will search the resource wait queue for a PCB that has requested the corresponding resource. Since JOB1 is waiting for resource 1, the indicated bit in its PCB bit string will be set and the PCB removed from the queue and made ready and then current by the dispatcher. The resource remains allocated so the SCB bit string remains unchanged.

7.4
Deadlocks

A demonstration of the general condition of deadlocked processes can be provided by continuing the example of LOCK and UNLOCK operations from Section 7.3. Assume that JOB1 performs an I/O with wait while resource 1 is still locked. JOB2 will again become current and will, in this example, use the LOCK service to acquire resource 2, as shown in Figure 7-10.

Next, suppose that JOB1 completes its I/O and is resumed, and that it now requests exclusive use of resource 2. This bit is already set in the system bit string, so JOB1 is added to the resource wait queue and JOB2 is again scheduled, since it is the highest-priority process on the ready list (see Figure 7-11).

Finally, let JOB2 again request use of resource 1. Since the system lock bit string already has this bit set, the request is saved in the JOB2 PCB and the process is placed in the resource wait queue. This causes a deadlock condition. JOB2 has use of resource 2 and is waiting for resource 1. JOB1 has use of resource 1 and is awaiting the release of resource 2 by JOB2. Since both processes are blocked, neither will ever execute and release the resource needed by the other. This final condition is shown in Figure 7-12.

Stated generally, **deadlock** is a condition in which processes are blocked, waiting for events that can never occur. When a deadlock occurs involving

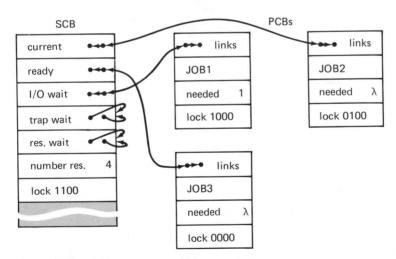

FIGURE 7-10 JOB2 Has Acquired Resource 2

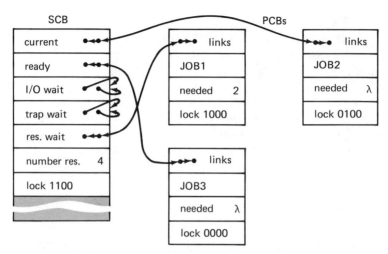

FIGURE 7-11 JOB1 Is Again Queued, This Time Waiting for JOB2 to Unlock Resource 2

more than one process, four conditions exist. (Recall from Chapter 6 that a simple form of deadlock occurs when a process enters a trap-wait state and no other process exists that will send a message satisfying the wait condition.) First, some nonshareable resources must exist together with a mechanism for exclusively allocating them to processes. Second, processes must be able to hold acquired resources even when blocked. Third, processes must not be able to confiscate resources held by other processes. Finally, there must be a circular wait condition; that is, each process involved in the deadlock must remain in a nonproductive state pending release of resources held by other processes in the same state.

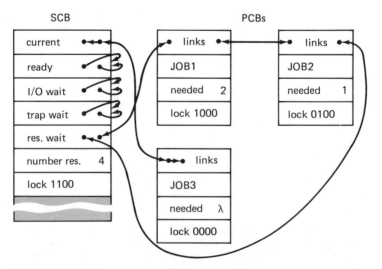

FIGURE 7-12 Deadlock Conditions Involving JOB1 and JOB2

7.4.1 Avoiding Deadlock

There are a number of ways of preventing the occurrence of multiple process deadlocks within a computer system. Five of the simplest approaches are single-semaphore serialization, ensuring adequate resources, preallocation of resources, fixed-order resource allocation, and detection and avoidance of potential deadlock conditions before they occur. Each has its attractions and detractions.

Single semaphore serialization uses only a single lock semaphore to serialize the access to all serially reusable resources. When using only one lock bit or counter, it is not possible for processes to hold non-CPU resources while waiting for others, and therefore, if busy-waiting techniques are not used, it is not possible to create a deadlock condition. The obvious disadvantage of this very effective technique is the needless serialization of processing caused when several processes, using unrelated resources, are forced into a serial processing sequence by use of the single lock facility, which, in effect, locks all resources simultaneously. (This approach is similar to that existing in the interrupt logic of the MOS architecture. When I/O structures are being updated, all I/O interrupts are disabled, thus serializing system processing of operations to all I/O devices.)

This technique is more attractive if it is extended by partitioning resources into several groups, each one of which has its access controlled by a single bit or counter. If processes are prohibited from concurrently having two locks set, deadlock conditions cannot arise and the degree of unnecessary serialization is reduced.

Another technique is that of **providing adequate resources** initially. This is usually impractical due either to the nature of the resources (e.g., the FSB list) or to their costs. The basis for this method is that if a computer system has enough tape drives, printers, and so on, to satisfy worst-case demands, no process will acquire part of its resources, then become blocked waiting for others to be released. No deadlocks will therefore occur. The fallacy here is that even if cost were not a factor, some serially reusable resources are not amenable to such a technique. For example, how can one build an integrated data base with an adequate number of duplicate copies of records which are modifiable by multiple processes? Even if the copies were generated, how could they be kept current and consistent? Similarly, what is the meaning or utility of multiple FSB lists?

The third technique is that of **preallocation** of all needed resources. Specifically, all resources that will be needed concurrently by any process must be allocated simultaneously and before the first resource is accessed. If memory management, a set of data base records, and two magnetic tape drives will be needed in some intermixed and overlapping way during a period of time, all must be acquired initially, so that the process will never become blocked due to lack of resources while it holds other resources in reserve. This technique can cause some resources to be locked for prolonged periods of time, thus degrading the performance of other processes in the system. This degradation occurs because resources are reserved even when not in actual use.

Several other methods exist for preventing the circular wait condition from developing. Establishing precedence or **fixed ordering** of the resources and requiring that they be acquired only in increasing numerical order relaxes the impact of simultaneous preallocation while maintaining a safe environment.

The LOCK service enforces the condition that if resource *n* is to be allocated, the process must not already have possession of any resource numbers greater than *n*. If JOB1 and JOB2 have locks in effect for resource numbers 1 and 2, respectively, and JOB1 requests resource 2, it will become blocked, as before. However, if JOB2 now requests resource 1, a deadlock is prevented since the LOCK service will deny the request. (Probably JOB2 will be aborted, thus releasing resource 2 and allowing JOB1 to resume.) Proof of the general case of deadlock prevention is left as an exercise.

As a final example of deadlock prevention, the LOCK algorithm could be extended to include **detection of potential deadlock** conditions. As in the fixed ordering method, this technique may refuse use of a resource in the interest of preventing a deadlock from occurring. LOCK could include logic to examine the entire PCB lock bit string of the calling process once it had been determined that the PCB was to be moved to the resource wait queue. Other bits being set indicates that the process had already acquired some resources. Examination of the queue would indicate if other processes were already blocked pending release of these allocated resources. By refusing to place a process in the wait queue while it holds resources needed by other waiting processes, the possibility of deadlock is avoided. If such a condition is detected, a status could be returned to the calling program, providing it with the option of either terminating or requesting the resource again at a later time. (It should be noted that placing the call to LOCK in a busy-waiting loop until the resource is available is not an appropriate option, as has already been demonstrated. In fact, delaying for a random period of time and issuing the request again will not guarantee acquisition in any finite number of attempts.)

To illustrate this simple algorithm extension, suppose that JOB1 and JOB2 again have locked resources 1 and 2, respectively. If JOB1 now requests exclusive use of resource 2, the following steps would be performed.

1. Bit 2 is determined to already be set in the SCB, indicating that the resource is already allocated.
2. The request for resource 2 is saved in the JOB1 PCB.
3. Examination of the JOB1 PCB lock string reveals that the process also has resource 1 allocated; therefore, a search of the wait queue is made to determine if other processes are waiting for resource 1, that is, to determine if JOB1 will be blocked while holding resources already blocking other processes. The search results are negative.
4. JOB1 is added to the rear of the resource wait queue.

Now if JOB2 requests resource 1, the first three steps above will be repeated except that the search for processes blocked awaiting resource 2, which is already held by JOB2, will yield a positive result. The lock request is then denied since placing JOB2 on the wait queue could result in a deadlock: JOB2 would be waiting for resource 1 while holding resource 2 for which other processes were already waiting.

7.4.2 Recovering from Deadlock

Finally, note that removing a deadlock condition frequently leads to loss of data and is potentially catastrophic to the function of some, or all, processes involved. When a deadlock exists, each process has already entered a critical section updating semaphore-controlled data. Successful completion of the functions depends on acquisition of still more resources. Since all processes are in this same predicament, the only way to break the deadlock is to release an acquired resource from one of the processes, even though it is not ready for releasing.

Releasing a lock held by a process can take one of two basic forms. The resource can be confiscated, either by directly unlocking it or by aborting the process, or the previous activities of the process can be backtracked, followed by a release of the lock. (Reversing actions of critical sections, thereby removing the effects of incomplete data manipulations, is a complex and perhaps impractical chore.)

Regardless of the technique used to release a resource involved in a deadlock condition, the first process waiting for it will resume execution and update the data. Unless earlier data states are restored by backtracking, the data may be inconsistent, due to the original activities of the process just victimized. Data inconsistencies, perhaps arbitrarily selected by the operating system or computer operator, can result.

7.5
A Final Look at Locks

Although LOCK and UNLOCK seem to provide relatively secure operations, an obscure problem still remains. The original example of the dangers of non-coordinated use of serially reusable resources involved not only access to the FSB list by processes, but also access by interrupt handlers. The resource wait queue and the algorithms that manipulate it were designed for use by processes exclusively. There is no provision in MOS for placing an interrupt handler in the resource wait queue. They are not processes and do not have PCBs to act as nodes in the queue. In addition, since they have various classes of interrupts temporarily disabled, it is inappropriate to have them blocked indefinitely. Therefore, other techniques must be used to avoid race conditions within the interrupt subsystem.

The memory management scenario, presented in Section 7.1, illustrated a very real problem. Some process was running, had invoked GET_MEMORY, and was interrupted. The interrupt handler, of necessity, invoked FREE_MEMORY to release space and the resulting interleaved execution garbled the FSB list. On the surface, LOCK and UNLOCK appeared to solve the problem, but now it is seen that the interrupt handler cannot call LOCK, because there is no way to block a handler. What now?

Several possibilities exist. In a kernel architecture, such modules as the FREE_MEMORY service could be implemented as separate processes together with the second-phase device interrupt handlers. This would allow the handlers to form messages to the FREE_MEMORY process to communicate the location and size of memory to be released, and then continue with the immediate handling of the interrupt. Eventually, the released memory would be collected into the FSB list when the FREE_MEMORY process was scheduled.

Even the kernel architecture approach can result in unnecessary serialization of processes, however. Many accesses to lockable resources are for read-only activities. It may be vital to obtain consistent data for calculations and reports via accesses that do not modify the data. In these cases, many processes should be granted concurrent access to the data, as long as none of them change it. Read-only processes thus need a LOCK service to prevent updates while allowing other read-only accesses to proceed. They do not need exclusive use of the resources. Of course, updating processes would still be required to gain exclusive use of each resource. (See Peterson and Silberschatz [1983] for a treatment of these reader and writer synchronization problems.)

Examination of the structure of various contemporary operating systems will reveal many complex mechanisms for communicating and queuing information between operating system components. Some systems have multiple execution states within the operating system which help to guarantee the integrity of the various structures. As stated in the introduction, MOS is highly simplified and designed to illustrate techniques, not necessarily to solve all system programming problems.

PROBLEMS

1. Illustrate the process-related MOS data structures after the times specified. The relative dispatching priorities of the processes in decreasing order are JOB1, JOB2, JOB3, and JOB4. There are four managed resources, all of which are initially available.

   Time = 1:
   (1) JOB1 starts and attempts to lock resources 1 and 2, then perform I/O with wait.
   (2) JOB3 starts and attempts to lock resources 3 and 4, then perform I/O with wait.
   (3) JOB2 starts and attempts to lock resource 2, then perform I/O with wait.
   (4) JOB4 starts and attempts to lock resource 3, then compute.

   Time = 2
   (1) JOB1 I/O completes, and the process attempts to unlock resources 1 and 2, then terminate.
   (2) JOB3 I/O completes, and the process attempts to start computing.

   Time = 3:
   (1) JOB2 I/O completes, and the process attempts to lock resource 3 and start another I/O with wait.   [DS]

2. Illustrate the process-related MOS data structures at the times specified. The relative dispatching priorities of the processes in decreasing order are LPSPOOL, CRSPOOL, JOB1, JOB2, JOB3, JOB4, and JOB5. There are six managed resources, all of which are available initially. Unless otherwise stated, process activities carry on from one time to the next.

   Time = 1:
   (1) LPSPOOL is in a trap wait pending receipt of messages identifying work.
   (2) CRSPOOL is copying cards to DSK1 using double buffering. It has CDR1 locked with resource 1.
   (3) JOB2 starts and attempts to lock resource 4, then read from DSK2 with wait.

Time = 2:
(1) JOB2 I/O completes and the process attempts to unlock resource 4, lock resource 5, and write to DSK2 with wait.
(2) JOB4 starts and attempts to compute.

Time = 3:
(1) JOB1 starts and attempts to lock PTR2 with resource 3, then initiate a write with wait to it.
(2) JOB4 completes and a message is sent to LPSPOOL to print the results.
(3) LPSPOOL receives the message trap and attempts to lock PTR1 with resource 2 and start copying data from DSK1 to PTR1 using double buffering.

Time = 4:
(1) JOB5 starts and attempts to compute.
(2) JOB1 stops printing and attempts to lock resource 5 and compute.

Time = 5:
(1) JOB2 I/O completes, and the process unlocks resource 5 and terminates.

Time = 6:
(1) JOB1 attempts to start a read to DSK1 with wait.
(2) JOB3 starts and attempts to lock resources 4 and 5, then compute.

Time = 7:
(1) JOB5 attempts to lock resources 6 and 4, then continue computing.
(2) JOB1 I/O completes and the process attempts to lock resource 6 and compute.
(3) LPSPOOL completes the disk-to-printer work and attempts to unlock resource 2 and reenter the trap-wait state.   [DS]

3. Give three distinct examples each of nonreusable resources, serially reusable resources (other than the FSB list), and concurrently reusable resources in computer systems. Explain briefly why each example is so classified.

[Ana]

4. Rewrite LOCK and UNLOCK of Algorithms 7-2 and 7-3 to remove the assumption regarding the valid current state of the input resource number.

[Alg]

5. Provide the design for LOCK and UNLOCK algorithms which use counting semaphores to control resources and maintain a separate PCB wait queue for each.   [Alg]

6. Rewrite LOCK of Algorithm 7-2 to support collective allocation of all needed resources via a single call. This approach is intended to avoid deadlock conditions; thus you should include all logic, assumptions, and data structure modifications necessary for its successful operation.   [Alg]

7. Show that forcing the allocation of resources in ascending numerical order and releasing them in descending order always avoids multiple-process deadlock from occurring. Ignore busy-waiting situations.   [Ana]

8. Does allocation of resources in ascending numerical order with releases in any order guarantee avoidance of multiple-process deadlock? Ignore busy-waiting situations and justify your answer.   [Ana]

9. Rewrite LOCK of Algorithm 7-2 to force ascending-numerical-order allocation. Make no assumptions regarding the state of the input resource number.   [Alg]

10. Rewrite LOCK of Algorithm 7-2 to detect and avoid potential deadlock conditions resulting from any order of resource allocation.   [Alg]

11. Identify the four necessary elements of deadlock in the traffic problem shown [Angier, 1983].   [Ana]

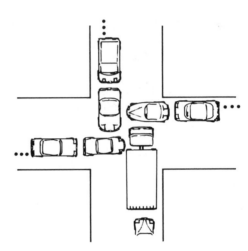

12. Assume that no deadlock prevention logic exists in LOCK. Provide the design for an algorithm that can be run independently to detect multiple-process deadlock conditions. Ignore busy-waiting situations.   [Alg]

13. Provide an analysis and discussion comparing the ordering of a PCB resource wait queue by first-in, first-out (as in MOS), process priority, and by nonincreasing number of resources already acquired by waiting processes.

[Ana]

14. Does ordering the PCB resource wait queue in nonincreasing order of process priority have an effect on deadlock potential? Explain why or why not.   [Ana]

15. Provide an analysis and discussion of the problems involved in attempting to use SEND, RECEIVE, WAIT_MESSAGE, and message traps to serialize execution of critical sections between two processes.   [Ana]

16. Using the logic outline given in Section 6.4.4 as a guide, provide the algorithm for the LPSPOOL main program and its asynchronous message trap handler. (Do not provide this for the DISK_TO_PRINTER support module.) Identify all points where race conditions occur in this program (a straightforward design has two such conditions). Analyze and propose solutions to these concurrency problems. Remember that this is a single process, not multiple processes.   [Ana]

17. Consider two cooperating processes as follows. The first process cooks hamburgers and places them in a burger bin which holds up to 10 burgers.

The second process removes burgers and sells them. Deadlock occurs if they gain concurrent access to the bin (they stop and hold hands indefinitely). Access to the burger bin is therefore a critical section of activity for both processes. The cook process must be prevented from cooking more burgers than the bin can hold and the salesclerk process cannot complete a sale when the bin is empty.

The following solution uses three counting semaphores and the *P* and *V* operations defined in Section 7.2.4. Does it solve the communications problem for the two concurrent processes and always avoid deadlock? Show that the algorithm is correct or correct it. (This is an example of a producer/consumer problem and is similar to two processes providing printed results. One process produces lines of output in a shared pool of buffers, while the other prints the buffer contents, then returns the empty buffers to the pool.)

Begin BURGER_BIN $\left[\begin{array}{l}\text{Use counting semaphores and P and V operations}\\ \text{to simulate hamburger production and sales}\end{array}\right]$

Initialize the REMAINING_CAPACITY of the bin to 10
Initialize the number of BURGERS_AVAILABLE to 0
Initialize the number of concurrent ACCESSES_ALLOWED to the bin to 1

BeginConcurrentProcess COOK
    Forever
    Do
        Cook a hamburger
        P(REMAINING_CAPACITY)
        P(ACCESSES_ALLOWED)
        Place the hamburger into the bin
        V(BURGERS_AVAILABLE)
        V(ACCESSES_ALLOWED)
    EndDo
EndConcurrentProcess COOK

BeginConcurrentProcess SALESCLERK
    Forever
    Do
        P(BURGERS_AVAILABLE)
        P(ACCESSES_ALLOWED)
        Remove a hamburger
        V(REMAINING_CAPACITY)
        V(ACCESSES_ALLOWED)
        Sell the hamburger
    EndDo
EndConcurrentProcess SALESCLERK

End BURGER_BIN

Will the algorithm operate properly if the two P-operations in the COOK process are interchanged? Explain why or why not. [Alg]

18. High in the San Juan mountains of Colorado is the ghost town of Chattanooga. In the valley beyond a ridge to the west lies the town of Telluride. It is over 60 miles from Chattanooga to Telluride by highway; however,

there is a shortcut: the Black Bear Road, a winding four-wheel-drive road over 13,000-foot-high Black Bear Pass. The sign identifying the road reads

TELLURIDE ——➤
"City of Gold"
12 miles · 2 hours
You don't *have* to be
crazy to drive this
road · but it helps

The road is so narrow and treacherous from the top of the pass to Telluride (a 4000-foot descent in 3.5 miles) that it must be considered a serially reusable resource where two-way traffic is concerned. Concurrent use by vehicles traveling in the same direction is acceptable, however.

Suppose that several solutions for managing the road resource had been tried. Analyze and discuss each.

a. Two mailboxes were mounted on posts, one at the top of Black Bear Pass and one at the bottom near Telluride. A single token existed and was transported back and forth between the mailboxes. The procedure posted on each mailbox was as follows:
   (1) Wait until the token is in the mailbox.
   (2) Remove the token and transport it in the last vehicle of the caravan.
   (3) Travel the road.
   (4) Place the token in the mailbox at the other end.
   Travelers found this solution unacceptable. Why?

b. An electrical wire was strung from the top of the pass to the bottom. Lights and switches were connected to each end such that the switch at either end could change the state of the lights. The procedure posted at each end was
   (1) Wait until the light is off.
   (2) Throw the switch.
   (3) Travel the road.
   (4) Throw the switch at the other end when the last vehicle of the caravan reaches the end of the pass road.
   One day two vehicles going in opposite directions met on the road. How did this happen? (No, the lights were not burned out.)

c. A second wire was strung from the top of the pass to the bottom. As with the first wire, lights and switches were connected to each end such that the switch at either end could change the state of the lights connected to that wire. The lights connected to one wire were labeled "up" and those connected to the other "down." The new procedure posted at each end was as follows:
   (1) Wait until the light indicating the other direction (the direction you don't want to go) is off.

(2) If the light for your direction is off, throw the switch for your direction.

(3) Travel the road.

(4) Throw the switch for your direction of travel at the other end when the last vehicle of the caravan reaches the end of the pass road.

Again two vehicles going in opposite directions met on the road. How did this happen?

d. Next, a new set of procedures was posted beside the lights and switches.

(1) Wait until neither light is on.

(2) Throw the switch for the direction you are going.

(3) Travel the road.

(4) Throw the switch for your direction of travel at the other end when the last vehicle of the caravan reaches the end of the pass road.

Once again two vehicles going in opposite directions met on the road. How did it happen this time?

e. The posted procedures were replaced again to redefine the meaning of the lights not only to indicate when the road was in use, and which direction, but also intent to use the road. The new procedures were as follows:

(1) Wait until the light indicating your direction is off.

(2) Throw the switch for the direction you are going.

(3) Wait until the light indicating the other direction is off.

(4) Travel the road.

(5) Throw the switch for your direction of travel at the other end when the last vehicle of the caravan reaches the end of the pass road.

No accidents happened, but soon, travelers were again dissatisfied. Why?

f. Finally, the wires, switches, lights, and mailboxes were removed. Today, on the posts where these once hung, are signs which read

UP ON THE HOUR

DOWN ON THE HALF-HOUR

There have been no accidents and few complaints. Discuss the advantages and disadvantages of this solution. [Ana]

19. Provide your own solution to problem 18 which will satisfy the travelers while preventing accidents. (*Hint:* Research Dekker's algorithm; restore the wires, switches, lights, and mailboxes; then post your procedure.)

[Ana]

CHAPTER 8

Timer Management

In this chapter we address time-related functions of MOS. The only additional hardware component necessary is an **interval timer,** a device that can be used to generate periodic timer-class interrupts. With such a timer, MOS is extended to support a time-slicing mode of operation, thereby providing a more typical time-sharing environment than that previously presented. Provisions are also be made for supporting other time-related functions.

The term **time sharing** is usually applied to interactive computer environments in which multiple users concurrently share the resources of the computer on a more-or-less equal basis. Time sharing is generally associated with multiprogramming and a preemptive scheduling policy based on a time slice or time quantum. (Since most computer systems, including the MOS system, support multiprogramming, the remainder of this chapter assumes multiprogramming exclusively.)

A **time slice** is a brief period of time (e.g., 60 milliseconds), assigned to a single process for its use of the CPU. It is the maximum duration of a process in the current state before the scheduling policies are reapplied. When the quantum expires, another process may become the current process. The dispatcher will decide which process is to be current for the next quantum period based on one of the scheduling policies discussed in Chapter 9.

8.1
The Interval Timer

8.1.1   Timer Operation

A basic element of most multiprogramming systems is the interval timer. Typically, the interval timer is a fast, high-resolution decrementing counter, which resides in a special processor register. Once it is initialized with an integer value it begins a high-speed countdown. When zero is reached, the timer generates an interrupt signal to the CPU (a timer-class interrupt in the case of the MOS hardware). A new countdown value is then loaded into the interval timer, and the cycle repeats. As with all other classes of interrupts, the MOS interrupt subsystem handles interrupts from the timer.

There are many applications of the interval timer and related software services. For example, this device is sufficient to allow an operating system to

1. Maintain the current time of day.
2. Support conventional time sharing rather than just simple multiprogramming.
3. Provide processes with other general time-related services (e.g., starting a process at a particular time of day and blocking a process for specified period of time).
4. Support real-time operations. (Real time is discussed in Section 8.5. Basically, it refers to the operation of computer programs in such a way as to allow interaction with external events at a pace consistent with the ongoing demands of those events.)

8.1.2 Keeping the Time of Day

Suppose that you were asked to simulate some of these functions in a human setting. What would you need, and how would you approach the problem?

First, you must have your own interval timer, the essential characteristics of which are that it

1. Can be assigned an initial value.
2. Will automatically decrement its value at a known, fixed rate.
3. Will signal you when its value reaches zero.
4. Can be reset to repeat this cycle indefinitely.

A conventional watch is not adequate for the task since it neither decrements nor signals. An hourglass uniformly decrements its supply of sand and is repeatable, but it emits no signal. The common kitchen timer, however, satisfies all four criteria. Turning its knob assigns an initial value which it reduces at a constant rate until the interval expires, whereupon it sounds a bell. Turning the knob again starts the cycle anew.

The other tools needed for the simulations are memory and a way of recording data in that memory. For simulation purposes, a pencil and paper will suffice for memory operations. Now, let us use these items to maintain the time of day by the following procedure.

1. Obtain the correct present time and record it. (To maintain the time, you must know it initially. So must the computer operating system. When daily operation is initiated, the operator is asked to supply the current time and date. These data are recorded and updated automatically by the operating system as operations proceed.)
2. Set the timer for a predetermined interval, for example, 15 seconds. (This will be the accuracy to which you maintain the time of day; that is, your time-of-day clock will advance once each 15 seconds.)
3. Do whatever productive work you wish until the bell sounds. (This corresponds to the period in which operating systems allow processes to execute.)

4. When the bell rings:
   a. Immediately reset the timer for another 15 seconds.
   b. Add the initial value, 15 seconds, to your recorded time, producing the new time of day. (You have now serviced a timer interrupt.)
5. Repeat the cycle starting with step 3.

Notice that these instructions keep the timer running at all times. This is accomplished by starting a new countdown immediately upon expiration of the previous one. If the activity ". . . immediately reset the timer . . ." were delayed until the end of step 4, your time-of-day value would accumulate an error and gradually fall behind the correct time at a rate equal to the addition and recording time required by step 4b. Keeping the timer running is an important concept in timer management and in real-time applications.

8.1.3 Time-Sharing Procedure

The second timer application to simulate is time sharing. To do this you should allow multiple users to time-share a serially reusable resource. For example, in addition to maintaining the time of day, use the timer, pencil and paper, and a manual control panel to operate a traffic light governing the flow of vehicles at the intersection of two streets.

The objective is to allow equal flow intervals on both streets while not significantly delaying traffic from one direction when no vehicles are arriving on the other street. It is also desirable not to inhibit flow on either street for more than 2 minutes (just as it is desirable for an operating system not to allow processes to be held in the ready queue for prolonged periods while a compute-bound process grinds away).

An acceptable, but not optimal, procedure for time sharing the intersection follows.

1. Obtain and record the current time of day.
2. Start the timer with its predetermined interval of 15 seconds.
3. Record a time-slice value of 2 minutes for traffic flow in the current direction (whichever direction has a green light).
4. Do whatever other work you wish until the bell sounds in 15 seconds.
5. When the bell rings:
   a. Immediately reset the timer for another 15 seconds.
   b. Add the initial value, 15 seconds, to your recorded time, producing the new time of day.
   c. Decrement the recorded time slice value for the current direction of flow by 15 seconds.
   d. If traffic is waiting on the other street and either the time slice is zero or no more vehicles are approaching on the current street, switch the light to the other street and zero the time slice.
   e. If the time slice is now zero, reset it for 2 minutes.
6. Repeat the cycle starting with step 4.

This procedure meets all requirements of the simulation while blocking waiting traffic no more than one 15-second-clock quantum when the other street is empty. Examples of simulating various process delays are left as end-of-chapter exercises, as is the improvement of the preceding procedure to eliminate the 15-second wait just identified.

8.1.4 Timer Components

Returning to the task of managing time within a computer system, let us examine the mechanics of the interval timer more closely. Implementation of time related functions is very dependent on the features of and interfaces to the timer hardware. MOS assumes an interval timer functionally similar to that used in the VAX computers manufactured by Digital Equipment Corporation [DEC, 1980a]. It contains three registers: a countdown register, an initial value register, and a control and status register. These are the timer functional equivalents of the data, control, and status registers in the I/O device controllers discussed in Chapter 4.)

The countdown register is the actual timing element. When a nonzero value is contained within this register, it is decremented according to the fixed frequency of an internal oscillator. For the purposes of this text we will assume that the decrementing frequency is 1 millisecond. Normally, when the count reaches zero, three events occur automatically:

1. An interrupt signal is sent to the CPU.
2. The value in the initial value register is copied into the countdown register, allowing the timer automatically to start its decrementing cycle again.
3. The occurrence of the interrupt is noted in the control and status register.

The status register may be read by a program to determine whether or not the interval timer followed this expected sequence. In the MOS hardware, reading the status of the timer will clear the interrupt-sent field, thus acknowledging the interrupt and allowing the next timer interrupt to occur.

If the counter decrements to zero a second time and the CPU has not acknowledged the previous interrupt, an error is noted in the control and status register. This allows MOS to recognize that at least one timer interrupt has been lost. The amount of lost time will be an integer multiple of the value in the initial value register, but in general is indeterminable.

8.2
Time-Related Services

MOS uses the timer to support five time-related services.

1. GET_TIME returns the current time of day, within the accuracy maintained by MOS.
2. DELAY_INTERVAL establishes a process unique logical timer to expire at a specified time from the current time. The delay can be repeated automatically with a specified frequency.
3. DELAY_TIME establishes a process-unique logical timer to expire at a specified time of day within the next 24 hours. The delay can be repeated automatically with a specified frequency.

4. WAIT_TIME blocks the calling process pending the expiration of the next logical timer as established by previous calls from that process to DELAY_INTERVAL and/or DELAY_TIME.

5. CANCEL_DELAYS purges all outstanding logical timer requests for the current process.

All of these services are available to processes through the system call, SC, interface to MOS. To illustrate their use, suppose that a process needs to perform some function four times per hour, on the quarter-hours. A simple procedure using three of the services can accomplish this as follows.

1. A system call to GET_TIME is made to determine the current time.
2. The program calculates the number of milliseconds from the current time until the next quarter hour.
3. A second system call is made, to DELAY_INTERVAL, to start a logical timer counting down for the required number of milliseconds. For efficiency, this call should also specify that subsequent intervals are to be established automatically at a 900,000-millisecond (15-minute) frequency.
4. Next, WAIT_TIME is invoked to block the process until the calculated time interval has expired.
5. When it is resumed from the wait state, the process may cycle, performing its function and repeating the WAIT_TIME call pending arrival of the next quarter hour mark.

An alternative, and potentially more accurate, approach replaces steps 2 and 3 above with a calculation to determine the time of day corresponding to an approaching quarter-hour and a call to DELAY_TIME rather than to DELAY_INTERVAL. This approach has the potential of improving accuracy because it begins to address an absolute time problem in the light of a non-dedicated CPU.

Two difficulties plague the first method, the effects of which are reduced by the suggested modifications. First, calculation 2 and system call 3 require time to complete. This means that the delay will actually be established to expire at the original current time plus the calculated number of milliseconds plus the time required to accomplish steps 2 and 3. (A bias could be built into the calculation to approximate this error, but another, more important, variant exists. Since processes do not have exclusive use of the CPU, the number of interrupts serviced and the amount of time allotted to other processes time-sharing the machine during this interval is not only unknown but also unpredictable. The original method is doomed to erratic behavior.

By using DELAY_TIME, the second method attempts to negate these unknown effects. It does not matter how long it is until the quarter-hour as long as the request is scheduled to occur at that time. But what if steps 2 and 3 were slowed to the extent that the calculated time of day had passed before the request is queued? The delay would be established to occur at the calculated time on the next day! Final solution of this problem is left as an exercise (see problem 4).

Implementation of the five MOS time services requires that the SCB data structure be extended to include a current-time-of-day field, a field containing the timer initial value (to govern the frequency of timer interrupts), a PCB

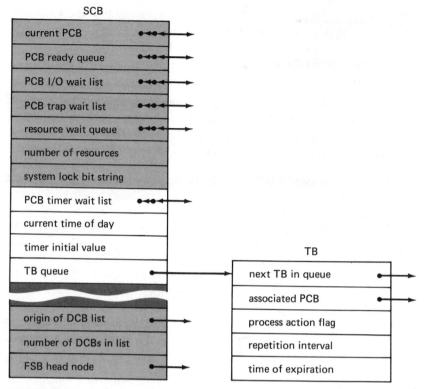

FIGURE 8-1   MOS Data Structure for Timer Management

timer wait list, and an ordered queue of time blocks. This structure is shown in Figure 8-1. It parallels the MOS input/output structure in that

1. There is a wait list in which to place blocked PCBs.
2. There is a group of device-related fields (these are incorporated directly into the SCB since there is only one timer device).
3. Process-specific time operations are tracked via a queue similar to the IOB queues.

The interval timer is always set to interrupt after a fixed period specified in the timer initial value field. (This is the same value maintained in the initial value register of the clock.) The time accuracy maintained by MOS is therefore equal to the value in the initial value field multiplied by the clock frequency. Thus, if the clock frequency is 0.001 second and a timer initial value of 20 clock cycles is selected, the precision of all time-related events in MOS will be

$$20(0.001 \text{ second}) = 0.020 \text{ second}$$

Timer interrupts will, therefore, occur 50 times each second.

A **time block** (TB) is established each time one of the delay services is called, just as an IOB is established for each I/O request. Each TB includes the time of day of expiration, a pointer to the associated process, an indicator of whether or not the process is to become unblocked when the time is reached, and a repetition field. If no repetition value is included in the delay request, the event is singular and the block will be deleted after the time event occurs. If repetition is requested, a new expiration time of day will be calculated and the modified TB automatically repositioned within the TB queue. This cycle will repeat either until the process uses the CANCEL_DELAYS service to remove all of its pending TBs or until the process terminates.

To illustrate the use of these data structure extensions, assume that the current time is 08:16:19.120 and that MOS is maintaining time to an accuracy of 20 milliseconds. Now let a process request to be resumed in 5 seconds, and every 10 seconds thereafter, a DELAY_INTERVAL call followed by a WAIT_TIME call. A TB pointing to the PCB of the process would be constructed containing the expiration time of

$$8{:}16{:}19.120 \ + \ 5.000 \ = \ 08{:}16{:}24.120$$

as shown in Figure 8-2. (Note that interval timers are generally binary counters and that time maintenance software must run exceedingly fast. Times are therefore not maintained in hours, minutes, and seconds, much less in character form, but rather in a time unit such as integer milliseconds since midnight. Thus, 8 hours, 16 minutes, and 19.120 seconds into the day would more likely be represented as

$$[(8{\cdot}60 \ + \ 16)60 \ + \ 19{\cdot}120]1000 \ = \ 29{,}779{,}120 \ \text{milliseconds}$$

in the clock registers and memory locations of the computer.)

✗ A major objective of introducing a timer into the MOS computer was to support time slicing and thereby improved time sharing. To do this, the dispatcher must be given control at regular intervals. But the dispatcher is not a process that can be identified by the address of its PCB. Therefore, by convention, when the dispatcher needs a time signal to trigger application of its scheduling policy, the defined TB will have a null PCB pointer, indicating that there is no particular process associated with the TB but that it is for the MOS dispatcher.

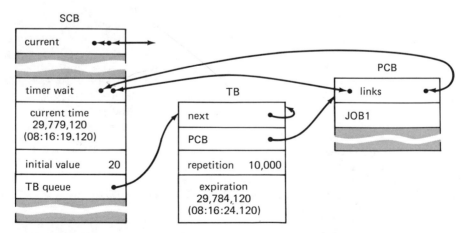

FIGURE 8-2 Five Second Delay Request by JOB1 with a Ten Second Repeat

We are now ready to address implementation of the time-related services. As with all other MOS services, these five functions are all called from the SC initial phase interrupt handler, SC_IH. The simplest of these, GET_TIME, need only retrieve the contents of the SCB current-time-of-day field and return it to the calling program. The current time field of the SCB will be maintained as part of the regular processing of timer interrupts defined in Section 8.3.

The logic of the second timer service, DELAY_INTERVAL, is presented in Algorithm 8-1. Notice that it has been divided into two routines. The DELAY_INTERVAL module performs all process-related activities, calling BUILD_TB to perform actual TB list management. The algorithm for DELAY_TIME is similar to that of DELAY_INTERVAL and is left as an exercise.

The fourth service, WAIT_TIME, has similarities to the WAIT_IO service of Chapter 5. WAIT_TIME examines the TB queue and either blocks or allows continuation of the current process, depending on whether or not unexpired logical timers exist for this process. (WAIT_IO examines the IOB queue for the appropriate device and either blocks or allows continuation of the current process, depending on whether or not any I/O operations for the current process are incomplete.) There are, however, significant philosophical differences between these routines when multiple queue nodes point to the current PCB.

After invoking WAIT_IO, following initiation of multiple I/O requests, a process is blocked until all operations have completed; however, it is not logical to assume that a process which has established multiple logical timers would

Begin DELAY_INTERVAL

Establish a logical timer for the specified number of time units, on behalf of the current process

Input   – DURATION of the delay in timer units, i.e., in milliseconds
               – Optional REPETITION interval, in timer units, for automatic scheduling of next delay
               – SCB and associated lists

Output   – SCB and associated lists

Assume – Memory address mapping is disabled
               – The CPU is operating in the system state

Note   – If DURATION or REPETITION is not an integer multiple of the timer initial value, the TB created will be serviced by TB_IH (Algorithm 8-4) while processing the first interrupt after the scheduled time

Calculate the expiration time of the interval by adding the SCB current time of day to the DURATION, modulo 24 hours
Get the address of the current PCB from the SCB
Call BUILD_TB to construct a TB and insert it into the TB queue

End DELAY_INTERVAL

ALGORITHM 8-1   Service for Establishing Timed Delays

Begin BUILD_TB

> Construct a TB and insert it into the TB queue ordered by nondecreasing expiration time
>
> Input   — Address of associated PCB or null if the TB is a time-slice signal for the MOS dispatcher
>   — EXPIRATION time
>   — REPETITION value, if any
>   — TB queue
> Output — TB queue
> Assume — Timer interrupts are enabled
>   — Memory address mapping is disabled
>   — The CPU is operating in the system state

Call GET_MEMORY to allocate space for a new TB

If the allocation was successful

Then [Build the TB and insert it into the queue]

    Store the address of the PCB and the REPETITION and EXPIRATION
        values in the new TB
    Clear the process action flag field of the new TB
    Disable timer interrupts to prevent TB queue changes
    Insert the new TB into the TB queue according to the expiration time
        (the queue contains TBs in nondecreasing order of expiration time
        except for a step decrease in queue values at the midnight point
        in queue)
    Enable timer interrupts

Else [Terminate the current activity]

    If the PCB address is not null, i.e., the TB is for a process
    Then
        Generate an error message to the standard process output file
        Call the process termination service to abort the current process
    Else [The dispatcher was requesting the TB, so crash the system]
        Display a system crash code to the operator
        Place the system in a wait state with all interrupts disabled (This
            will preserve the contents of all registers and memory locations.
            The state can be changed only by reloading the operating system.
            Frequently, the reload is with a system dump program.)
    EndIf

    EndIf

End BUILD_TB

ALGORITHM 8-1 continued

wish to be awakened only after all have expired. Rather, it is assumed that the process should be awakened upon expiration of each unexpired time request. To support this approach, WAIT_TIME searches only for the first occurrence of a TB for the current process. Finding such a node results in blocking the process with the notation in the PCB action field of the TB that the process is to be unblocked when the related interrupt is processed. If no TB exists for the process, it is allowed to continue execution. The logic for WAIT_TIME is shown in Algorithm 8-2.

Begin WAIT_TIME

> Ensure that there are no unexpired logical timers for the current process
>
> Input   – TB queue
>   – SCB and associated lists
> Output   – SCB and associated lists
>   – Process state via the dispatcher
> Assume – Timer interrupts are enabled
>   – Memory address mapping is disabled
>   – The CPU is operating in the system state

Disable timer interrupts to prevent TB queue updates
Examine the TB queue for a TB associated with the current PCB
If a TB for the current process was located
Then [Force the process to wait for expiration of the TB]
        Change the PCB action flag field in the located TB to indicate that
           the process is to be unblocked when this TB is removed
        Notify the dispatcher that the current process is to be blocked placing
           it in the timer wait list

> The dispatcher will be called from SC_IH upon completion of WAIT_TIME

Else [Any previous TBs for this process have been cleared by TB_IH; therefore, execution is allowed to continue]

        EndIf
Enable timer interrupts

End WAIT_TIME

ALGORITHM 8-2   Wait-Time Service Module

8.3
Timer-Interrupt Processing

Servicing interrupts from the interval timer is divided into two parts:

1. Updating the time of day stored in the SCB.
2. Processing any expired nodes in the TB queue.

As with all other MOS interrupt handlers, the logic for timer interrupts has both an initial phase and a second-phase, as shown in Algorithms 8-3 and 8-4. Even though there is only one second-phase handler, this partitioning is maintained for timer interrupts.

In keeping with the decision to block a process only until the first of its queued TBs expires, TB_IH clears the action flag field while unblocking a process. This ensures that a TB reinstated with a new expiration time will function the same as a newly created TB.

Notice also that provision is made for notifying the dispatcher when its time-slice TB has expired. It is through this logic that MOS is able to wrestle control of the CPU from a compute-bound process and allow other processes to be scheduled in a true time-sharing manner.

Begin TIMER_IH

Provide initial-phase interrupt handling for timer interrupts, including maintenance of the current time of day

Input — STATUS from the interval timer
— Old PSW from the timer element of the interrupt vector
— SCB and associated lists

Output — The interval timer interrupt is acknowledged
— SCB and associated lists

Assume — The interval timer was started during MOS initialization
— The current time of day was initialized during MOS initialization
— The interval timer automatically restarts itself from the initial value register after generating the interrupt signal
— The timer control and status register indicates whether or not interrupts were lost
— Timer and lower priority interrupts are disabled
— Memory address mapping is disabled
— The CPU is operating in the system state

Save all general register values in a local save area
Increment the value of the SCB current-time-of-day field by the timer initial value, modulo 24 hours
Retrieve the STATUS of the interval timer, thus resetting the control and status register and acknowledging the interrupt
If the STATUS indicates that a timer interrupt was lost, i.e., processing of a previous timer interrupt took too long
Then
    Increment the current-time-of-day value again to offset the minimum amount of lost time
    Notify the operator of the potential time loss
EndIf
If the interrupted activity was a process (determined by examining the old PSW system/process state bit)
Then
    Copy the old PSW and saved register values into the appropriate save areas of the current PCB
    Call the second phase interrupt handler, TB_IH
    Enable timer interrupts and call the dispatcher to accomplish any PCB list updates and to schedule some process to run (the dispatcher will not return to the interrupt handler)
Else [Some other interrupt handler was active]
    Call the second-phase interrupt handler, TB_IH
    Return to the interrupted activity in the appropriate interrupt state by restoring the general register values from the local save area and the PSW from the old PSW field of the interrupt vector
EndIf

End TIMER_IH

ALGORITHM 8-3   Initial-Phase Timer-Interrupt Handler

Begin TB_IH

> Complete interrupt processing for the timer by servicing
> any and all expired TBs
> Input   – TB queue
>   – SCB current-time-of-day field
> Output – TB queue
>   – Process states via the dispatcher
> Assume – Timer and lower-priority interrupts are disabled
>   – Memory address mapping is disabled
>   – The CPU is operating in the system state

While the TB queue is not empty and the front TB is due to expire (recall that
   there is a step decrease in value at the midnight point in the queue;
   therefore, a simple comparison to the current time of day is not sufficient)
   TB ≤ the current time of day
Do [Process the front TB]

   Remove the front TB from the queue

   If the TB is marked to unblock a waiting process
   Then
        Notify the dispatcher that the associated process is to be removed
                from the timer wait list
        Clear the process action flag field of the TB
   Else
        If the TB is a time slice TB for the dispatcher, i.e., the PCB field = λ
        Then
             Notify the dispatcher that the time slice has expired
        EndIf
   EndIf

   If no repetition interval is specified in the TB
   Then
        Call FREE_MEMORY to release the TB space
   Else
        Increment the expiration time of the TB by the repetition value,
             modulo 24 hours
        Reposition the modified TB in the queue according to the new expiration
             time
   EndIf

   EndDo

End TB_IH

ALGORITHM 8-4 Second-Phase Timer-Interrupt Handler

   Recall from the study of SC, I/O, and program-error interrupts that there
are two advantages to partitioning interrupt processing into two phases.

1. Common logic for saving the state of the interrupted activity, manipulating the interrupt vector, and returning from interrupt processing is
   factored from the interrupt specific routines.
2. In many cases MOS can run more efficiently if the second-phase logic
   resides in a privileged system process rather than as a callable module
   within the interrupt subsystem. This efficiency is derived from the fact
   that interrupts can be enabled during most, or all, of the process execution

time, thus allowing important events of the same or lower interrupt priority to gain access to computing resources sooner. Even with interrupts enabled, events serviced by these second-phase interrupt-handling system processes are still serialized since each process obtains work from its process message queue, one task at a time.

Even though there is only one source of timer interrupts, eliminating the first of these advantages, the second reason is even more important when time is involved.

Recall that MOS I/O devices operate with one interrupt signaling completion of a single I/O operation (or channel program execution) and with only one activity per device at any time. A monolithic system, operating with I/O interrupts disabled, may delay service to other devices but interrupts from these devices are not lost since the controller hardware automatically queues one pending interrupt per device. Eventually all requests for I/O service will be met. However,

> Time and tide stayeth for no man. *(Brathwaite)*

Neither do they wait for software.

If the time of day is to be accurately maintained, and if time blocks are to be serviced on schedule, timer interrupt handling must be designed to keep pace. Most important, the periodic timer interrupts must not be lost. Recall from Section 8.1.4 that the MOS interval timer operates continuously, automatically restarting itself and detecting any software failure to keep pace (i.e., a software failure to read the control and status register before the countdown register reaches zero again).

Since only higher-priority machine-malfunction and power-failure interrupts can preempt timer interrupts (see Table 5-1), both of which are beyond the control of the timer logic, the only performance concern of timer interrupt processing is to avoid losing subsequent interrupts while processing the current one. Thus periods of operation during which timer interrupts are disabled should be minimized.

There are two important design points in Algorithms 8-3 and 8-4. First, loss of time (loss of timer interrupts) can be detected but not reliably corrected. The first **If** structure in TIMER_IH detects that at least one interrupt was lost and corrects for this event. It cannot, however, determine how many, if any, other interrupts were not processed. Notifying the operator of a potential problem is the only recourse left.

The two conditions most likely to precipitate time loss are that interrupts are being generated too frequently, due to a small timer initial value, and that there are too many TBs to process during a single timer countdown. These conditions are related and can be addressed by running TB_IH as a process rather than as the interrupt subsystem callable module presented in Algorithm 8-4.

This brings us to the second important design point: TIMER_IH maintains the current time of day while all TB queue operations are accomplished in TB_IH. Queue processing time is obviously the most unpredictable part of the interrupt processing task. The division of functions between the two modules allows TB_IH to be implemented as a process executing with timer interrupts enabled. Such an organization leaves only a brief period during which interrupts are disabled and reduces the risk of TIMER_IH losing an interrupt. The speed increase comes from replacing the calls to TB_IH with logic to queue messages to the TB_IH process, so that TIMER_IH need no longer wait for TB_IH to complete its TB queue work. The restructured interrupt-handling logic is the subject of several problems at the end of this chapter.

8.4
Using Time Management Functions

There are many system and computer operation uses for time-related services, in addition to implementing time sharing.

1. The duration of activities can be timed by differencing the starting time of day and ending time obtained from calls to GET_TIME.
2. The dispatcher can account for CPU usage by accumulating the total time a process occupies the current process state.
3. The creation or update of items such as disk files can be time-stamped to assist in record-keeping and backup procedures.
4. Daily events such as disk file backup to magnetic tape can be scheduled automatically.
5. Periodic reports of equipment errors, resource utilization, and job throughput can be generated.

Applications can make similar use of these services.

1. Data base updates can be time-stamped.
2. The labels for periodic reports and graphs can include the time.
3. Computer-aided instruction programs can limit the time allowed for students to answer questions or solve problems.
4. Interactive games can provide the appearance of continuous movement by the computer-simulated opponent.

As an example of the use of the MOS timer services, consider a design for a simplified version of the popular Pac-Man arcade game. This game is played on a fixed maze background. The player moves a pac-man to attack or run from computer moved ghosts. In the simplified game, when two tokens occupy the same position, the attacker (last to enter the position) wins. Since this program will be designed to run on the multiprogramming MOS computer, it is unacceptable for the program to spin in a calibrated delay loop to allow time for the human being to move the pac-man. Rather, the program should use the MOS time-delay and wait services. Algorithm 8-5 solves the general problem given these ground rules.

Notice that the game will proceed at a constant speed of one move per 0.1 to 1.0 second, depending on the players skill level. This assumes that the longest path through the **While** loop can be reliably completed in 0.1 second. Otherwise "real time" cannot be maintained and the human player will have an unfair advantage of a prolonged think time between moves. The constant cycle time is maintained by the automatic reinstatement of the logical timer by TB_IH. The DELAY_INTERVAL call requested perpetual regeneration of the

Begin PAC-MAN   [Provide token movement and an adversary for a
                             simplified Pac-Man game
                             Input   – Skill level of player and pac-man moves
                             Output – Maze and token positions   ]

   Initialize the maze, including the starting positions of the ghosts and
      pac-man tokens

   Establish the slowest speed (longest cycle time for human input) as 1
      second
   Obtain the players skill level in the range 1 to 10
   Calculate the cycle time by dividing the slowest speed by the skill level
   Call DELAY_INTERVAL to start a logical timer to expire in one cycle time
      with a one-cycle-time repetition factor

   Initiate a read of the player's pac-man move (no WAIT_IO is associated
      with this read)

   While both pac-man and ghosts tokens remain in the maze
   Do [Play one cycle of the game]

         Call WAIT-TIME to allow a delay for the player's input (the next cycle
            will be started automatically via the timer repetition factor)

         If the read operation is complete, i.e., the player input a move for
            this cycle

      Then
            Initiate a read for the next pac-man move (again there is no WAIT_IO
               associated with the read)
            Move the pac-man token as requested, attacking any ghost token
               previously occupying the new position
      EndIf

         Compute moves for all remaining ghosts tokens, attacking the pac-man
            token if it occupied any of the new ghost positions

   EndDo

   Call CANCEL_DELAYS to terminate the perpetual regeneration of the game-
      cycle logical timer

End PAC-MAN

ALGORITHM 8-5   Using Time Functions to Pace an Interactive
Game Program

program's logical timer. Not until the CANCEL_DELAYS at the end of the
program would TB_IH cease to automatically reinstate the expired TB.
    Notice also that the PAC-MAN program runs its logical timer, user input
operation, and move calculation logic concurrently. Through the DELAY_
INTERVAL service and the timer interrupt logic, the logical timer operates
continuously. Each time a user's input has been received, another read operation is initiated. Since the program is never waiting for read completion, and
since only at the beginning of a cycle does it wait for timer expiration (to pace
the program to the human player), the timer runs while the player responds
with a move request and the program computes and implements its moves.

8.5
Real-Time Processing

Another time-related mode of system operation is known as real time. **Real time** refers to much more stringent time dependencies than does time sharing. Real-time systems are frequently used in computer monitoring and control of continuing physical activities. Applications range from air-conditioning and heating control to air traffic control and from controlling petrochemical refining processes to spacecraft guidance and navigation. Common to such applications is the need for dependable and responsive computer interaction with the physical activities, since control of such functions is dependent on changing input parameters supplied to the computer system. Real-time systems must complete their tasks within application dependent time constraints or they fail in their objective of keeping pace with their environment.

Real-time systems are typically characterized by periodic scheduling of processes which read and analyze input parameters, then determine and output control signals that will affect future values of the input parameters. Such processes may execute in cycles with frequencies ranging from a few milliseconds for spacecraft guidance to several minutes for air-conditioning control. The frequency of the real-time program execution depends on the rate with which input values can change and the reaction time between sending an output signal and realizing corresponding changes in the related input parameters. Is the MOS timer capability adequate to support real-time application processes? Does it conveniently meet the service demands of typical real-time programs?

In addition to completing their computations and I/O in a timely manner, real-time processes typically must perform such functions as:

1. Determining whether or not they are behind schedule, i.e., whether or not periodic logical timers have expired without a WAIT_TIME call actually delaying the process.
2. Sending synchronization messages to other real-time processes and receiving the answering signal within a short interval. Failure of such a message exchange within the interval indicates failure to complete the real-time tasks, and thus requires that alarm messages be sent to the operator.
3. Detecting the malfunction of external devices through their failure to complete requested operations within a specified "time-out" limit. Time-outs are important because they allow programs to detect device failures under conditions existing when the failure interrupts cannot be generated (e.g., power loss to or failure in a controller). When a response from an external device has not been detected for a given number of milliseconds or seconds, associated interface software may conclude that it has failed or been powered-down. The normal way of timing out a device is to send a signal that requires a response, then to schedule a timer interrupt to occur after the appropriate delay. The process then enters a wait state. If the timer expires before a response from the device is received, the device is assumed to have failed.

Can MOS support these activities efficiently? No, it cannot. Try to design straightforward process logic to accomplish these three functions (see problems

14 through 19 at the end of the chapter). Although some of these functions have both serial and concurrent program solutions, they are complicated by a significant short coming in the MOS design: it does not allow a single process to wait for multiple events. For instance, in the message exchange function above, the sending process cannot wait for either receipt of the reply or the timer expiration. If it waits for either without the other, there are potential adverse effects.

1. When it waits for the message with the intent of checking the time after receipt of the message, it could fall even further behind the real-time schedule if the receiving process is slow to respond.

2. When it waits for the timer but the reply is received quickly, both synchronization and valuable processing time could be lost due to the timer delay.

A common operating system aid to real-time processes is the use of a single blocked state list, that is, a single wait list regardless of the reason(s) for the process suspension. Each PCB might then contain an event wait mask, each bit of which would correspond to one of the MOS blocked states, I/O, trap, lock, timer, and so on. The WAIT_IO, WAIT_MESSAGE, WAIT_TIME, and similar services could then be combined into perhaps two blocking services:

```
WAIT_OR (list of events)
```

and

```
WAIT_AND (list of events)
```

These services would cause the process to wait for completion of any event in the list or completion of all of them, respectively.

Simply adding multiple-event wait features to MOS would not make it a comprehensive real-time operating system, however. MOS is first an instructional tool and it is missing many other mechanisms important to real-time processing. For example, there is no method of prohibiting a process from being swapped to secondary storage. (High-frequency real-time processes probably could not meet their objectives if swapped.) There are also no provisions for establishing and directly sharing impure, memory-resident data areas (e.g., a real-time data base) or for allowing multiple, simultaneous read-only locks on shared data resources.

PROBLEMS

1. Define the recording methods and procedures for simulating a hotel switchboard operator providing the following time-related services on demand using only an interval timer and data recording items.

   a. Provide the time of day upon request.
   b. Provide a wake-up call at any time of day requested.
   c. Provide a wake-up call after an elapsed interval of time.
   d. Cancel any pending wake-up call. [Ana]

2. When a process can no longer productively use the CPU, MOS blocks it immediately and selects a new current process. (The MOS dispatcher gains control as a result of events other than time-slice expirations.) Adjust the intersection time-sharing simulation in Section 8.1.3 to include a similar feature and thus improve throughput. [Ana]

3. Describe the operation of the clock hardware in your computer or some other non-VAX machine. [OS]

4. Correct the example procedures of Section 8.2 to guarantee process resumption on an approaching quarter-hour and every quarter-hour thereafter. Explain how your approach works regardless of the length of time required to complete any of the steps in the method. (You may assume that your program receives adequate CPU time to execute one cycle in less than 15 minutes of elapsed time.) [Ana]

5. Illustrate the pertinent elements of the MOS data structure at the two following times.

   Time = 10:00:00.150:
   (1) The system started at exactly 9:00:00.000 with a timer initial value of 25 milliseconds.
   (2) The dispatcher time slice is 50 milliseconds.
   (3) JOB1 has logical timers set to expire at 10:30:00.000 and 10:45:00.000.
   (4) JOB2 is receiving timer expirations each minute, on the minute.

   Time = 10:01:00.025:
   (1) JOB3 has just requested a 2-minute logical timer countdown.
   (2) JOB4 is blocked until 10:05:00.000. [DS]

6. Provide a design for the DELAY_TIME service. [Alg]

7. Algorithm 8-1 contains a notation that TBs not aligned with timer interrupts will be processed during the first interrupt following their calculated expiration time.

   a. Explain this note with an example.
   b. Outline changes to MOS necessary to eliminate this time error.
   c. What are the disadvantages, if any, of implementing the changes specified in part (b)? [Ana]

8. Provide a detailed design of the BUILD_TB logic for inserting a new TB into the ordered TB queue. [Alg]

9. Specify a new version of TB_IH to execute as a process with minimal special privileges. Be thorough in your statement of assumptions. [Alg]

10. Explain how TB_IH, executing as a process, would gain access to the CPU to notify the dispatcher of a time-slice expiration, even if the previous current process were compute bound. [Ana]

11. Does implementing either TB_IH, DELAY_INTERVAL, DELAY_TIME, WAIT_TIME, or CANCEL_DELAYS as a process require any, or all, of the others to be processes also? Contrast the various design alternatives for coordinating use of the TB queue among these modules, if all are processes. Do not require the disabling of timer interrupts. [Ana]

12. There are a number of alternative approaches to implementing TB_IH, DELAY_INTERVAL, DELAY_TIME, WAIT_TIME, and CANCEL_DELAYS as processes. Provide the designs for TB_IH, DELAY_INTERVAL, and CANCEL_DELAYS using some consistent approach. [Alg]

13. Use the logical timer services of your computer system to implement the Pac-Man program of Algorithm 8-5. (Refer to problems 7 and 14 in Chapter 1 for assistance with the interfaces.) [OS]

14. Modify Algorithm 8-5 to determine whether or not it has maintained a constant playing rate (i.e., whether or not a periodic logical timer expired other than when it was in the timer wait state). [Alg]

15. Redesign Algorithm 8-5 using a concurrent programming approach to ensure that no logical timer expirations are lost. If the program gets behind in its processing, your design should support getting back on schedule given adequate CPU resources. [Alg]

16. What MOS changes would allow Algorithm 8-5 not to lose logical timer expirations? Justify your answer. [Ana]

17. Design two real-time processes that synchronize their operations via exchanging messages. Either process should detect failure to maintain a real-time pace. What are the shortcomings of your solution, if any? [Alg]

18. Explain a set of MOS design changes supporting more efficient operation of the programs in problem 17. [Ana]

19. Explain how MOS I/O routines (services and/or interrupt handlers) could be modified to time-out a device connected to a failed controller. [Ana]

20. Provide a revised MOS data structure design that supports waiting for the occurrence of multiple events using both WAIT_OR and WAIT_AND facilities. [Ana]

21. Discuss changes to the second-phase interrupt handlers (e.g., TB_IH), if the capabilities of problem 20 were adopted. [Ana]

22. Explain how MOS could accumulate and bill CPU usage on a process-by-process basis. How would it efficiently distribute SC, I/O, program, and timer-interrupt processing time? Is your method accurate? Is it fair? Explain why or why not. [Ana]

CHAPTER 9

Process Scheduling and the Dispatcher

9.1
System List Management

In preceding chapters, the functions of the dispatcher were repeatedly referenced at key points during the management of various resources. From these
references sufficient detail is available to define the requirements for the MOS
dispatcher. In general, the interrupt and service subsystems of MOS levy two
requirements on the dispatcher. First, it must implement the necessary state
changes for processes. Specifically, no PCB is ever added to or removed from
any SCB list by any service or interrupt subsystem module; rather, the dispatcher is always notified to accomplish the state change. **Process-state management** is thus the first function of the MOS dispatcher.

The second responsibility of the dispatcher is that of process scheduling.
Process scheduling is the management of the CPU itself. In this activity, the
dispatcher must determine when the current process should relinquish control
of the processor and which, if any, process should become the new current
process.

Process-state management requirements are derived from service and interrupt subsystem calls defined in the preceding four chapters. Chapter 5 required
that process state transitions be accomplished between the current, ready, and
I/O wait states: WAIT_IO requested movement from the current list to the I/O
wait list, DEVICE_IH unblocked the process by requesting movement from
the wait list to the ready queue, and both SC_IH and IO_IH could invoke the
dispatcher for scheduling (transitions between the ready and current states).

Among other things, Chapter 6 defined the procedures for the creation and
termination of processes. Creating a process caused a new PCB to be added to
the ready queue while terminating a process removed the PCB from any list
and destroyed the PCB.

Chapter 6 also introduced the concepts of process traps and the handling of program error interrupts. Since processes could wait for a trap event and then be resumed when it occurred, transitions from the current state to the trap-wait state, then to the ready state, were used.

The LOCK resource allocation service of Chapter 7 required blocking the current process and placing its PCB in the resource wait queue whenever a requested resource was unavailable. When the owner of such a resource unlocked it, the dispatcher was invoked to place the new owner in the ready state from which it could be scheduled.

Similarly, in Chapter 8, WAIT_TIME used the dispatcher to accomplish the actual blocking of a process. Unblocking was done by references to the dispatcher from the interrupt module TB_IH.

From this review of dispatcher references, we see a pattern for process transitions as illustrated in Figure 9-1.

1. Frequently, service modules request blocking of the current process and movement of its PCB to the proper wait list (e.g., WAIT_IO, WAIT_MESSAGE, LOCK, and WAIT_TIME).
2. Frequently, second-phase interrupt handlers and some service modules request unblocking of specified processes and movement of their PCBs to the ready queue [e.g., DEVICE_IH, SEND (Chapter 6, problem 3), UNLOCK, and TB_IH].
3. The lowest priority of the active initial-phase interrupt handlers always transfers control to the dispatcher for scheduling (e.g., SC_IH, IO_IH, PROGRAM_ERROR_IH, or TIMER_IH).
4. Processes are created and introduced in the ready state by actions of the CREATE service.

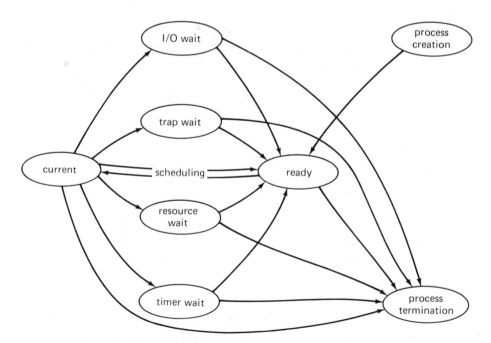

FIGURE 9-1 Process State Transitions

TABLE 9-1 Events Requiring Notification of
the Dispatcher

1. Create a process in the ready queue.
2. Block the current process, moving it to the
   a. I/O wait list.
   b. Trap wait list.
   c. Resource wait queue.
   d. Timer wait list.
3. Unblock a process, moving it to the ready queue.
4. Terminate a process, destroying its PCB.
5. Perform end-of-time-slice process scheduling.

5. Processes are destroyed from any state by actions of the process termination function.

With the exception of scheduling, these transitions are all accomplished by specific requests to the dispatcher. (When transfer is made for the dispatcher to perform scheduling, it is at the discretion of the dispatcher as to whether or not changes between the current and ready states will actually be accomplished.) Table 9-1 and Figure 9-2 illustrate the four basic requests that result in specific process-state changes. In addition to these requests, timer management functions notify the dispatcher when a time slice has expired. There are, therefore, five event types that must be communicated to the dispatcher.

Due to the priority structure of interrupt handling (interrupts of higher priority may interrupt processing of those of lower priority), and the potential for

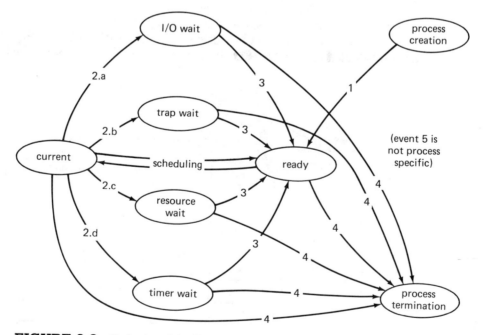

FIGURE 9-2 Relationship Between Notification Events and Process State Transitions

simultaneous expiration of multiple time blocks, it is possible, even likely, that several of the transitions shown in Figure 9-2 will occur at approximately the same time. The likelihood of such occurrences necessitates the processing of events by the dispatcher in groups, or batches. When the dispatcher is invoked at the completion of processing for the lowest-priority interrupt, all pending state changes will be implemented. Only then will scheduling policies be applied.

The concurrent generation of events dictates that many elements of MOS must be able to communicate requests to the dispatcher in a secure fashion. The management of the process-state lists is itself a critical section, updating the serially reusable SCB list resources. It is therefore important to avoid race conditions for the dispatcher functions. (One interrupt handler must not interfere with event notification by another.)

Consider an example that will illustrate the problem. Given the initial conditions shown by solid lines in Figure 9-3, suppose that the I/O associated with the last IOB for JOB2 completes. DEVICE_IH will request that JOB2 become ready, and possibly current, as indicated by the dashed line from the JOB2 PCB. Since timer interrupts have a higher priority than those for I/O, the task of requesting the list change could be interrupted when a timer interrupt occurs. While processing this second interrupt, TB_IH determines that both JOB1 and JOB6 should transition from the timer wait list to the ready state, after which JOB1 might become the current process. Two interrupt handlers are now concurrently attempting to move three processes to the ready queue.

Considering the interrupt-handling activities independently, two of the processes, JOB1 and JOB2, could each displace JOB3 and become the current process. How can all of this be accomplished in a reliable and orderly way? A queue is the appropriate list structure for accomplishing the communication of events to the dispatcher and serializing the processing.

Activities causing process-state transitions and time-quantum expirations are defined as MOS dispatcher events. **Event communication blocks** (ECBs), are used by all elements of MOS to communicate with the dispatcher. Each ECB

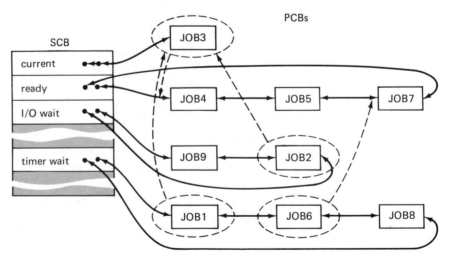

FIGURE 9-3 Concurrent Requests for Process State Changes by Interrupt Handlers

is a node in a linked queue and indicates the type of event, the associated process, if any, and the next ECB in the circular queue. Note that the time-quantum-expiration event has no associated process, since this is only a signal to the dispatcher that the quantum has ended.

Using the ECB queue eliminates the race conditions for the dispatcher, but what is to prevent races for the queue itself? What is to prevent two modules from attempting to add ECBs at the same time? The ECB queue could be designated as a controlled resource and assigned a bit in the lock bit string. Such a solution unfortunately introduces the possibility of blocking a requesting interrupt handler. As has been previously explained, this is not a feasible condition. ECB queue updates must therefore be serialized by briefly disabling all interrupts. This could easily be accomplished by providing a common module, BUILD_ECB, which would disable all maskable interrupts, construct the ECB, add it to the rear of the queue, then reinstate interrupts (see Section 9.5).

From the beginning of this text, there has been a gradual development of the 10 data structures needed to support MOS. With the ECB queue, accessed via a queue head element in the SCB, and PCB priority and time-slice fields, the data structure for this simplified operating system is complete. Figure 9-4 presents the final MOS data structure, including items specified previously.

9.2
Communication with the Dispatcher and Event Handling

Returning to the example of Figure 9-3, removing JOB2 from the blocked state is initiated in DEVICE_IH, Algorithm 5-5, by the phrase "Notify the dispatcher that the associated process is to be removed from the I/O wait state." This is implemented by calling BUILD_ECB to place an ECB in the queue for later processing by the dispatcher. In this case, the associated PCB field of the ECB will point to the JOB2 PCB as indicated in the IOB, that is, the process on whose behalf the I/O was performed, and which is now to be removed from the I/O wait list. (The ECB is allocated, formed, and queued in an uninterruptible environment, thus serializing use of the queue.) The event attributes field of this ECB will specify that the process is to be unblocked and made ready (event type 3 in Table 9-1).

Assuming that the timer interrupt discussed with Figure 9-3 occurs just after queuing of the first ECB, TB_IH (Algorithm 8-4) will "Notify the dispatcher that the associated process[es are] to be removed from the timer wait list" by construction of two ECBs, also of type 3. Control would then return to the TIMER_IH routine (Algorithm 8-3), then back to DEVICE_IH, and finally to IO_IH (Algorithm 5-4).

Since the I/O interrupt was the first interrupt in the processing sequence, IO_IH would then transfer to the dispatcher to implement all pending process state changes and to apply its scheduling policy. At the time of this transfer, the PCBs and ECB queue would appear as shown in Figure 9-5.

The first function of the dispatcher is to process the ECB queue sequentially, implementing all process-state changes. Figure 9-2 shows that once the event type is specified and the location of the PCB determined, movement of the PCB from one list to another is a straightforward activity. For example, if an I/O completion event, type 3, is detected, the PCB specified by the ECB can

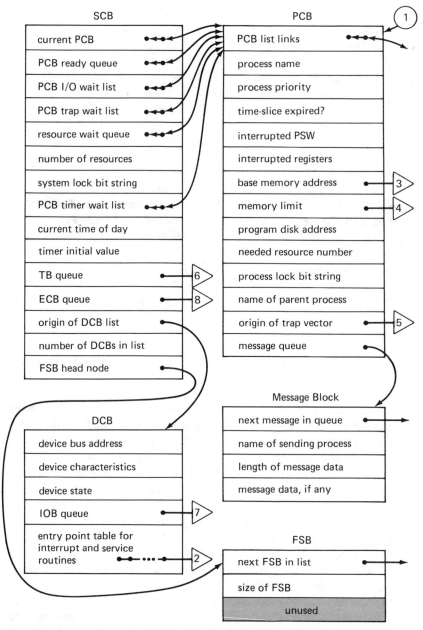

FIGURE 9-4 Complete MOS Data Structure

easily be delinked from the doubly linked I/O wait list and moved to the ready queue. (Note that, for now, we are still assuming priority scheduling, so the ready queue is ordered by process priority.) Algorithms 9-1 and 9-2 present the overall logic of the dispatcher and its list management subfunction.

After its scheduling policy has been applied, the DISPATCHER must change the state of the CPU appropriately. One of two conditions will exist at this time: either some process will be in the current state or the current PCB list will be empty. When a current process exists, the DISPATCHER reverses the

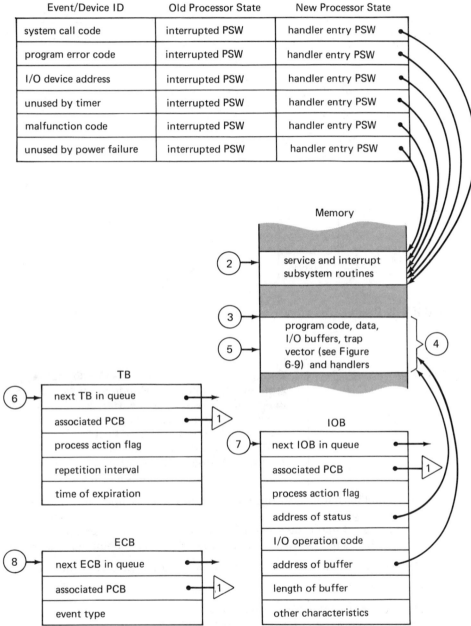

Interrupt Vector

Event/Device ID	Old Processor State	New Processor State
system call code	interrupted PSW	handler entry PSW
program error code	interrupted PSW	handler entry PSW
I/O device address	interrupted PSW	handler entry PSW
unused by timer	interrupted PSW	handler entry PSW
malfunction code	interrupted PSW	handler entry PSW
unused by power failure	interrupted PSW	handler entry PSW

Memory

service and interrupt subsystem routines

program code, data, I/O buffers, trap vector (see Figure 6-9) and handlers

TB

next TB in queue

associated PCB

process action flag

repetition interval

time of expiration

IOB

next IOB in queue

associated PCB

process action flag

address of status

I/O operation code

address of buffer

length of buffer

other characteristics

ECB

next ECB in queue

associated PCB

event type

FIGURE 9-4 continued

actions of the interrupt subsystem taken at the time the process was suspended. When the interrupt occurred, the values of the general registers and the PSW were saved in the PCB of the interrupted process, the process now being resumed. The DISPATCHER therefore restores the general registers, mapping registers, and PSW from the current PCB. This restores the process to exactly the condition that existed prior to the interrupt.

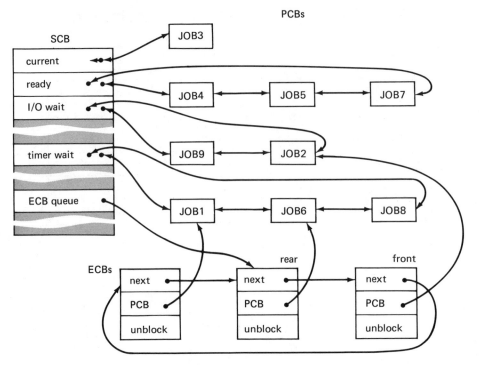

FIGURE 9-5 ECBs for Communicating Transitions Shown in Figure 9-2

Begin DISPATCHER

Perform all process-state transitions requested,
implement the process scheduling policy, and resume
execution of the resulting current process, if any
Input — SCB and associated lists
Output — SCB and associated lists
— CPU register contents
Assume — Memory address mapping is disabled
— The CPU is operating in the system state

Disable all maskable interrupts to prevent the interrupt handlers from
encountering incorrect process states while the ECB queue is being
processed and scheduling is in progress (the final interrupt state
is established below by loading the PSW after scheduling is completed)

Call EVENT_HANDLER to accomplish all pending process-state transitions

Call SCHEDULER to select some process from the ready queue to be current

If the current PCB list is not empty
Then [Resume the current process]
Restore the general registers, base and limit registers, and PSW from
the current PCB
Else [Wait for something to do]
Load the PSW with values that place the CPU in an interrupt-enabled
wait state
EndIf

End DISPATCHER

ALGORITHM 9-1   General Logic for the MOS Dispatcher

210

Begin EVENT_HANDLER

> Perform all process-state transitions requested
> Input   − SCB and associated lists
>   − PCBs for any newly created processes
> Output   − SCB and associated lists
> Assume − Memory address mapping is disabled
>   − The CPU is operating in the system state
>   − All maskable interrupts are disabled
> Note   − Event types are defined in Table 9-1

While the ECB queue is not empty
Do
   Remove the front ECB from the queue
   If the time slice has expired, i.e., event type = 5
   Then
      Indicate expiration in the time-slice field of the current PCB,
         if any
   Else [The ECB is requesting a process-state transition]
      If the process is starting, i.e., event type = 1
      Then
         Insert the associated PCB at the proper position within the ready
            queue
      Else [Move an existing PCB]
         Delink the PCB from its present list
         If the process is terminating, i.e., event type = 4
         Then > The process has already been disengaged by the
                  > termination function
            Call FREE_MEMORY to release the PCB memory space
         Else [The PCB is being moved to another list]
            If the process is now unblocked, i.e, event type = 3
            Then
               Insert the PCB at the proper position within the ready
                  queue
            Else > The process is to be blocked, i.e.,
                     > event type = 2
               Add the PCB to the appropriate list, either in FIFO order
                  or priority order, depending on the list
               If the process did not use its entire time slice, as indicated
                  in the PCB
               Then
                  Call CANCEL_DELAYS to remove any dispatcher time
                     quantum TB
               EndIf
            EndIf
         EndIf
      EndIf
   EndIf
   Index to the next ECB in the queue, if any
   Release the ECB memory space
EndDo
End EVENT_HANDLER

ALGORITHM 9-2   Event-Handling Logic of DISPATCHER

If no process is current, the CPU must be left idle (it has nothing to do). The MOS computer has a bit in the PSW which allows the CPU to do nothing: the run/wait bit (see Figure 1-5). Loading the appropriate value into this field stops the CPU. It is important that the interrupt mask, loaded at the same time, enable interrupts (generally all of them) so that the first event requiring service will remove the CPU from its "do nothing" state and allow execution of the interrupt-handling software.

The EVENT_HANDLER must insert PCBs into two types of lists: unordered wait lists and queues. The resource wait queue is maintained in FIFO order as defined in the algorithms of Chapter 7. The ready queue is some type of ordered list, as determined by the process scheduling policy. The order of all other lists is immaterial since the order in which processes will be removed is generally unpredictable. The EVENT_HANDLER therefore uses several versions of the logic for inserting a node into a doubly linked list, depending on the organization of the target list.

Notice that near the end of the EVENT_HANDLER logic is a call to CANCEL_DELAYS to remove any outstanding time-slice TB for the dispatcher. This call is executed when a process voluntarily relinquishes the CPU and becomes blocked without using all of its allotted quantum. The dispatcher's TB is removed from the TB list to prevent the new current process from being short-changed when it begins executing with its quantum. Similar logic exists in the SCHEDULER to handle the case of the current process being preempted from the CPU before its quantum has expired (see Algorithm 9-3 in Section 9.4).

When a process terminates or is aborted (event type 4), the standard MOS process termination function must guarantee the orderly disengagement of the process before queuing the termination ECB to the dispatcher. Disengagement activities include disposing of all outstanding I/O, timer, and lock requests, releasing all acquired resources, and notifying related processes, if appropriate.

All IOBs associated with a terminating process must be located. Those with operations not yet begun can be deleted; however, if an I/O operation is already in progress and the device controller does not support a halt command, the activity must be allowed to complete normally. Many computers support a halt-I/O, **HIO,** instruction, which can be used to cancel any current operation to an I/O device, thus expediting the termination task.

Similar steps apply to TB cleanup. Any TBs for the process should be canceled so that TB_IH will not encounter nodes whose associated PCB has been deleted.

Next, any requests for resources must be canceled and all resources locked by the process released. This allows the resumption of processes blocked by the locked resources.

Other processes must be notified of a process termination. If the process has a parent process, the parent is notified via a message indicating that the sub-process has terminated. Also, since the process may have been using SPOOL files, the SPOOL processes must be notified so that input files can be deleted and print files can be copied to the printer, then deleted.

Finally, all program space associated with a terminating process must be released. Queued message blocks and the region of memory occupied by the program must be returned to the FSB list. The secondary storage swap area must also be returned to the pool of available space.

9.3
Scheduling Policies

After the PCB lists have been updated as requested by the various ECBs, the scheduling function of the dispatcher is invoked to determine which process, if any, should be current. We have assumed that the ready queue is ordered such that the ready process with the highest priority will be at the front of the queue. The original current process may or may not still be indexed by the current list pointer. (Recall that all event type 2 transitions require that the current process become blocked.) However, if the original current process is not blocked or terminated, it will still be on the current list, and it may or may not have a higher priority than the PCB at the front of the ready queue.

The dispatcher is now ready to implement its scheduling policy by manipulation of the current list and ready queue. But there are many process scheduling policy options, each of which presents some computer facility with an advantage relative to the job mix and management objectives of that business, project, or institution. The following paragraphs provide an overview of several popular scheduling policies. This is followed in the next section by a sample design for implementing a policy for MOS.

In general, the dispatcher module of most operating systems can be used to collect process statistics supporting any of the following policies. This activity should generally be independent of the rest of the operating system, just as memory management tactics should be independent of other functions. Policies can therefore be changed with limited impact on nondispatcher system elements.

Priority scheduling is among the simplest of scheduling policies. It has a very low overhead and is frequently used in real-time applications. Processes are provided with unlimited use of the CPU on a priority basis (i.e., the highest priority unblocked process executes first). Once a process has been given control of the CPU, it remains current until becoming blocked or terminating or until a higher-priority process becomes ready. Processes of equal priority are generally run in first-come, first-served (FCFS) order, based on when they entered the ready queue.

Pure **FCFS scheduling,** also known as FIFO scheduling, ignores priority and treats the ready queue not as a priority queue but as a standard FIFO queue. Processes becoming ready are always added to the rear of the queue and the front of the queue is always the new current process. A process remains current until becoming blocked or terminating.

Time-sharing systems frequently use a **round-robin scheduling** policy to provide more equitable distribution of the CPU resource. The intent of time sharing is to have each process receive frequent allotments of CPU time so that the responsiveness of the computer system is adequate for all users. The accepted mechanism for accomplishing this objective is the time quantum. At the end of this brief period, if the current process has not voluntarily relinquished control of the processor, the dispatcher will move that process to the end of the ready queue and select the process from the front of the queue as the new current process. In this way, processes are serviced at more-or-less equal intervals and no process is allowed to dominate use of the processor. This is a time-limited version of FCFS scheduling.

A great deal of study has been devoted to analyzing the effects of quantum size on system performance. As the quantum value is decreased, the relative overhead associated with handling the timer interrupt and applying the scheduling policy increases. Therefore, less and less productive work is accomplished. On the other hand, as quantum size increases, round-robin scheduling approaches the FCFS policy.

Peterson and Silberschatz [1983] suggest choosing a quantum value with the general objective of allowing about 80 percent of the scheduled processes to voluntarily relinquish control of the CPU before the quantum expires. Such a value must be determined by carefully analyzing the characteristics of the work being processed.

The three simple techniques discussed above operate without regard to the changing conditions within the system, and, in particular, without regard for the resource consumption rates and ratios of the processes. When process priority is involved, it is static; that is, the priority of a process does not change as the process executes and uses resources.

There are several, more complicated, strategies that utilize feedback from the process environment to adjust the effects of the scheduling algorithm. As expected, these methods are more expensive to use due to the overhead involved in collecting process statistics and selecting a new process to run. Nonetheless, in may cases such increases in overhead are justified by improved throughput and/or response time.

Dynamic priority methods adjust the priority of the processes based on various criteria. For instance, since a goal of multiprogramming is increased utilization of equipment, and since such increases are frequently related to increases in the degree of multiprogramming, priorities can be increased when sharing of resources is attributed to some processes, and decreased when lack of resource sharing is detected. Under this objective, a process might use a small memory partition, require very few dedicated devices, and perform considerable input and output, thereby frequently relinquishing the CPU to other processes. By increasing the priority of this process, overall resource utilization can be increased. This happens because very little CPU time is required to keep I/O devices busy and, when I/O completes, the process will quickly resume execution and start other I/O operations.

Conversely, processes that are compute bound, or require significant amounts of memory and other scarce resources, will typically have their priorities lowered to release more CPU time and, if they are swapped to disk, more memory. This will allow processes more compatible with multiprogramming to execute. However, arguments can also be made for raising the priority of such ''bad'' processes. The idea being to give them what they need so they will complete as soon as possible and thus cease to perturb the balance of the system. (Such arguments are not widely accepted.)

As a final example of policies utilizing feedback, consider the **shortest-remaining-time scheduling** technique. This policy is intended to move jobs through the system as quickly as possible, thus making room for more work. Hopefully, this will increase the job throughput rate of the system. When shortest-remaining-time is used, each process is required to have an estimated maximum amount of CPU time for completion of its work. Each time the process receives control of the CPU, the amount of time actually used is decremented from the original maximum time estimate. As processes are removed from blocked states and returned to the ready queue, they are inserted into the queue based on the estimated CPU time remaining to complete the job. If a process enters the ready queue having a shorter time estimate than the current process, the new ready process would displace the current process in the running state. Thus jobs with the greatest likelihood of completing quickly are given preference over longer jobs.

Round-robin scheduling can be viewed as a form of the shortest-remaining-time policy. Since CPU time estimates are not known, round-robin must determine them by sampling job execution. This is done by cyclically applying the quantum, thus allowing the shortest jobs to finish first since they require fewer quantums. For a more complete treatment of basic scheduling policies, see Bunt [1976].

9.4
Implementing Process Scheduling in MOS

Deitel [1983] summarizes the objectives of a scheduling discipline, stating that it should

> Be fair . . . Maximize throughput . . . Maximize the number of interactive users receiving acceptable response times . . . Be predictable . . . Minimize overhead . . . Balance resource use . . . Achieve a balance between response and utilization . . . Avoid indefinite postponement . . . Enforce priorities . . . Give preference to processes holding key resources . . . Give better service to processes exhibiting desirable behavior . . . [and] Degrade gracefully under heavy loads. . . .

Since it is unlikely that such an ''all things to all people/processes'' algorithm could be realized, in view of the inherent conflicts between the members of this set of objectives, a more simplistic approach is taken for MOS: a combination of priority and round-robin scheduling. With this technique, processes are scheduled first by priority, then, when processes of equal priority exist in the ready queue, scheduling uses the round-robin technique. The ready queue is, in effect, a prioritized collection of round-robin subqueues. Each subqueue contains processes of the same priority which are of lower priority than the jobs of the preceding section of the ready queue. Only when no jobs of higher priority are ready will the round-robin scheduling of a lower-priority group be accomplished.

System processes such as SWAP_IN, Algorithm 3-1, should have priority over interactive users' processes, all of which should have priority over batch jobs. Batch jobs receive use of the CPU only when there are no system or interactive processes ready to execute.

A time quantum will be used so that a process cannot monopolize the CPU when processes of equal priority are ready to run. This mixture of priority and round-robin scheduling is a very common policy in computer systems dedicated to time-sharing environments. If the ready queue is maintained in proper order, implementing this scheduling policy only requires knowledge of the attributes of the current process, if any, and the attributes of the front process on the ready queue, if any. Table 9-2 is a state transition matrix detailing actions for

TABLE 9-2   State Transitions for Priority/Round-Robin Scheduling Combination

Current Process	λ	Process at the Front of the Ready Queue		
		Priority Lower Than Current	Priority Equal to Current	Priority Higher Than Current
λ	Conitnue doing nothing	Start the front process	Start the front process	Start the front process
Time slice completed	Continue with a new time slice	Continue with a new time slice	Start the front process*	Start the front process*
Time slice not completed	Continue the current time slice	Continue the current time slice	Continue the current time slice	Start the front process†

*Insert the old current process at the end of its priority group.
†Insert the old current process at the beginning of its priority group

all possible combinations of these two list positions. The matrix considers priority first and then round-robin scheduling.

By systematically testing for the conditions listed in the table, the scheduling policy can be concisely specified and implemented. The logic for this policy is given in Algorithm 9-3. Notice that a single test of the PCB pointer stored in the current process list isolates the first row of the table and a second test for an empty ready queue differentiates the two actions of that row.

Testing the time-slice expiration field of the current PCB will determine if conditions of the middle row exist. (Remember that the ECB_HANDLER will indicate an end-of-slice condition in the PCB when the time quantum has expired.) In either case a comparison of priorities of the current process and the one at the front of the ready queue partitions the options between the two alternatives given in the row.

There are two conditions in the SCHEDULER that warrant special attention. First, if the current process has not completed its time slice and is being preempted by a higher-priority process, it is returned to the ready queue ahead of all other processes of its priority. This ensures that the preempted process will receive its full allotment of time before being placed at the rear of its priority group.

Tracing the logic for this case reveals, however, that such a process could receive more than its share of CPU time by being returned repeatedly to the front area of the queue and allowed to restart its quantum. Alternative logic is explored in the problems at the end of the chapter.

The second SCHEDULER condition needing attention is the assumption that all ready processes are memory resident. As discussed in Section 3.3, when memory requirements exceed capacity, the MOS system process SWAP_IN is used to copy processes back and forth to secondary storage, thus accommodating a larger number of processes. But the current process must be resident in memory in order to execute. However, the entire set of ready processes need not be in memory simultaneously. Ideally, SWAP_IN should ensure that the first several processes in the ready queue are swapped in so that each will be ready to execute when reaching the front position.

Begin SCHEDULER

[
Implement a combined priority and round-robin scheduling policy
Input   − Current PCB list and ready queue
           − TB queue
Output − Current PCB list and ready queue
           − TB queue
Assume − Memory address mapping is disabled
            − The CPU is operating in the system state
            − All maskable interrupts are disabled
            − The front process in the ready queue, if
              any, is memory resident
]

If the current list is empty
Then [Implement actions of first row of Table 9-2]
     If the ready queue is not empty
     Then
         Move the front PCB in the ready queue to the current list
         Indicate a time-slice start in the new current PCB
         Call BUILD_TB to generate a dispatcher TB for the next quantum
     Else [No scheduling action is appropriate]
     EndIf
Else [Switch processes as necessary]
     If the current PCB time slice has expired, as indicated in the PCB
         time slice field
     Then [Start a new time slice for some process as indicated by the middle row of Table 9-2]
         If the ready queue is not empty and the front PCB has an equal or
            higher priority than that of the current PCB
         Then
            Move the current PCB to the rear of its priority group in the
                ready queue
            Move the front PCB in the ready queue to the current list
         EndIf
         Indicate a time-slice start in the current PCB
         Call BUILD_TB to generate a dispatcher TB for the next quantum
     Else [Implement actions of last row of Table 9-2]
         If the ready queue is not empty and the front PCB has a higher priority
            than that of the current PCB
         Then
            Move the current PCB to the front of its priority group in the
                ready queue
            Call CANCEL_DELAYS to remove the unexpired time-quantum TB
            Move the front PCB in the ready queue to the current list
            Indicate a time-slice start in the current PCB
            Call BUILD_TB to generate a dispatcher TB for the next quantum
         Else [Continue the time slice of current PCB (this requires no specific scheduling action)]
         EndIf
     EndIf
EndIf

End SCHEDULER

ALGORITHM 9-3   Scheduling Logic of DISPATCHER

Alternatives governing the execution of SWAP_IN include:

1. Selecting a threshold value for the minimum desired number of memory-resident ready processes and scheduling SWAP_IN by means of a repeating periodic logical timer. SWAP_IN would then examine the ordered ready queue attempting to restore any of the nonresident front processes until the threshold was reached.
2. Selecting a threshold value for the minimum desired number of memory-resident ready processes and having the DISPATCHER examine the front area of the ready queue between the calls to the EVENT_HANDLER and the SCHEDULER. If swapped processes were detected before the threshold was reached, SWAP_IN would be scheduled in an attempt to restore the ready processes to memory.
3. Each time the EVENT_HANDLER logic unblocked a process (type 3 ECB), the PCB base memory address field would be examined. If the process was not in memory, a message would be sent adding it to a queue of pending work for SWAP_IN, which would then receive a trap and begin running.

Each of these suggestions has advantages and shortcomings. None of them guarantee that the front PCB in the ready queue will be resident when needed by the SCHEDULER. Several problems at the end of the chapter continue the analysis.

SWAP_IN is itself a scheduler, and its policies could actually take precedence over those coded into the CPU SCHEDULER. The SCHEDULER performs short-range scheduling of the CPU based on the set of ready, memory-resident processes, while SWAP_IN determines which processes will be memory resident. SWAP_IN therefore schedules processes over a longer range than does the SCHEDULER.

Although not included in MOS, computer systems that run batch jobs frequently have an even higher-level scheduler, the job scheduler. Its function is to determine which processes are allowed to start from the input spool files. Such systems therefore have three levels of scheduling. Again, SWAP_IN schedules memory for that set of processes started by the job scheduler, and the CPU scheduler selects the current process from those ready and swapped into memory.

9.5
A Final Look at Events and Internal
Operating System Communications

Once again, in the interest of clarity, some of the simplifying assumptions for MOS are inadequate for operational use. Although not stated explicitly, it was implied that ECB memory space is acquired and released using the memory management services GET_MEMORY and FREE_MEMORY. A moment of reflection should convince the reader that this is probably not appropriate.

Generally, memory management services operate in a partially enabled interrupt state. Suppose that a process is in the midst of allocating memory, perhaps for stack space for a recursive call, or for an IOB, and a higher-priority interrupt occurs. Ultimately, an ECB might be formed, notifying the dispatcher that an associated process is to be unblocked. How can space for the ECB be acquired while GET_MEMORY is executing for the interrupted process? (Remember, the FSB list is a serially reusable resource.)

Similar examples can be defined for the release of ECB memory space by the EVENT_HANDLER. In practice, space for ECBs is needed during critical times, when becoming blocked awaiting availability of memory management resources is neither appropriate nor possible. Frequently, the problem of system space allocation and deallocation is resolved by defining the maximum number of each type of block needed as part of the operating system generation. (**System generation,** popularly referred to as **sysgen** is the assembly and linking of the operating system modules and data structures into a configuration tailored to the specific needs of a computer facility.) If facility management had determined that the maximum number of concurrent processes ever needed was 40, for example, the system could be generated with 40 PCBs preallocated in memory. Unused PCBs could be linked into an availability stack and acquired and returned as needed without the services of GET_MEMORY and FREE_MEMORY.

If this were the case with MOS, examination of the set of process-state transitions in Figure 9-2 would reveal that 2(number of PCBs) + 1 is the maximum number of events that could ever be outstanding to the dispatcher. (Each process could have a event signaled and could also be terminated. In addition, the end of a time quantum could be signaled.) Therefore, the maximum number of ECBs could be preallocated (81 in the example) and managed with an ECB stack.

Finally, some improvement in efficiency could be gained in a time-sharing system by depending on the frequent handling of dispatcher time-slice interrupts. Under this philosophy most initial-phase interrupt handlers would simply add their ECBs to the queue but not call the dispatcher, the exception being the timer-interrupt handler, TIMER_IH. The ECB queue would thus be allowed to grow longer before being cleared by the dispatcher when invoked by TIMER_IH. Since fewer executions of the dispatcher would occur over a given period, lower operating system overhead would result in a potential overall increase in productivity. The critical assumption in this modification is that most events are not sufficiently important to warrant an immediate call to the dispatcher. Of course, this is not a valid assumption for high-priority processes that must run at maximum possible speed.

Systems programming activities are replete with subtle concurrency problems similar to the ECB allocation problem. Failure to recognize and properly resolve them will lead to intermittent catastrophic failures, which are extremely difficult to recreate and expensive to correct. Some of the most important software development investments made by systems programmers are in analyzing design and looking for points of failure due to process and interrupt-handler concurrency in the multiprogramming environment.

PROBLEMS

1. Illustrate all relevant MOS data structures after the times specified. Use the MOS scheduling policy provided in Section 9.4. There are three priority groups. LPSPOOL is the highest-priority process. JOB1, JOB2, JOB3, and

JOB4 are all equal in priority and in the middle group. JOBX and JOBY are equal in priority and in the lowest-priority group.

Time = 1:
(1) LPSPOOL starts a write to the printer followed by a read with wait to the disk.
(2) JOB1 starts a read to the disk with wait.
(3) JOB2 calls DELAY_INTERVAL for three time intervals followed by a WAIT_TIME call.
(4) JOB3, JOB4, JOBX, and JOBY are all attempting to compute.

Time = 2:
(1) The read for LPSPOOL completes generating an interrupt that invokes IO_IH, which then calls DEVICE_IH. DEVICE_IH completes and returns to IO_IH.
(2) The time-quantum TB expires, generating an interrupt that invokes TIMER_IH, which then calls TB_IH. TB_IH completes and returns to TIMER_IH.

Time = 3:
(1) TIMER_IH completes, thus reactivating IO_IH, which completes and transfers to the DISPATCHER. The DISPATCHER then calls the EVENT_HANDLER.

Time = 4:
(1) Dispatching completes.
(2) LPSPOOL waits for its write to complete.
(3) The timer for JOB2 expires and the resulting interrupt is serviced completely, including all dispatcher functions.   [DS]

2. Computer facility management objectives vary. Some computers should be tuned to guarantee that certain work be completed as quickly as possible, whereas others should strive for the shortest response time for interactive users (time from user entry of a command to completion of that command by the system). Still other objectives are maximum job throughput and minimum average turnaround time for jobs. Considering these four independent objectives, compare each of the following scheduling policies to the others.

   a. Priority scheduling.
   b. First-come, first-served scheduling.
   c. Round-robin scheduling.
   d. Shortest-remaining-time scheduling.   [Ana]

3. Assume that a system is using a 1-second time quantum and that context switching (interrupt processing and dispatching) is accomplished with zero overhead. Given the relative arrival times and processing needs of the seven compute-bound jobs listed below, determine the order in which the jobs are completed, the average turnaround time, and maximum ready-queue length using

   a. First-come, first-served scheduling.
   b. Round-robin scheduling.
   c. Shortest-remaining-time scheduling.

Jobs with the same arrival time are to be considered in the order listed.

[Ana]

Job	Time of Arrival	CPU Requirements
JOB1	1	5
JOB2	1	3
JOB3	1	1
JOB4	3	2
JOB5	4	4
JOB6	4	3
JOB7	6	1

4. Produce a histogram (either graphically or tabular) of CPU activity as the interactive job transactions given below are performed. Produce four histograms, one each for priority; first-come, first-served; round-robin; and the MOS combined priority/round-robin scheduling policies. For each of these policies, calculate the mean transaction response time, job throughput rate, mean turnaround time (average time from start to completion of a job), and process-state CPU utilization (fraction of the total time actually spent doing useful work).

Each job consists of several transactions of varying length as provided in the table. All jobs start at the same instant. Allow a constant user think time of 5 seconds between the end of computation for one transaction and the command to start the next. Assume a 0.1-second context switching time (interrupt processing and dispatcher overhead) and, when appropriate, a time quantum of 2.0 seconds. When priority is important, assume that JOB1 and JOB2 are of equal high priority and that JOB3 is of low priority. Compare the service received by JOB1 and JOB2 to that of JOB2.

Job	Transaction CPU Requirements (seconds)					
JOB1	1	1	1	1	1	1
JOB2	1	1	2	5	2	
JOB3	7	7	7			

If JOB1 were running alone, the beginning of its histogram would appear as

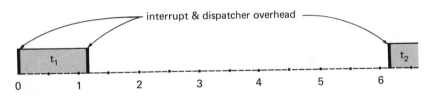

At time = 0, the JOB1 user would enter the first command. Processing of the interrupt and dispatching would require a 0.1-second context switch; such that processing for the first transaction would occur between time = 0.1 and time = 1.1. This would be followed by a 5-second think time and then the cycle would repeat. Upon completion of the sixth and final transaction, JOB1 would have averaged a 1.1-second response time and have had a turnaround time of 31.6 seconds. The CPU process-state utilization would be about 19 percent (6/31.6).

All of your histograms are to contain three jobs rather than one. Using priority scheduling, the first histogram begins as follows. (Remember the 2.0-second quantum and 0.1-second context switch time.)   [Ana]

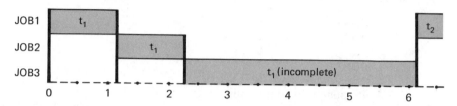

5. Repeat the round-robin histogram from problem 4 using both a shorter and a longer time quantum in the range 1 to 5 seconds. Discuss the effects of quantum size on response time, throughput, and turnaround time.   [Ana]

6. Design and implement a program to simulate and evaluate the performance of various job mixes using one of the scheduling policies given below. Your program should be able to run the data given in problem 4. Specifically, it should allow input of

- (1) Context switch time.
- (2) Time quantum, if needed by the policy.
- (3) Think time.
- (4) Number of processes/users.
- (5) Priority of each process, if needed by the policy.
- (6) Number of transactions and the CPU requirements of each, on a process-by-process basis.

Write a program simulating one of the following:

a. Priority scheduling.
b. First-come, first-served scheduling.
c. Round-robin scheduling.
d. Priority and round-robin scheduling as used in MOS.   [Ana]

7. Develop the equivalent to Table 9-2 for each of the scheduling policies listed in problem 2.   [Ana]

8. Compare the MOS scheduling policy of combined priority and round-robin to each of the options in problem 2, considering each of the four management objectives independently.   [Ana]

9. Prove or disprove that with accurate CPU time requirements, the shortest-remaining-time scheduling policy minimizes mean turnaround time. [Ana]

10. A proposal is made to use a dynamic-priority, time-sharing, process scheduling policy based on ordering the ready queue as an inverse function of the amount of time remaining in the quantum when a process is removed from the current list. (Using only a small part of an allotted quantum results in a position in the queue close to the front, while using all of the quantum places the process at the rear. Processes with equal quantum remainders are treated FIFO.) What are the advantages and disadvantages of this approach when compared to simple FIFO and round-robin policies?   [Ana]

11. Specify the changes to the MOS data structures and the EVENT_HANDLER module and provide the complete detailed design of a new SCHEDULER module to implement the process scheduling policy of problem 10. [Alg]

12. The last activity of the MOS DISPATCHER is to load the PSW register. Describe the importance of each of the following fields of the PSW to this final action. What are the contents of these fields under each of the two possible SCHEDULER exit conditions?

   a. Run/wait bit.
   b. System/process bit.
   c. Interrupt mask.
   d. Memory address mapping bit.
   e. Program counter.   [Ana]

13. Design a TERMINATE service for MOS which satisfies all orderly disengagement activities appropriate to a MOS process.   [Alg]

14. Compare the advantages and disadvantages of returning a preempted current process to the front of its priority group as opposed to maintaining strict FIFO queuing within a priority group using the MOS scheduling policy. (Refer to the discussion accompanying Algorithm 9-3.)   [Ana]

15. Modify the MOS data structures and the dispatcher algorithms as necessary to return a preempted current process to the front of its priority group while ensuring that it receive only the remainder of its unused quantum upon being scheduled again.   [Alg]

16. Explain why SWAP_IN (Algorithm 3-1) should execute as a system process rather than as a subprogram called by the SCHEDULER when the front process in the ready queue is not resident.   [Ana]

17. Explain why none of the SWAP_IN strategies proposed in Section 9.4 guarantee that the front process in the ready queue will be memory resident when referenced by the SCHEDULER.   [Ana]

18. Provide any necessary design modifications for DISPATCHER, EVENT_HANDLER, SCHEDULER, and SWAP_IN to use a logical timer to execute SWAP_IN periodically as stated in the first option in Section 9.4. Remember that the SCHEDULER cannot assume that all ready processes are in memory.   [Alg]

19. Work problem 18 allowing the DISPATCHER to determine when SWAP_IN should execute as defined in the second option of Section 9.4.   [Alg]

20. Work problem 18 allowing the EVENT_HANDLER to cause SWAP_IN execution when swapped-out processes become unblocked.   [Alg]

21. Propose and discuss your own option for scheduling SWAP_IN (see Section 9.4). (*Hint:* What method does your computer system use?)   [Ana]

Process Design Language Definition

The value of top down structured design and structured coding has repeatedly been demonstrated as a superior technology. Those who carefully and consistently practice this discipline generally produce correct and efficient software much quicker than do those who use less systematic approaches. Generally, the programmer-to-programmer communication through structured logic is far superior to that of flow-diagram-type documentation and therefore better suited to supporting software maintenance activities.

The following pages contain syntax, flow figures, examples, discussions, and coding suggestions for an English-oriented Process Design Language, PDL. This appendix is not intended as a comprehensive treatment of the software design techniques. What is intended is the documentation and brief presentation of the design language methodology used in this book which has evolved from practical use over several years and has been used successfully in the development of several hundred thousand lines of near error-free computer code for several large software systems.

The reader will notice immediately that this PDL has marked differences from the currently popular, and more symbol oriented, software engineering methodologies. Justification for this follows two premises.

1. In many cases it is more important to communicate ideas, concepts, and approach to a wide readership without a common background of standardized training, rather than meticulously to communicate details of data operation.
2. In most applications it is more important to communicate logic structure clearly than to support formal proof of correctness procedures.

Many of the basic structures presented herein are similar to those suggested by Linger, Mills, and Witt [1979], the primary difference being a more English-like and less symbolic syntax. A very valuable set of additions to the PDL can be found in Forthofer [1981]. These additions are a comprehensive set of search structures useful for expressing logic to examine a list and take different actions depending on whether or not a desired item is located. Forthofer's paper also presents correctness proofs for the search structures.

A.1
Structure and Notation

All PDL structures are delimited. Each structure has associated with it a key word that identifies the type of structure and marks its beginning or single point of entry. Similarly, each has a terminal key word which bounds the logic and marks the single point of exit. Terminal key words are generally of the form **Endkw,** where **kw** is the beginning key word. Thus **If** and **EndIf** form a delimiter pair that bounds a conditional structure (see Section A.3).

Symbols used in the syntax definitions are as follows:

1. $F, F_e, F_1, F_2, \ldots, F_n$ denote any set of complete structures or functions.
2. p and q are predicates or statements of condition and are either true or false.
3. i is an index.
4. $v, v_1, v_2, \ldots, v_m$ are values.
5. ? indicates a decision among options specified on the emanating paths.
6. [and] are used to delimit functional statements (logical commentary). These blocks of comments are used to state functions or conditions of subsequent detailed logic and are thus used to abstract details of the design. Such commentary is optional but should be used when the function of the logic is complex.
7. { } indicates optional syntax.

A.2
Implementation

For those who are not familiar with the translation of structured design into computer code using an unstructured language such as assembler or simple FORTRAN, implementation examples in FORTRAN, generic assembler language, and Pascal are frequently included with the structure. The coding style used is meant to illustrate a way to implement the logic and does not imply that other valid implementations do not exist.

One final note: structured programming has often been interpreted to mean ''GO TO''-less code. This is not a valid view! Structured programming implies ''GO TO''-less design with parallel code, but not necessarily ''GO TO''-less implementation. The advantages of discipline in design are modularity, clarity, reduced potential for error, easier verification, and reduced cost of maintenance. As will be seen in the sample implementations, code for many of the structures requires internal branching. Indeed, how could we code most assembler routines without branches? The significant point is that there are no external branches into or out of the structures. Flow always enters at the beginning and no branches or GO TO's leave the confines of a structure. The key to structured programming is to produce a strictly structured design, then faithfully translate it into the target implementation language. The resulting code should exactly parallel the design.

A.3
Nonrepeating Structures

The largest logic unit in the design language is the **module**. A module is implemented as a separately assembleable or compilable element such as a main program or subprogram. Modules are delimited by the key words **Begin** and **End** and have the form

Begin module_name

```
Module function
Input    − . . .          define all externally
Output − . . .           referencable data here
{Assume − . . .  }
```

F

End {module_name}

There are four elements of this structure.

1. "**Begin** module_name" marks the entry of the structure. The module may be entered either by invocation by the operating system, or the "Call" of the subprogram by some other module.
2. The logical commentary, enclosed in brackets specifies global information regarding the structure—specifically, its general function or purpose, its input and output, and any fundamental understanding needed by users of the module.
3. The F denotes the body of the module and is the site of the logic design. In practice, F will be replaced with a sequence of other PDL structures.
4. "**End** {module_name}" marks the point of exit from the module.

Schematically, the module structure is denoted by

$$\longrightarrow F \longrightarrow$$

which indicates that the logic unit represented by F is entered at one point and has a single exit.

As an example, suppose that a subprogram were needed which would display the square of a number. Its design might be

Begin SQUARE

```
Display the square of a number.
Input    − Real NUMBER to be squared
         − Logical I/O UNIT on which to display the square
Output − Display of SQUARE
Assume − The display logical unit has been opened by the
         calling program
```

Compute the SQUARE of NUMBER
Write the SQUARE to the display UNIT

End SQUARE

The logic of the preceding SQUARE routine was expressed as a **sequence** of two functions such that F was replaced by the two-phase sequence

Compute the SQUARE of NUMBER
Write the SQUARE to the display UNIT

The general structure of the sequence is

$$\{[\text{ Sequence function }] \}$$
$$F_1$$
$$F_2$$
$$\vdots$$
$$F_n$$

corresponding to the static flow

$$\longrightarrow F_1 \longrightarrow F_2 \longrightarrow \cdots F_n \longrightarrow$$

For example, consider the sequence of human events in the early morning.

[Get up]
Turn off the alarm
Turn on the light
Get out of the bed
Stretch
$\vdots$
[Eat breakfast]
Open the refrigerator
Find the milk
$\vdots$

Here the two major functions, Get up and Eat breakfast, have been abstracted from the detailed sequence for specific actions.

Most logic is not static sequential flow, however. In PDL, **Conditional** execution of a function F_1 or choosing between two functions F_1 and F_2 is indicated with the **If** structure.

If p
Then [F_1 function]
F_1
{ **Else** [F_2 function]
F_2 }
EndIf

which is schematically represented as

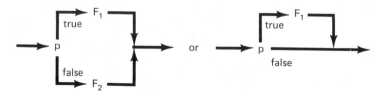

PDL	FORTRAN
If the stack is empty	`If (STKPTR .NE. NIL )GO TO 10`
Then	
Set the status to failure	`STATUS = .FALSE.`
	`GO TO 20`
Else [Pop data from the stack]	`10 CONTINUE`
Set the status to success	`STATUS = .TRUE.`
Decrement the stack index	`STKPTR = STKPTR - 1`
Copy the data from the	`DATA   = STACK (STKPTR)`
indexed stack element	
Endlf	`20 CONTINUE`

FIGURE A-1   Implementing a Conditional Structure in Simple FORTRAN

If the predicate p is true, F_1 alone is executed. Otherwise, F_1 is skipped and F_2 is executed, if it is present.

This is a case of effective use of branching statements of a lower-level implementation language within the confines of the PDL structure. For example, see Figure A-1. Notice that there are two GO TO statements, yet the code is still structured and exactly parallels the design. The logic block has one entry, at the IF statement, and one exit, at statement 20.

One of the unfortunate effects of a nonstructured implementation language is the frequent necessity of inverting the predicate. In the example, it was necessary to test for the stack being not empty. Assuming that a value equal to the variable NIL means that the stack is empty, two alternative ways of coding this decision are

```
    IF ( .NOT. (STKPTR .EQ. NIL) ) GO TO 10
        STATUS = .FALSE.
        GO TO 20
10 CONTINUE
        etc.
```

and

```
    IF ( STKPTR .EQ. NIL ) GO TO 5
        GO TO 10
 5 CONTINUE
        STATUS = .FALSE.
        GO TO 20
10 CONTINUE
        etc.
```

The general approach to implementing the logic of Figure A-1 in assembler follows the FORTRAN example very closely, as shown in Figure A-2.

As logic becomes more complex, nesting of structures within other structures occurs. If many functions are to be considered for mutually exclusive execution

Assembler

	LOAD	STKPTR	If the stack is empty
	COMPARE	NIL	
	BRANCH_NOT_EQUAL	ELSE	Then
	LOAD	=FALSE	Set the status to failure
	STORE	STATUS	
	BRANCH	ENDIF	Else [Pop data from the stack]
ELSE	LOAD	=TRUE	Set the status to success
	STORE	STATUS	
	LOAD	STKPTR	Decrement the stack index
	SUBTRACT	=1	
	STORE	STKPTR	
	LOAD_INDEXED	STACK,STKPTR	Copy the data from the indexed
	STORE	DATA	stack element
ENDIF	etc.		EndIf

FIGURE A-2   Implementing a Conditional Structure in Generic Assembler Language

depending on various conditions, specification with many nested PDL **If** structures tends to obscure the simplicity of the overall function, for example,

```
[ Approach a traffic-light-controlled intersection ]
If the light is red
Then
    Stop
Else
    If the light is green
    Then
        Proceed with care
    Else
        If the light is yellow
        Then
            Exercise caution
        Else ⎡ The light must be out of order, so use the rules for an ⎤
             ⎣ uncontrolled intersection                          ⎦
            Take evasive action
        EndIf
    EndIf
EndIf
```

As with most procedural languages, a Case, computed GO TO, or branch table capability is provided for clarity. With this **extended conditional** structure, the previous example can be more clearly specified as

```
[ Approach a traffic-light-controlled intersection ]
Case ( color of light )
Part ( red )
    Stop
Part ( green )
    Proceed with care
Part ( yellow )
    Exercise caution
```

Else $\begin{bmatrix} \text{The light must be out of order, so use the rules for an} \\ \text{uncontrolled intersection} \end{bmatrix}$

Take evasive action
EndCase

Now it is clear that there are several equally likely conditions. The structure of the **Case** and its flow are

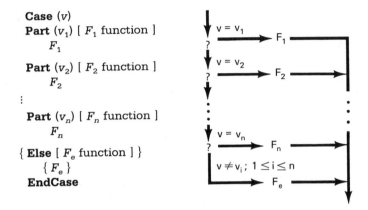

Case (v)
Part (v_1) [F_1 function]
    F_1

Part (v_2) [F_2 function]
    F_2
$\vdots$

Part (v_n) [F_n function]
    F_n
{ **Else** [F_e function] }
    { F_e }
EndCase

A.4
Repeating Structures

Repeated performance of a function a specified number of times is an **iteration**. Iterations are the purpose of the BASIC FOR statement and the FORTRAN DO. The corresponding PDL and flow structures are

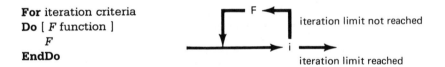

For iteration criteria
Do [F function]
    F
EndDo

where the iteration criteria may take many forms depending on the need. For example, the iteration might cycle for all names in the telephone directory, or from 20 to 0 in steps of -2. (Note that if the limit is satisfied initially, the function F is never executed.)

In addition to the fixed cycle iteration, there are three useful **loop** structures. As with the **If** and **Case** structures, the full set is not necessary for specifying any particular design. Collectively they do, however, permit more concise and obvious logic under different conditions. All loops terminate conditionally and differ only in the placement of the test and the termination on true versus false predicates. With this set we can either indicate

1. Performance of a function until a condition is met,
2 While a condition is met the function is performed, or
3 Performing one function and, while a condition is met, continuing the loop and performing a second function as well.

PDL	*FORTRAN*
| **Do** [ *F* function ]<br>　　*F*<br>**Until** *p*<br>**EndDo** | ```
10  CONTINUE
       code for implementation of F
    IF (not condition p) GO TO 10
``` |
| **While** *p*<br>**Do** [ *F* function ]<br>　　*F*<br>**EndDo** | ```
10  CONTINUE
       IF (not condition p) GO TO 20
       code for implementation of F
       GO TO 10
20  CONTINUE
``` |
| **Do** [ $F_1$ function ]<br>　　$F_1$<br>**AndWhile** *p*<br>**Continue** [ $F_2$ function ]<br>　　$F_2$<br>**EndDo** | ```
10  CONTINUE
       code for implemenation of F1
       IF (not condition p) GO TO 20

       code for implementation of F2
       GO TO 10
20  CONTINUE
``` |

The respective flow of the **Do Until, While Do**, and **Do AndWhile** loops are shown below. Notice that the **Do AndWhile** structure is a combination of the **Do Until** and the **While Do** in that in each cycle it executes F_1 prior to testing for completion and F_2 after the test. It repeatedly cycles through two functions with the controlling test between them.

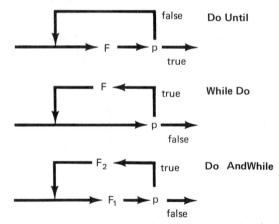

The **Do AndWhile** loop is certainly a luxury, but again, with the extended structures, logic is often clearer, for example,

PDL	*Assembler*
| **Do**<br>　Read a card<br>**AndWhile** an end-of-run<br>　sentinel was not detected<br>**Continue** [Process for . . . ]<br>　Print the card<br>⋮<br>**EndDo** | ```
Do      (instructions to read
           the card)
        LOAD          SENTINEL
        COMPARE       END_OF_RUN
        BRANCH_EQUAL ENDDO
        (instructions to print
           the card, etc.)
        BRANCH        DO
ENDDO etc.
``` |

as opposed to

PDL	*Pascal*

Do
    Read a card
    If and end-of-run sentinel
        was not detected
    Then [Process for . . .]
        Printcard
        ⋮
    EndIf
Until and end-of-run sentinel
    was detected
EndDo
	`Repeat`
	    `Read(card);`
	    `If not end_of_run`
	
	    `Then begin (*Process for ... *)`
	        `Writeln (card);`
	        ⋮
	    `End(*If*)`
	`Until end_of_run;`

or

PDL	*Pascal*

Read a card
While an end-of-run sentinel
    was not detected
Do [Process for . . .]
    Print card
    ⋮
    Read the next card
EndDo
	`Read (card);`
	`While not end_of_run`
	
	`Do begin (*Process for ... *)`
	    `Writeln (card);`
	    ⋮
	    `Read (card)`
	`End(*Do*);`

A.5
Module Abstraction

As discussed with the module structure, **Begin** . . . **End**, the basic unit of design is the subprogram. By convention the verb call is used to reference subprograms. For each subprogram referenced by a call, there should in general be a **Begin** . . . **End** module structure (the exception being reference to standard library routines).

Normally, the call statement should indicate what is accomplished by executing the subject routine, that is, it should briefly repeat the function from the referenced module. This is an important aid to design continuity by the reader.

The block

    [Process next transaction]
    Call DATA_IN to read a card and add all strings to the directory
    While symbol table is not empty
    Do
        ⋮

might mystify the reader for some time if he was not familiar with DATA_IN and if the function of DATA_IN were not included with the Call.

A.6
Example

The module shown in Figure A-3 appears in a different form as Algorithm 3-1. It is repeated here with a slightly different structure to illustrate the differences between the **Do AndWhile** and other looping structures.

Notice the complete lists of items in the input and output portions of the function statement commentary. Every item is listed that is accessible by both this module and the invoker. If an item is referenced before it is assigned a value, it is defined as an input. Similarly, externally accessible items that have values determined by execution of the module are defined as outputs.

Since this module has no error logic for failures in read and write operations, this significant assumption is listed to all who might apply the module.

Begin SWAP_IN 　　　　Attempt to bring the program for a specified process
　　　　　　　　　　　　into memory from a swap area of secondary storage
　　　　　　　　　Input 　　– PCB of the process needing memory
　　　　　　　　　　　　　– SCB and associated lists
　　　　　　　　　　　　　– Process swap file
　　　　　　　　Output 　– Base field of the input PCB
　　　　　　　　　　　　　– Base field of PCBs for processes swapped out
　　　　　　　　　　　　　　to accommodate the specified process
　　　　　　　　　　　　　– Swap files of processes removed from memory
　　　　　　　　Assume – No errors occur during input/output operations

Determine the amount of memory required for the process from the limit
　　　　register field of the input PCB
Do ⎡Attempt to bring the program into memory or locate an⎤
　　　⎣area of memory to confiscate　　　　　　　　　　　　　　⎦
　　　Call **GET_MEMORY** to request the needed space
　　　If allocation was successful
　　　Then [Swap the program into memory]
　　　　　Locate the program on secondary storage
　　　　　Copy the program image into the allocated area
　　　　　Set the PCB base register field to the origin of the allocated area
　　　Else
　　　　　Look for a process to swap out (consider blocked processes first,
　　　　　　　then ready processes of lower priority)
　　　EndIf
AndWhile swap-in was not accomplished and a process to swap out was
　　　located
Continue [Move the identified process to secondary storage]
　　　Copy the program area of the located process to secondary storage
　　　Call **FREE_MEMORY** to return the vacated area to the available memory
　　　　　pool and merge it with any adjacent free areas
　　　Clear the base register field of the located PCB to indicate that the
　　　　　process is no longer in memory
EndDo

End SWAP_IN

FIGURE A-3   Alternative SWAP_IN Module of Algorithm 3-1

APPENDIX **B**

MOS Simulator

B.1
Overview

The **MOS simulator** (MOSSIM) is a set of FORTRAN subroutines that provide
a simulated programming environment consistent with the MOS design presented in the text. There are program elements that simulate

Memory.
The CPU interrupt hardware and the interrupt vector.
The interrupt mask and program counter fields of the PSW.
Indirect I/O controllers using DMA.
Machine instructions for accessing and changing PSW and I/O controller
   registers.
An SC machine instruction for calling system services.
MOS data structures, including SCB, PCB, DCB, IOB, and FSB.
The MOS first-level interrupt handler for SC interrupts.
Dispatcher functions for process management and scheduling.

The simulator is constructed so that students can implement missing portions
of the operating system, then test them in a reasonably realistic environment
which includes unpredictable timing of events and device malfunctions. Exactly
how the simulator behaves is under the control of the instructor.

Some programming problems in the chapters require students to write main
programs and supporting subroutines that interface with MOSSIM subroutines
to accomplish various operations. The operations that have simulator counterparts will be acted on appropriately. Those operations that are missing from
the simulator (e.g., memory management) will be passed on to subprograms
supplied by the students.

For example, if an application routine needs to allocate a block of memory, a call to the MOSSIM SC instruction routine must be made with the appropriate code to identify the type of request. Since the memory management functions are not part of MOSSIM, the simulator calls the appropriate student-supplied module. On the other hand, if a process is to be blocked, a call to the MOSSIM NOTIFY and DISPATCHER subroutines will accomplish the function directly.

While executing within MOSSIM, various operations and asynchronous events are simulated which frequently require additional action on the part of the student programs. For example, during the processing of an SC call, MOSSIM might allow an active I/O operation to complete. Such an event could invoke the student's I/O interrupt-handling logic before completing the call to GET or FREE. Actually, several interrupts could occur during this time.

Complete programs include three parts:

1. Student-supplied main programs and application subprograms called by them (i.e., a main program and a CARD_TO_DISK or DISK_TO_PRINTER subroutine).
2. MOSSIM subroutines linked from an object file provided by the instructor.
3. Service subsystem and interrupt subsystem modules supplied by the students and called by MOSSIM (i.e., GET, FREE, INITIO, WAITIO, IOIH, and DEVICE_IH).

The next three sections describe the various simulated components of MOSSIM. Section B.5 contains a complete summary of all elements of MOSSIM that are callable by student programs, along with detailed interface definitions.

MOSSIM contains a "stub" routine for the first-phase I/O interrupt handler, IOIH. When the programs of Chapter 4 are written, this routine will acknowledge, then ignore all I/O interrupts, thus permitting the programs to pole the simulated device controllers. More advanced logic for asynchronous interrupt handling is developed in the problems of Chapter 5.

Since student programs are simulated as processes with priorities higher than other work existing within MOSSIM, no dispatching will ever occur in the programs from Chapter 4. This means that for the duration of these simulations, a high-priority student process will have full control of the simulated computer. When the programs are extended by the interrupt concepts of Chapter 5, a full multiprogramming environment is automatically provided. Table B-1 is a summary of what students should know about the simulator to be able to work the related problems in the text.

B.2
Simulated Hardware and Data Structures

The simulated hardware includes memory, the interrupt hardware, the PSW, and eight indirect I/O controllers. **Memory** is represented as a 2000-element array of 16-bit words in the FORTRAN labeled COMMON block MEMORY. All student modules should therefore contain the following statement, or equivalent:

```
COMMON / MEMORY / MEMORY(2000)
```

TABLE B-1 What You Need to Know About MOSSIM and When

When	What
Chapter 1	(No problems related to the simulator)
Chapter 2	MEMORY is 2000 16-bit words. The FSB head node is in MEMORY(19) through MEMORY(23) (you also need its format). FSB node format. Interface requirements for system service calls (see Section B.4).
Chapter 3	(No problems related to the simulator)
Chapter 4	Use of MOSUP to initialize MEMORY and to obtain SC_PARAMETER_INDEX. Use of SC to interface to your GET, FREE, INITIO, and WAITIO modules. Use of GETDSK or GETJOB, depending on the problem. Types and block sizes of devices 1 through 4. Use of SIO and TIO instructions.
Chapter 5	Structure of the SCB and interrupt vector. Structure of the DCBs and IOBs. Use of DISPATCHER and NOTIFY. Structure of the PSW interrupt mask field. Use of SETMASK and XCHANGEMSK instructions. Use of MOSDMP.
Chapter 6	(No problems related to the simulator)
Chapter 7	(No problems related to the simulator)
Chapter 8	(No problems related to the simulator)
Chapter 9	(No problems related to the simulator)

Since this represents all of the memory within the simulated computer, many parameters to be communicated to or from MOSSIM must reside within this array. With the exception of the SCB and the interrupt vector, all of MEMORY is dynamically managed. The SCB and interrupt vector reside in the fixed locations defined in Table B-2. No other fixed references may be made to the MEMORY array.

The other three MOS data structures that are needed when running the simulator are the FSB list, the sequentially allocated DCB list, and an IOB queue for each device. The FSB list is accessed through the head node at index 19 within the SCB. Its node structure is shown in Table B-3.

Relative location 17 in the SCB points to the device control block list. There is one five-word DCB for each device, each of which may have a circularly linked IOB queue. IOB nodes are seven words each. The node structures of these lists are shown in Tables B-4 and B-5.

Since most simulator data are 16-bit integer values, it is recommended that the following statement, or equivalent, be used throughout the programs:

```
IMPLICIT INTEGER*2 ( A—Z )
```

TABLE B-2   MOSSIM Fixed Address Data Structures

MEMORY Index	Definition
1–23	**SCB** as follows:
1, 2	PCB current list (backward and forward links)
3, 4	PCB ready queue (backward and forward links)
5, 6	PCB I/O wait list (backward and forward links)
7-16	Reserved
17	Index to the sequentially allocated DCB list
18	Number of DCBs in the list
19-23	FSB head node link, size, rover, maximum limit of managed memory = 2000, and a minimum limit of managed memory
24-53	**Interrupt vector** for 6 classes of interrupts each with 5 words containing the interrupt code, old PSW mask, old PSW program counter, new PSW mask, and new PSW program counter as follows:
24-28	SC identifying code and old and new PSW fields
29-33	Program error code and old and new PSW fields
34-38	I/O device address and old and new PSW fields
39-43	Unused code field and timer old and new PSW fields
44-48	Malfunction code and old and new PSW fields
49-53	Unused code field and power fail old and new PSW fields

All student application programs operate as simulated processes within MOSSIM. Therefore, the simulated MOS computer is assumed to be "up and running" when the student's code is executed. This operational environment must be established as one of the initial actions of all main programs by calling MOSUP, for example,

```
CALL MOSUP ( MAX_SECTORS, MAX_OPERATIONS,
             SC_PARAMETER_INDEX )
```

The call should appear very early in each main program and should be executed only once. This will cause complete initialization of MEMORY and will start the simulation. The parameters MAX_SECTORS and MAX_OPERATIONS are inputs that allow students to optionally control when various failures are to occur. MOSSIM has default values for these parameters, but students are encouraged to override the defaults while debugging their programs to ensure that all failure conditions have been properly addressed. Default values should be used for final execution of the programs. (See Section B.5 for MOSUP interface definitions.)

TABLE B-3   FSB Node Structure

Relative Index	Definition
1	Link to the next FSB in the circular list
2	Size of this FSB, including these two fields
3-size	Unused

TABLE B-4   DCB Node Structure

Relative Index	Definition
1	Device address (1–8)
2	Maximum block size (record length) in characters
3	Access mode, 0 if sequential, 1 if random
4	Device state (recorded by software), 0 for ready, 1 for busy, 2 for hard failure, and 3 for soft failure
5	Index to the rear IOB in the circular queue or zero if the queue is empty

The MOSUP call will also supply an output to the caller, the address within MEMORY of an eight-word calling packet array for use in issuing SC calls. Students are free to acquire other SC packet areas by calls to the GET service.

The **interrupt hardware** allows MOSSIM to simulate system call and I/O interrupts. SC interrupts can occur only when the simulated SC instruction is executed. I/O interrupts are asynchronous to code execution and may occur whenever the random-speed devices complete simulated operations. The occurrence of all interrupts is governed by the **interrupt mask** in the simulated **PSW**. The mask is stored in the least significant 6 bits of a 16-bit integer word. Within this field, each class of interrupt is enabled (1) or disabled (0) by its corresponding bit. The bit assignments from left (most significant) to right (least significant) are

power failure	malfunction	timer	I/O	program error	SC

A mask value of $56_{10} = 111000_2$ has power-failure, machine-malfunction, and timer interrupts enabled while I/O, program error, and SC interrupts are disabled.

The interrupt mask field of the PSW can be changed either automatically, by the simulated interrupt generation hardware when the new PSW fields are loaded from the interrupt vector, or explicitly by the student's code, by executing either a SETMASK or XCHANGEMSK privileged instruction (see Section B.5).

TABLE B-5   IOB Node Structure

Relative Index	Definition
1	Index to the next IOB in the circular queue for this device
2	Index to the associated PCB
3	Process action flag, 0 if no action is required when the I/O completes, nonzero if the process is to become unblocked
4	Index of the status variable to be updated upon completion of the I/O operation
5	OPERATION code for the SIO instruction
6	BUFFER_INDEX for the SIO instruction
7	LENGTH of the transmission for the SIO instruction

TABLE B-6   Simulated Physical Devices

Address	Device Description
1	64-column card reader
2	80-column line printer
3	Disk with 192 character positions per sector
	Disk with 192 character positions per sector
5	Tape drive with block sizes of up to 640 characters
6	Tape drive with block sizes of up to 640 characters
7	Terminal without internal buffering (transmission of one character per operation)
8	Terminal without internal buffering

MOSSIM uses two words to simulate two fields of the PSW: the interrupt mask (discussed above) and the program counter. However, since MOSSIM has no control over the execution of instructions within student-written code, a true program counter cannot be maintained. This field in the simulated PSW is used only to maintain the address of the calling parameter area passed to the SC instruction as part of a simulated system call. In general, the student need not be concerned with the program counter field of either the PSW or the corresponding positions within the interrupt vector.

The other fields of the PSW are also missing from MOSSIM. There is no run/wait bit, memory addressing mapping bit, system/process state bit, and so on. This means that student-supplied interrupt handlers must improvise when these fields are needed. Specifically, initial-phase interrupt handlers must determine whether they interrupted other interrupt logic by examining the interrupt mask field of the old PSW, rather than trying to reference the old system/process state bit. For example, if the simulator was previously operating in the process state, all interrupts should have been enabled and the interrupt mask from the old PSW would be 63_{10} ($3F_{16}$). If another interrupt handler was interrupted, the old mask would be less than this value, since some interrupts would then be disabled.

Eight **indirect I/O controllers** exist within MOSSIM. They are at bus addresses 1 through 8 and have devices attached as shown in Table B-6. Each controller has the internal configuration defined in Chapter 4: separate registers for control, status, address, count, and data values. The registers of these eight controllers may be accessed only by the SIO and TIO instructions (see Sections B.3 and B.5).

Once activated by the SIO instruction, the controllers operate independently of the simulated CPU and thus independently of the code in the student's program. When I/O operations complete, interrupts will occur subject to the state of the appropriate bit in the interrupt mask field of the PSW.

B.3
Simulated Machine Instructions

There are five machine-level instructions simulated within MOSSIM. These instructions are implemented as FORTRAN-callable subroutines.

SC
: Generates an SC interrupt to call the first-phase SC interrupt handler, which in turn calls the service module indicated.

SIO
: Initiates an I/O operation to the controller specified. It stores values provided into the control, address, and count registers.

TIO
: Retrieves the contents of the status register from the controller specified and acknowledges any outstanding interrupt from that controller.

SETMASK
: Replaces the interrupt mask field of the PSW with the value specified.

XCHANGEMSK
: Exchanges the contents of the interrupt mask field of the PSW with the value specified (i.e., the original mask value is returned and the input value is placed into the mask).

With the exception of SC, these instructions are privileged and executable only from within service subsystem and interrupt subsystem modules. Section B.5 contains a complete interface definition for all instructions simulated.

B.4
System Calls and Interrupts

In Chapters 2, 4, and 5 students are asked to develop subprograms that are consistent with the interrupt-handling environment of MOS. These routines include GET and FREE in Chapter 2, simplified versions of INITIO and WAITIO in Chapter 4, and more complex versions of INITIO and WAITIO as well as IOIH and DEVICE_IH in Chapter 5.

The first four routines operate as second-phase interrupt handlers for SCIH. As such, they are classified as service subsystem routines. They must be FORTRAN callable with one to seven simple integer variables in their parameter lists. Within these restrictions, students are free to define the subroutine interfaces. SCIH will unpack the parameter packet array supplied by the calling program, invoke the indicated service, and reload the packet with output values before returning to the application program.

Recall that the SC instruction is the method by which processes invoke operating system functions to perform privileged operations. Processes may not execute the routines of the service subsystem directly. This restriction does not apply, however, to elements of MOS itself. Code executing as part of MOS is already in a privileged state; therefore, direct calls to the services are appropriate (see Figure 1-2). In the programming problems assigned, this means that INITIO, WAITIO, IOIH, and DEVICE_IH should call GET and FREE directly and should not use the SC interface to these services. However, CARD_TO_DISK and DISK_TO_PRINTER must use SC calls.

Finally, there are the interface requirements to IOIH and DEVICE_IH. These routines are members of the interrupt subsystem. IOIH is a first-phase interrupt handler. It is called by the interrupt hardware of the simulated CPU and not by other software modules. It can have no calling parameters, but rather must retrieve all its inputs from the interrupt vector in MEMORY. As stated earlier, the complete set of MOS PSW fields is not represented in MOSSIM. IOIH must use the old interrupt mask value to determine the system or the process state, depending on whether or not some interrupts were disabled previously.

Algorithm 5-4 indicates that the version of DEVICE_IH to be called is designated in the entry-point table within the located DCB. In MOSSIM all devices can be serviced by the same DEVICE_IH routine. There is no need to implement multiple versions of the second-phase handler and no need to obtain an entry-point address from the DCB to complete the call from IOIH.

B.5
MOSSIM Subroutine Interface Summary

Table B-7 contains a list of all control sections in the MOSSIM object file. Unless the problem assigned specifically requires replacing one of these modules (e.g., IOIH), student programs should avoid defining external symbols with any of these names other than the MEMORY common area.

The following simulator modules are directly callable by student programs.

DISPATCHER

MOS module to perform PCB list management as requested by previous NOTIFY calls and to select the highest-priority process on the ready queue, if any, to be the new current process.

GETDSK (SECTOR_NUMBER, STATUS)

MOS module for dynamic allocation of sectors on the disk device 3.

SECTOR_NUMBER	Output integer number of the device 3 sector allocated, if any.
STATUS	Output integer status of the allocation request. A value of 0 indicates a successful allocation; a value of 1 indicates allocation failure.

TABLE B-7   MOSSIM Externally Defined Symbols

CANCHK	ENLINK	IOINT	POWIH	SETMASK
CNTEOF	ENQ	LIST	PRGINT	SIO
CNTIN	GETDSK	MALIH	PRIQ	STRIN
CNTOUT	GETJOB	MEMORY	PROGIH	STROUT
CNTREW	HLTIO	MOSDMP	PRTCTL	SUSPEND
CNTSKP	HWSIM	MOSOPN	RESUME	TAPCTL
CRDCTL	INTCHK	MOSUP	SC	TIMEIH
DELINK	INTCKR	NEXTNO	SCDISPATCHER	TIO
DISPATCHER	INTCLR	NOTIFY	SCHED	TRMCTL
DSKCTL	IOIH	PHANTM	SCIH	XCHANGEMSK
DUMP				

`GETJOB` (STATUS, STARTING_SECTOR, NUMBER_OF_LINES)

MOS module for removal of the next print job, if any, from the queue of pending print work. It provides the caller with the size of the job and the number of the first sector on disk device 4 containing the print lines.

STATUS	Output integer status of the request. A value of 0 indicates success; a value of 1 indicates that no more jobs are in the queue.
STARTING_SECTOR	Output integer number of the first sector in a block of consecutive sectors containing the print job.
NUMBER_OF_LINES	Number of lines in the print job. Lines are stored two per sector in consecutive sectors beginning with STARTING_SECTOR.

`MOSDMP` (DISPLAY_TITLE)

MOS module providing a formatted display of all data structures in MEMORY which are accessible from the SCB, the interrupt vector, and the I/O status values returned to all nonstudent processes.

DISPLAY_TITLE	Input CHARACTER*16 string containing a student-selected title used to label the display.

`MOSUP` (MAX_SECTORS, MAX_OPERATIONS, SC_PARAMETER_INDEX)

Initialization module to begin a simulation by completely initializing MEMORY, providing an array in MEMORY for SC calling parameter values, and optionally overriding default failure limits for the number of successful disk sector allocations and device operations.

MAX_SECTORS	Input value for the maximum number of disk sectors to be successfully allocated by GETDSK prior to causing an allocation failure. To use the default value, enter a value of zero. The final execution of all programs should be with the default value.
MAX_OPERATIONS	Input array of 16 values for the maximum number of read and write operations to each of the eight simulated devices. This array should be dimensioned (2,8). The second index corresponds to the device address (devices 1 through 8) and the first index indicates a read or write limit (1 = read, 2 = write). For example, if MAX_OPERATIONS(2,3) has a value of 4, simulated device 3 will be allowed to complete a maximum of 4 successful write operations before failing. To use the default values, enter zeros. The final execution of all programs should be with all values defaulted (i.e., 16 zeros).
SC_PARAMETER_INDEX	Output index into MEMORY of a block of eight words provided to allow initial calls to the SC

instruction simulator. Use of this array is necessary since acquiring memory requires execution of the SC instruction to access the GET memory service, and the call to SC must itself use a parameter packet within MEMORY (see the interface to SC, which follows).

NOTIFY (PCB_INDEX, ACTION)

MOS module for notifying the dispatcher that the PCB at the indicated location in MEMORY is to be moved to the appropriate list as indicated by ACTION. PCB list management does not actually occur at the time of the call; rather, the dispatcher is notified that the action should be taken when DISPATCHER is next invoked.

PCB_INDEX	Input integer index into MEMORY of the first word of the PCB for the process to undergo a state change.
ACTION	Input integer code indicating the desired action. A value of -1 indicates that a suspended process is to become unblocked and moved to the PCB ready queue. A positive value indicates that a process is to be blocked and moved to the corresponding wait list. The value indicates the location of the list within the SCB. Therefore, a value of 5 indicates that the process is to be blocked and placed on the PCB I/O wait list (see Table B-2).

SC (SC_CODE, PARAMETER_INDEX)

Simulated system call instruction, including the generation of an SC interrupt, if enabled, and the transfer of control to the first-phase SC interrupt handler, SCIH. SCIH will then select the appropriate service routine, unpack the calling parameters from the parameter packet array, and call the service. Upon returning to SCIH, it will store output parameters in the packet array and transfer to the dispatcher for PCB list management and process scheduling as specified in Algorithm 5-1.

SC_CODE — Input code identifying the service to be called as follows:

SC_Code	Service Routine to Be Invoked
1	GET dynamic memory management allocation service
2	FREE dynamic memory management release service
3	INITIO I/O operation initiation service
4	WAITIO service to ensure I/O completion

PARAMETER_INDEX — Input index into MEMORY of a packet (array) of calling arguments for the indicated service. The packet may be one to eight words in length, is located at MEMORY(PARAMETER_INDEX), and is structured as follows:

Word	Definition
1	Number of arguments in the calling sequence of the indicated service. This value must be in the range 1 to 7.
2	Value of the first calling parameter. If this is an output parameter, the value will be placed in this location after execution of the service.
3	Value of the second calling parameter, if any.

etc.

As an example, suppose that a parameter packet had been allocated at MEMORY(100) and was to be used to call the GET memory service with three arguments to allocate 17 words. PARAMETER_INDEX would therefore have a value of 100 and the packet might have the structure

100	number of arguments = 3
101	input size of GET request = 17
102	output location of block will be stored here
103	output status will be stored here

to interface with the student-supplied service routine defined by

SUBROUTINE GET (SIZE, LOCATN, STATUS)

Upon returning to the calling program, the outputs from GET would then be available in the last two words of the packet.

SETMASK (NEW_MASK)

Simulated instruction to replace the interrupt mask field of the PSW with the value specified.

NEW_MASK   Input integer value of 1 to 63 (decimal) which is to replace the current contents of the PSW interrupt mask field.

SIO (DEVICE_ADDRESS, OPERATION, BUFFER_INDEX, LENGTH)

Simulated instruction to replace the current contents of the control, address, and count registers of the controller specified with the input operation code, index into MEMORY of the buffer, and length of the data transfer. This action then starts the controller.

DEVICE_ADDRESS   Input integer address of the device to be started (1 to 8 inclusive).

OPERATION	Input decimal integer command code to be given to the controller. A value of 1 starts a read operation, 2 starts a write, n1 seeks to sector n of a disk and starts a read, and n2 seeks to sector n and starts a write operation. For example, if the data on sector 45 are to be read, the value of OPERATION would be 451. (Seek to sector 45 and then perform operation 1.)
BUFFER_INDEX	Input index into MEMORY of the first word of a block of at least LENGTH characters to accommodate the transfer, two characters per word.
LENGTH	Input number of characters to be read or written.

TIO (DEVICE_ADDRESS, STATE)

Simulated instruction to retrieve the contents of the status register from the specified controller and acknowledge any outstanding interrupt from the device.

DEVICE_ADDRESS	Input integer address of the device to be tested (1 to 8 inclusive).
STATE	Output value from the status register of the controller. A value of 0 indicates a ready device, 1 a busy state, 2 a hard device failure, and 3 a soft failure (e.g., printer out of paper).

XCHANGEMSK (NEW_MASK, OLD_MASK)

Simulated instruction which copies the current contents of the PSW interrupt mask field into the OLD_MASK variable, then replaces the PSW mask with the value contained in NEW_MASK.

NEW_MASK	Input integer value of 1 to 63 (decimal) which is to replace the current contents of the PSW interrupt mask field.
OLD_MASK	Output value of the original contents from the PSW interrupt mask.

Bibliography and Reading List ▬▬▬▬▬

Angier, R. C. 1983. "Lecture notes for CSCI 5531: Analysis of Operating Systems." University of Houston–Clear Lake.

Attwood, J. W. October 1976. "Concurrency in Operating Systems." *IEEE Computer*, Vol. 9, No. 10, pp. 18–26.

Bartlett, J. F. January 1978. "A 'Nonstop' Operating System." *Proceedings of the Eleventh Hawaii International Conference on System Science*, pp. 103–117.

Bays, C. March, 1977. "A Comparison of Next-fit, First-fit, and Best-fit." *Communications of the ACM*, Vol. 20, No. 3, pp. 191–192.

Beck, L. L. October, 1982. "A Dynamic Storage Allocation Technique Based on Memory Residence Time." *Communications of the ACM*, Vol. 25, No. 10, pp. 714-724.

Bourne, S. R. January 30, 1978. "The UNIX Time Sharing System: The UNIX Shell." *The Bell System Technical Journal*, Vol. 57, No. 6, Part 2.

Bowen, B. A. and Buhr, R. J. A. 1980. *The Logical Design of Multiple Microprocessor Systems*. Prentice-Hall, Inc., Englewood Cliffs, N.J.

Brinch Hansen, P. April 1970. "The Nucleus of a Multiprogramming System." *Communications of the ACM*, Vol. 13, No. 4, pp. 238–241, 250.

Brinch Hansen, P. July 1972. "Structured Multiprogramming." *Communications of the ACM*, Vol. 15, No. 7, pp. 574–578.

Brinch Hansen, P. 1973. *Operating Systems Principles*. Prentice-Hall, Englewood Cliffs, N.J.

Brinch Hansen, P. 1977. *The Architecture of Concurrent Programs*. Prentice-Hall, Englewood Cliffs, N.J.

Brooks, F. P. 1978. *The Mythical Man-Month, Essays of Software Engineering*. Addison-Wesley Publishing Company, Inc., Reading, Mass.

Brown, R. L., and Denning, P. J. October 1984. "Advanced Operating Systems." *IEEE Computer*, Vol. 17, No. 10, pp. 173–190.

Bull, G. M. 1971. *Time Sharing Systems*. McGraw-Hill, London.

Bunt, R. B. October 1976. "Scheduling Techniques for Operating Systems." *Computer*, Vol. 11, No. 10, pp. 10-17.

Busch, John R. 1981. "The MPE IV Kernel: History, Structure and Strategies." *Proceedings of General Systems Users Group, 1981 International Meeting*. Vol. 1, INTEREX, Mountain View, Calif.

Calingaert, P. 1979. *Assemblers, Compilers, and Program Translation*. Computer Science Press, Potomac, Md.

Coffman, E. G., Elphick, M. J., and Shoshani, A. June 1971. "System Deadlocks." *ACM Computing Surveys,* Vol. 3, No. 2, pp. 67–68

Coffman, E. G., and Denning, P. J. 1973. *Operating Systems Theory.* Prentice-Hall, Englewood Cliffs, N.J.

Courtois, P. J., Heymans, F., and Parnas, D. L. October 1971. "Concurrent Control with 'Readers' and 'Writers,'" *Communications of the ACM,* Vol. 14, No. 10, pp. 667–668.

Davis, D. J. M. August 1984. "Memory Occupancy Patterns in Garbage Collection Systems." *Communications of the ACM,* Vol. 27, No. 8, pp. 819–825.

Davis, W. S. 1983. *Operating Systems, A Systematic View.* Addison-Wesley Publishing Company, Inc., Reading, Mass.

DEC. 1980a. *VAX Hardware Handbook.* Digital Equipment Corp., Bedford, Mass.

DEC. 1980b. *VAX Software Handbook.* Digital Equipment Corp., Bedford, Mass.

DEC. 1980c. *VAX Technical Summary.* Digital Equipment Corp., Bedford, Mass.

Deitel, H. M. 1983. *An Introduction to Operating Systems.* Addison-Wesley Publishing Company, Inc., Reading, Mass.

Denning, P.J. May 1968. "The Working Set Model for Program Behavior." *Communications of the ACM,* Vol. 11, No. 5, pp. 323–333.

Denning, P. J. September 1970. "Virtual Memory." *ACM Computing Surveys,* Vol. 2, No. 3, pp. 153–189.

Denning, P. J. January 1980. "Working Sets Past and Present." *IEEE Transactions on Software Engineering,* Vol. SE-6, No. 1, pp. 64–84.

Dijkstra, E. W. 1968a. "Cooperating Sequential Processes," in *Programming Languages,* F. Genuys (ed.). Academic Press, Inc., New York.

Dijkstra, E. W. 1968b. "The Structure of "THE"—Multiprogramming System." *Communications of the ACM,* Volume 11, Number 5.

Doran, R. W. October 1976. "Virtual Memory." *IEEE Computer,* Vol. 9, No. 10, pp. 27–37.

Elson, M. 1975. *Data Structures.* Science Research Associates, Inc., Chicago.

Frank, H. October 1969. "Analysis and Optimization of Disk Storage Devices for Time-Sharing Systems." *Journal of the ACM,* Vol. 16, No. 4, pp. 602–620.

Ferrari, D. 1978. *Computer Systems Performance Evaluation.* Prentice-Hall, Englewood Cliffs, N.J.

Forthofer, M. J. April, 1981. *Extending PDL to Include a Superstructure.* IBM Technical Report FSD 81-0010. International Business Machines Corporation, White Plains, N.Y.

Freeman, P. 1975. *Software Systems Principles.* Science Research Associates, Inc., Palo Alto, Calif.

Gomaa, H. September 1984. "A Software Design Method for Real-Time Systems." *Communications of the ACM,* Vol. 27, No. 9, pp. 938–949.

Graham, R. M. 1975. *Principles of Systems Programming.* John Wiley & Sons, Inc., New York.

Habermann, A. N. July 1969. "Prevention of System Deadlocks." *Communications of the ACM,* Vol. 12, No. 7, pp. 373–377, 385.

Habermann, A. N. 1976. *Introduction to Operating System Design.* Science Research Associates, Inc., Chicago.

Hall, D. E., Scherrer, D. K., and Sventek, J. S. September 1980. "A Virtual Operating System." *Communications of the ACM,* Vol. 23, No. 9, pp. 495–502.

Haverder, J. W. 1968. "Avoiding Deadlock in Multitasking Systems." *IBM Systems Journal,* No. 2.

Hoare, C. A. R., and Perrott, R.H. (editors) 1972. *Operating Systems Techniques.* Academic Press, London.

Hoare, C. A. R. October 1974. "Monitors: An Operating System Strcuturing Concept." *Communications of the ACM,* Vol. 17, No. 10, pp. 549–557 (erratum in *Communications of the ACM,* Vol. 18, No. 2, p. 95).

Hoare, C. A. R. August 1978. "Communicating Sequential Processes." *Communications of the ACM,* Vol. 21, No. 8, pp. 666–677.

Holt, R. C. September 1972. "Some Deadlock Properties of Computer Systems." *ACM Computing Reviews,* Vol. 4, No. 3, pp. 179–196.

Holt, R. C., Graham, G. S., Lazowska, E. D., and Scott, M. A. 1978 *Structured Concurrent Programming with Operating Systems Applications.* Addison-Wesley Publishing Company, Inc., Reading, Mass.

Holt, R. C. 1983. *Concurrent Euclid, The Unix System, and Tunis.* Addison-Wesley Publishing Company, Inc., Reading, Mass.

Horning, J. J., and Randell, B. March 1973. "Process Structuring." *ACM Computing Surveys,* Vol. 5, No. 1, pp. 5–30.

Horowitz, E. and Sahni, S. 1976. *Fundamentals of Data Structures.* Computer Science Press, Inc., Rockville, Md.

IBM Systems Reference Library. November 1969. *IBM System/360 Operating System, Linkage Editor and Loader.* GC28-6538-8. International Business Machines Corporation, White Plains, N.Y.

IBM. 1972. *Introduction to Virtual Storage in System/370.* International Business Machines Corporation, White Plains, N.Y.

IBM. 1973a. *IBM System/370 Principles of Operation.* GA22-7000-3. International Business Machines Corporation, White Plains, N.Y.

IBM. 1973b. *OS/VS1 System Data Areas.* SYS28-0605-2. International Business Machines Corporation, White Plains, N.Y.

IBM. May 1978. *OS/VS2 MVS System Programming Library: Initialization and Tuning Guide.* GC 28-0681-3. International Business Machines Corporation, White Plains, N.Y.

IBM. 1979a. *OS/VS2 System Logic Library,* Volume 3. SY28-0715-2. International Business Machines Corporation, White Plains, N.Y.

IBM. August, 1979b. *OS/VS2 System Programming Library: Supervisor.* GC28-0628-3. International Business Machines Corporation, White Plains, N.Y.

IBM. October, 1979c. *Systematic Design Workshop "A" (SDWA) (79-V1).* FSD Software Engineering Education, International Business Machines Corporation, White Plains, N.Y.

IBM. January 1980. *OS/VS1 Programmer's Reference Digest.* GC24-5091-6. International Business Machines Corporation, White Plains, N.Y.

IBM. March 1984. *OS/VS1 Data Management for Systems Programmers.* GC26-3837-3. International Business Machines Corporation, White Plains, N.Y.

Intel. September, 1975. *Intel 8080 Microcomputer Systems User's Manual.* Intel Corporation, Santa Clara, Calif.

Interdata. 1977. *Dynamic OS/32 MT Program Reference Manual.* 29-613. Perkin-Elmer Data Systems, Oceanport, N.J.

Isloor, S. S., and Marsland, T. A. September 1980. ''The Deadlock Problem: An Overview.'' *IEEE Computer,* Vol. 13, No. 9, pp. 58–78.

Jones, C. B. 1980. *Software Development: A Rigorous Approach.* Prentice-Hall. Englewood Cliffs, N.J.

Kenah, L. J., and Bate, S. F. 1984. *VAX/VMS Internals and Data Structures.* Digital Press/Digital Equipment Corp., Bedford, Mass.

Knuth, D. E. 1975. *The Art of Computer Programming,* Vol. I: *Fundamental Algorithms.* Addison-Wesley Publishing Company, Inc., Reading, Mass.

Kobayashi, H. 1978. *Modeling and Analysis: An Introduction to System Performance Evaluation Methodology.* Addison-Wesley Publishing Company, Inc., Reading, Mass.

Kurzban, S. A., Heines, T. S., and Sayers, A. P. 1975. *Operating System Principles.* Petrocelli/Charter, New York.

Kutti, S. October 1984. ''Why a Distributed Kernel?'' *ACM Operating Systems Review,* Vol. 18, No. 4, pp. 5–11.

Lampson, B. W., and Redell, D. D. February 1980. ''Experience with Processes and Monitors in MESA.'' *Communications of the ACM,* Vol. 23, No. 2, pp. 105–117.

Leibson, S. 1982a. ''The Input/Output Primer, Part 1: What is I/O?.'' *BYTE,* Vol. 7, No. 2.

Leibson, S. 1982b. ''The Input/Output Primer, Part 2: Interrupts and Direct Memory Access.'' *BYTE,* Vol. 7, No. 3.

Levy, H. M. and Eckhouse, R. H. April, 1980. *Computer Programming and Architecture, The VAX 11.* Digital Press/Digital Equipment Corp., Bedford, Mass.

Linger, R. C., Mills, H. D., and Witt, B. I. 1979. *Structured Programming Theory and Practice.* Addison-Wesley Publishing Company, Inc., Reading, Mass.

Lister, A. M. 1975. *Fundamentals of Operating Systems.* Macmillan, London.

Madnick, S. E. and Donovan, J. J. 1974. *Operating Systems.* McGraw-Hill Book Company, New York.

Nielsen, N. R. November, 1977. ''Dynamic Memory Allocation in Computer Simulations.'' *Communications of the ACM,* Vol. 20, No. 11, pp. 864–873.

Peterson, J. and Silberschatz, A. 1983. *Operating System Concepts.* Addison-Wesley Publishing Company, Inc., Reading, Mass.

Presser, L. March 1975. ''Multiprogramming Coordination.'' *ACM Computing Surveys,* Vol. 7, No. 1, pp. 21–44.

Ritchie, D. M. January 6, 1978. ''The UNIX Time Sharing System: A Retrospective.'' *The Bell System Technical Journal,* Vol. 57, No. 6, Part 2.

Ritchie, D. M. and Thompson, K. April 3, 1978. ''The UNIX Time Sharing System.'' *The Bell System Technical Journal,* Vol. 57, No. 6, Part 2.

Shah, A. C. 1974. *The Logical Design of Operating Systems.* Prentice-Hall, Englewood Cliffs, N.J.

Sleator, D. D., and Tarjan, R. E. February 1985. ''Amortised Efficiency of List Update and Paging Rules.'' *Communications of the ACM,* Vol. 28, No. 2, pp. 202–208.

Sloan, M. E. 1983. *Computer Hardware and Organization,* 2nd ed. Science Research Associates, Inc., Chicago.

Stephenson, C. J. October 1983. ''Fast Fits: New Methods for Dynamic Storage Allocation.'' *ACM Operating Systems Review,* Vol. 17, No. 5, pp. 30–32.

Stone, H. S., et al. 1980. *Introduction to Computer Architecture.* Science Research Associates, Inc., Chicago.

Tanenbaum, A. S. 1984. *Structured Computer Organization.* Prentice-Hall, Englewood Cliffs, N.J.

Teorey, T. J. and Pinkerton, T. B. March, 1972b. ''A Comparative Analysis of Disk Scheduling Policies.'' *Communications of the ACM,* Vol. 15, No. 3, pp. 177–184.

Thompson, K. December 5, 1977. ''The UNIX Time Sharing System: UNIX Implementation.'' *The Bell System Technical Journal.* Vol. 57, No. 6, Part 2.

Tremblay, J. P. and Sorenson, P. G. 1976. *An Introduction to Data Structures with Applications.* McGraw-Hill Book Company, New York.

Tsichritzis, D. C., and Bernstein, P. A. 1974. *Operating Systems.* Academic Press, Inc., New York.

Wallace, J. J., and Barnes, W. W. August 1984. ''Designing for Ultrahigh Availability: The Unix RTR Operating System.'' *IEEE Computer,* Vol. 17, No. 8, pp. 31–39.

Welsh, J., and Mckeag, M. 1980. *Structured System Programming.* Prentice-Hall, Englewood Cliffs, N.J.

Wicklund, T. L. 1982. ''MINI-EXEC: A Portable Executive for 8-bit Micro-computers.'' *Communications of the ACM,* Vol. 25, No. 11.

Wilkes, M. V. 1975. *Time-Sharing Computer Systems,* 3rd ed. Macdonald, London.

Witt, B. I. January 1985a. ''Communicating Modules: A Software Design Model for Concurrent Distributed Systems.'' *IEEE Computer,* Vol. 18, No. 1, pp. 67–77.

Witt, B. I. February 1985b. ''Parallelism, Pipelines, and Partitions: Variations of Communicating Modules.'' *IEEE Computer.,* Vol. 18, No. 2, pp. 105–112.

Wulf, W. A., Levin, R., and Harbison, S. P. 1981. *HYDRA/C.mmp: An Experimental Computer System.* McGraw-Hill Book Company, New York.

Yourdon, E., and Constantine, L. L. 1979. *Structured Design: Fundamentals of a Discipline of Computer Program and System Design.* Prentice-Hall, Englewood Cliffs, N.J.

Index ▬▬▬▬▬▬▬▬▬▬▬▬▬▬▬▬▬▬▬▬▬